Carolyn J. Mullins

THE
Complete
Writing Guide
TO PREPARING
- Reports
- Proposals
- Memos, Etc.

A SPECTRUM BOOK

PRENTICE-HALL, INC, Englewood Cliffs, NJ 07632

Library of Congress Cataloging in Publication Data

MULLINS, CAROLYN J
    The complete writing guide to preparing reports,
proposals, memos, etc.

    (A Spectrum Book)
    Bibliography: p.
    Includes index.
    1.–Report writing. I.–Title.
PE1478.M78   808'.0666021   80-24075
ISBN 0-13-164665-6
ISBN 0-13-164657-5 (pbk.)

*To Elizabeth Eddy Johns and Corydon Thayer Johns,
for understanding why they get more of my words
in books than in letters*

© 1980 by Prentice-Hall, Inc., Englewood Cliffs, New Jersey 07632

Editorial/production supervision and interior design by Donald Chanfrau
Cover design by Ira Shapiro
Manufacturing buyer: Barbara A. Frick

A Spectrum Book

10 9 8 7 6 5 4 3 2 1

Printed in the United States of America

PRENTICE-HALL INTERNATIONAL, INC., *London*
PRENTICE-HALL OF AUSTRALIA PTY. LIMITED, *Sydney*
PRENTICE-HALL OF CANADA, LTD., *Toronto*
PRENTICE-HALL OF INDIA PRIVATE LIMITED, *New Delhi*
PRENTICE-HALL OF JAPAN, INC., *Tokyo*
PRENTICE-HALL OF SOUTHEAST ASIA PTE. LTD., *Singapore*
WHITEHALL BOOKS LIMITED, *Wellington, New Zealand*

Contents

Preface

Brilliant research, useful inventions, and ingenious proposals benefit no one unless their creators can explain them to others. When you don't write clearly and persuasively, good ideas don't bring either raises and promotions or the satisfaction of seeing your work get results. Technical writers and editors can help with writing, but they can't take full responsibility because they didn't do the work.

Even if you have already had trouble with writing, set aside the unpleasant experiences and try again with this book as a guide. Readers accept neat, crisply and precisely written documents as the result of sound reasoning and careful observation; they reject poorly written documents as the result of carelessness or incompetence. Readers form these opinions solely on the basis of writing, not on the quality of your work or thinking.

The students in my night classes have convinced me that most books on technical writing are too detailed and too concerned solely with writing. Most writers lack the time to sift through detail; a deadline is nearly upon them and getting the document written in any form is more important than getting it written effectively. To help resolve this problem, this book is shorter than most others on similar topics. It presents necessary steps in order (and thus acts as a checklist), summarizes information on support systems, and provides many outlines, examples, and time-saving suggestions.

I am grateful to Indiana University's Wrubel Computing Center for providing the text processing system on which I wrote the book, and to IU's Institute for Urban Transportation, where I developed and tested many of the ideas in the book. The university's Management Systems group used a draft of the book as a text for workshops in writing computer documentation. I owe a debt to the people in that group and in my night classes; many of them took the time to comment, criticize, and suggest improvements.

I am also grateful to E. Wainright Martin, Jr., who gave advice and helped with documentation; to Martha B. Dawson, who introduced me to the concept of working smarter; to Marjory Z. Bankson, Donald Graves, Luann J. Tennant, and Thomas W. West, who read the last rough draft and offered many valuable suggestions; to Norma Carr-Ruffino (San Francisco State University) and Alton V. Finch (University of Mississippi), who offered some of the most thoughtful and helpful criticism I have ever received from referees; to Stan Page and George W. Bostick, who prepared the illustrations for Chapter 6 and loaned me books on how to prepare illustrations; and especially to Corydon T. Johns (my father) and Nicholas C. Mullins (my husband), both fellow writers, who have always been my most lovingly persistent critics. Our children—Nick, Rob, and Nancy— spent many hours collating and stapling pages and babysitting the printer. I thank them for both their work and for their patience with a preoccupied mother.

The dedication is to my parents; they raised me to think clearly and independently, to take risks, and to respect the English language.

1 | Introduction

Why Write?

1.1 For many individuals in all organizations and jobs, writing is a necessary evil, to be avoided whenever possible. However, the cost of poor writing is high. It might cost you a job, a raise, or a promotion. It might cost your employer a contract or a sale. You and your employer will both suffer when people who depend on your writing keep interrupting your current work to get clarifications. If you are a reluctant writer, consider some of the more important functions of good writing.

Reports

1.2 Reports are an essential concluding step to any project because someone, somewhere must have needed the results or the project wouldn't have been planned. The report:

1. Presents results in an accurate, orderly manner to help those immediately interested in the work and to acquaint others, such as executives and foundation officials, with general progress on a subject.
2. Helps people decide whether the work is interesting and important enough to be continued.

3. Records results for future use to prevent expensive duplication of time and effort.
4. Gives manufacturing and advertising departments factual material to help them produce and advertise a product that has come from a project.
5. Preserves a record of methods and steps so the work can be evaluated and repeated in the future when necessary.
6. Provides a history of development, which may be needed as background for patent applications.
7. Helps people identify and analyze problems, make decisions, and design policies and programs.
8. Persuades readers to adopt a recommended course of action.

Proposals

1.3 Often written proposals constitute the beginning of a project. Sometimes they are the only way to:

1. Get a job or contract.
2. Get money for research or development.
3. Start a change in organization or procedure.
4. Persuade people to accept a new idea.

The proposal needn't be long, and doesn't always include a request for funds. In one organization, the employees' campaign for flexible work hours began as a simple, two-page proposal that opened with the request and then listed reasons, benefits to the organization, and a detailed plan. In another organization, the personnel department set up car pools and van pools in response to a proposal from employees. In a nonprofit organization, one determined group of parents even wrote a proposal that convinced a firm to sponsor the city's youth soccer teams and pay their travel expenses for weekend games in other cities.

Documentation and Other Instructions

1.4 Written, step-by-step instructions are the most efficient way to:

1. Tell people how to use a new product as safely, efficiently, and fully as possible.
2. Preserve your time for new projects.

For example, when you have developed a new product, such as a new computer program, you are the person others will ask when instructions on how to use the product aren't clear. Vaughn (1979) put the situation well when he remarked that programmers who were spending more than 5 percent of their time answering questions were well on their way to *becoming* the documentation they had never written, or had not written clearly enough. Constant demands for explanation are particularly likely when the product is for use in and by your organization, which puts you only a telephone call away at most.

What Can This Book Do for You?

1.5 This book can help you learn how to analyze problems and write faster, more easily, and more effectively and efficiently. Included are many sections on efficient planning and management of writing projects, but even if you are not yet in a management position, reading the suggestions will help you to understand a supervisor's viewpoint and to prepare for promotion to a management position. Equally important, the book tells many ways computers can help you to write better and ways to design text pages so that a document's nonverbal message supports and enhances the written message.

Basic Framework and Ideas

1.6 Each chapter gives useful suggestions, often in step-by-step lists, in the order in which writers need them. Each paragraph is numbered so you can find cross-referenced information quickly. The number before the decimal is the chapter number; the number after is the number of the paragraph in that chapter. For example, this is the sixth paragraph in Chapter 1. Discussions of many topics include cross-references, by paragraph number, to related information elsewhere in the book; and the index is by paragraph number, not by page. As a result, you'll never have to skim more than a few lines to find the specific information you are looking for. If you are not naturally well organized, following the steps and the chapters in order will help keep you organized and working efficiently. The book gives lots of help on writing, but when you need more, especially on grammar, try one of the writing books listed in the bibliography (for example, Tichy 1966; Perrin 1972; Lesikar 1974; and Fischman 1975).

1.7 In this book, detailed information is distributed somewhat unevenly because writers' needs usually are distributed unevenly. For example, more time is spent on tables, illustrations, and sentence clarity than on grammar because most writers have relatively fewer problems with grammar. (Also, those with severe problems need a book devoted solely to grammar.) If you already are proficient in the techniques discussed in detail, simply skip the discussion and go on to the next topic.

1.8 Most of the techniques in this book, such as how to write clear sentences, apply to all documents from one-page memos to lengthy documents of several volumes intended for wide distribution. Some, such as the need for careful scheduling and the use of computer programs for analysis, apply primarily to longer documents and especially to reports. Some, such as use of headings, apply differently depending on length of document. When differences exist, they are described and explained in terms of what they apply to and how to apply the techniques under special conditions.

1.9 The basic themes are: work smarter, not harder; write simply; and don't try to vary your prose or in other ways practice the techniques of creative writing. Unlike creative writing and even much expository writing, the purpose of reports, proposals, and other technical documents, whether written in short memos or as formal documents, is primarily to inform. Persuasion is often appropriate, but entertainment rarely is. The goal is to communicate all the information needed—but only that information and nothing extraneous—in a reasonably unbiased manner that is faithful to the data, and as clearly, briefly, neatly, and simply as possible.

Ethics in Writing

1.10 It isn't possible or even appropriate to eliminate all bias. Every writer biases every document by the simple act of including some information and throwing some away. Good business and scientific ethics forbid throwing away data because they contradict a theory or fail to support a proposal. However, you will always have to study information and then make the most informed and representative choice of what to present. And when information forces you to conclude that you must recommend a specific course of action, often you will want to make the recommendation in the most persuasive way possible. You will want to use the briefest, clearest prose you can muster, the most effective organization, the strongest nonverbal messages, the most compelling format, and the best timing you can manage. Throughout this book, different ways of handling text are described and explained according to purpose, so you will have a variety of tools for persuasion at your disposal. Your responsibility, having learned the tools, will be to use them in ethically sound ways.

Simplicity and Systems

1.11 Don't worry about writing too simply. Referring to his engineering firm, one technical writer commented, "We have never had a report submitted . . . in which the explanations and terms were too simple" (Richards and Richardson 1941, p. 9). Writing in any other style, even writing that is eloquent, entertaining, and unique to the writer, may detract from the purpose of writing. Use these criteria as guidelines for writing reports and proposals:

1. Write simply.
2. Choose plain words.
3. Correct grammatical errors.
4. Avoid long sentences.
5. Use the active voice.

The requirement of simplicity applies not only to words but to tables, illustrations, equations, format, and editorial style. If you work at writing long enough, you may develop enough skill to venture into a few of the complexities of writing. Until that time, however, simplicity will save time and effort and will help you to get the best results possible from the time available.

1.12 Although good writing always requires hard work and clear thinking, hard work by itself does not always produce good results. You must also think clearly, organize well, use human and mechanical resources intelligently, and work efficiently. For example, when you can apply to a report a general outline that you have used before, do so. That saves you the effort of developing an outline. When sections of other reports—such as a description of specific state laws—must be included in every report you write, develop a "boiler plate," as such sections are called. Have it professionally edited so that it is as accurate, brief, clear, and smoothly written as possible; and use it, unchanged, as often as you need. When firms have word processing equipment, using boiler plates can be as easy as flipping the switch to turn on a light. Copying is easier than creating from scratch.

Where Do We Go from Here?

1.13 Chapter 2 discusses schedules for writing and production of longer documents. It includes suggestions to help writers know when and how to cut corners when time is short. Chapter 3 describes efficient procedures for gathering data, keeping records, and analyzing problems before you begin to write. These procedures will help you keep information organized in the way you will need it when you start writing a draft. Chapter 4 tells how word processing systems can automate writing and lower an organization's investment of time and money in the writing process.

1.14 Part II, on organizing and standardizing information, begins with Chapters 5 and 6 on when and how to use tables and illustrations, respectively, and how to prepare them. Chapter 7 tells how to organize textual information, how to develop outlines, why some writers have trouble outlining, and how to correct the difficulties. Chapter 8 describes why and how to use standard outlines, tells how to develop them, and gives many examples. Chapter 9 describes the purposes, kinds, and preparation of boiler plates, and tells how use of word processing can enhance the effectiveness of boiler plates.

1.15 Part III, on writing and revising, begins with a variety of ways to write first drafts, titles, and summaries. Chapter 11 highlights three useful, general tools for revision: readability measures, writing partnerships (especially useful on longer documents), and nonverbal messages created by thoughtful use of editorial style, page format, and artwork. Chapters 12 and 13 take you through the most efficient way to revise a draft. The emphasis is on smooth integration of text, tables, illustrations, and equations, and on development of a clear, brief writing style. In addition, Chapters 11 and 13 point out many ways that computers can help you write more effectively.

1.16 Part IV describes the mechanics of production. Chapter 14 details steps in editorial checking, especially necessary on longer and more important documents, and lists the multitude of questions about style and format to which all typists need answers before they can do fast, accurate work with a minimum of supervision. Chapter 15, designed to help your typists help you, lists answers to questions about typing, gives instructions for proofreading, and provides checklists for reproduction, binding, and mailing.

I. SUPPORT SYSTEMS

2 | Schedules: Why, When, and How; Ways to Save Time

2.1 On longer documents, plan a detailed schedule for writing and production so that you budget time and money wisely, avoid promising completion in too short a time, and avoid competition with work on other writing projects. In proposals, of course, a detailed schedule for the proposed project has at least two additional uses: it tells the reader you have thought carefully about the proposed project, and it keeps you from making promises that are unrealistic for the time and money involved. Then, when a contractor wants a cheaper or faster job, you have a basis for estimating trade-offs. For example, you could finish the report on a management audit a month earlier *if* the contractor were willing to pay for technical editors' and writers' overtime during the last six weeks of the contract. Or you could finish a month earlier for the same amount of money *if* the contractor agreed to a more limited scope for the study. Agreements in advance prevent hard feelings later. This chapter tells how to plan realistic writing schedules, where to spend money to buy extra time, and which steps are likely to conflict with work on other projects.

How to Plan a Schedule

Step-by-Step Tasks

2.2 Because most writers have never been editors or proofreaders, typists or clerks, they usually underestimate the amounts of time needed to edit, type, proofread, correct, and reproduce a report.

11

Because they have never learned systematic steps in writing and revising, they don't estimate accurately the amount of time needed for writing. Building a realistic schedule requires allocating realistic amounts of time not only for research and analysis, but also for writing, revising, editing, typing, proofreading, correcting, reproducing, binding, and mailing.

2.3 Table 2.1 lists the possible steps in chronological order because that is the way they are easiest to visualize. However, when you plan a schedule, work backward from the date a report or proposal is or would be due. Then compare the draft schedule with a master schedule for your organization to locate and eliminate potential

TABLE 2.1 *List of Scheduling Tasks from Beginning to End*

1. Data gathering.
2. Analysis.
3. Arranging for publicity.
4. Outlining.
5. Preparation of boiler plate appendixes.
6. Writing a first draft.
7. Revision to improve organization and clarity.
8. Typing a rough draft.
9. Getting criticism.
10. Using criticism and correcting grammar.
11. Editing.
12. Preparation of cover.
13. Final typing.
14. Proofreading.
15. Preparation of front matter.
16. Corrections.
17. Reproduction of cover and text.
18. Binding.
19. Mailing.

conflicts with work on other projects. In the list that follows, which contains the items in Table 2.1 in reverse order, the time estimates are very rough. It is assumed that the document has a normal priority (neither high nor low), that the organization's regular staff members usually have a full workload with little spare time, and that management doesn't want to hire temporary staff to help with writing, editing, typing, or proofreading. With documents shorter than 50 pages, some steps may take even less time than the lowest estimate in the allowed range; and some steps, such as binding and production of front matter, may be unnecessary. Documents for in-house distribution might not require mailing and publicity. Figures 2.1 through 2.3 show sample schedules for documents of different lengths, with different requirements, and with different typing equipment.The steps are:

1. Mailing; allow two to five days, depending on distance of contractor.
2. Binding; allow a week. Actual time can vary from one day to a month or more, depending on type of binding and the bindery's workload.
   SUGGESTION: Keep on hand a list of estimates (time and cost) from all binderies in your area, broken down by types of binding, length of manuscript, and number of copies. The actual time may vary a bit depending on time of year, but general estimates still will be reasonably accurate.
3. Reproduction of cover and text; allow two days for xerographic copy and up to two weeks for offset.
   SUGGESTION: As with binding, ask possible suppliers for estimates broken down by type of reproduction, number of pages in manuscript, and number of complete copies.
4. Corrections; for correction of typographical and other errors in text and tables, from the title page through the appendixes, allow 25 pages per day. The amount will vary with the number of errors, the typist, the amount of other work the typist has, and the type of equipment. Corrections on word processing equipment are always faster than corrections on a regular typewriter.
   SUGGESTION: Get actual estimates for each typist, both with other work to do and with only the corrections on a single manuscript. When the opportunity arises, also get estimates for temporary typists.
5. Preparation of front matter; allow seven days for writing, typing, proofreading, and correcting front matter—the release page, title page, table of contents, lists of tables and illustrations, preface,

SCHEDULE FOR REPORT ON SMALLCITY'S TRANSPORTATION SYSTEM

Interim report due: 3-21-80   Staff:

Type: First of several, requires questionnaire; 100 pages, double
       spaced, perfect binding, others to begin in 3 months; no word
       processing equipment; contractor in another state

Task	Due Date
Data gathered by	8-6
Analysis done by	9-6
Outline drafted by	9-20
Outline revised by	10-03
First drafts to typists:	11-11 to 2-6-78
Chapter One (inventory)	11-1
Chapter Two (problems)	12-1
Chapter Three (alternatives)	1-9
Chapter Four (analysis)	1-23
Chapter Five (recommendations)	2-3
Introduction (complete)	2-6
Clean drafts to editor and staff;	11-18 to 2-6-78
ask 7-day response from staff	
Chapter One	11-8
Chapter Two	12-8
Chapter Three	1-12-78
Chapter Four	1-30
Chapter Five	2-9
Front matter (modified boiler plate)	2-23
Confirm date of final typing; request one	2-13
typist only	
Complete final draft to typist; also	2-27
order cover for report	
Final typing, one typist	2-27 to 3-9
Proofreading out loud; pick up cover	3-2 to 3-13
Corrections; front matter thru appendixes	3-10 to 3-14
Deliver complete report for duplication	3-14
Have report bound	3-16
Mail by (to arrive by 3-21)	3-17

FIGURE 2.1 Sample schedule No. 1

acknowledgments, and other elements that may go before the
first page of text in the body of a document.

6. Proofreading; allow one day for every 40 pages of manuscript.
   SUGGESTION: To get accurate estimates for your staff, find out
   the number of proofed pages each pair of proofreaders can turn
   out in a single day; measure output both when they have other

work to do and when they can work just on the manuscript.

7. Final typing; allow one day for each 30 pages. Speed can vary with typist, workload, equipment, and condition of draft. SUGGESTION: Under ordinary work conditions, measure each typist's output both with and without other work to do. Measure

---

```
              SCHEDULE FOR REPORT ON MANAGEMENT AUDIT


Report due:  12/31/82               Staff:


Type:  Final, single-spaced, no computer analysis, first of several, 100
       pages; typed  on  word  processing  system;  contractor  is
       out-of-state
```

Task	Due Date
Data gathered by	8-30
Analysis done by	9-30 (Fri.)
Outline drafted by	10-21(Fri.)
Outline revised by	10-26 (Wed.)
First drafts to typists:	10-7 to 11-28
Chapter One (environment)	10-28 (Fri.)
Nat'l and state env.	10-7 (Fri.)
Local environment	10-14
Transp. resources	10-21
Attitudes	10-28
Chapter Two (board of directors)	10-11 (Tues.)
Chapter Three (analysis)	10-14 to 11-23 (F,W)
Chapter Four (more analysis)	10-14 to 11-4 (F)
Introduction (complete)	11-28 (Mon.)
Clean drafts to editor and staff; ask staff for comments within 7 days	10-12 to 12-4
Introduction	10-29 and 12-4
Chapter One	10-11 to 11-1 (Tues.)
Chapter Two	10-18 (Tues.)
Chapter Three	11-11 (Fri.)
Chapter Four (lots of tables)	10-21 to 30 (F,W)
Chapter Five	10-21 to 11-11 (Fri.)
Front matter (modified boiler plate)	12-06
Confirm date of final typing	11-3 (Thrs.)
Final draft to typist; order cover	12-2 to 12-09
Proofread changed sections	12-5 to 12-15
Corrections; front matter thru appendixes	12-8 to 12-15
Deliver complete report for duplication	12-16 (Fri.)
Have report bound	12-23 (Fri.)
Mail report	12-26 (Mon.)

FIGURE 2.2 Sample schedule No. 2

SCHEDULE FOR PRODUCING SMALL REPORT

Report due: 7-08-78   Staff:

Type: Final, 70 single-spaced pages, including all illustrations,
       tables, appendixes, etc., typed on word processing system, using
       boiler plates for the title page, contents, introduction, Chapter
       Three, and appendixes; offset reproduction, perfect binding

Task	Due Date
Writing	2-17 to 4-14
Chapter One	2-17 (Fri.)
Chapter Two	3-31 (Fri.)
Chapter Three	4-14 (Fri.)
First drafts edited by:	3-03 to 4-28
Chapter One	3-03 (Fri.)
Chapter Two	4-14 (Fri.)
Chapter Three	4-28 (Fri.)
Order Cover	3-10 (Fri.)
Boiler plates supplied by:	3-03 (Fri.)
Typing finished by	3-17 to 5-12
Chapter One	3-17 (Fri.)
Chapter Two	4-28 (Fri.)
Chapter Three	5-05
Appendixes	5-12
Author check entire report by:	5-19 (Fri.)
In-house review finished by:	5-26 (Fri.)
Return to editorial department by:	6-2 (Fri.)
Edit additions and changes	6-9
Prepare table of contents	6-12 (Mon.)
Type corrections	6-13 (Tues.)
Proofreading corrections	6-25 (Thrs.)
Print; take to maxi	6-16 (Fri.); 6-19
Add cover and take to bindery	6-26 (Mon.)
Pick up bound report; mail	7-03 (Mon.); 7-05

FIGURE 2.3 Sample schedule No. 3

by number of words (number of pages will vary with type pitch,
width of margins, and double or single spacing).

8. Preparation of cover; allow one day to two weeks, depending
   on whether you use a standard cover that needs only a change
   in title or whether you want a designer to prepare something
   unique.

   SUGGESTION: Get estimates of time and cost from designers in
   your organization or area, broken down by type and complexity

of design (for example, title and logo only, hand-drawn illustration, use of photographs, black and white versus one or more other colors).

9. Editing; allow one hour for every three pages for very light copy editing, and one hour or more per page for heavier editing and rewriting. (Sections 13.2, 13.34, 13.57, and Chapter 14 describe types of editing.)

    SUGGESTION: Measure the work done by editors on your staff under normal working conditions, with and without other work to do, by types of editing (See Chapter 14 for help). Take the same measures when you use temporary editors.

10. Using criticism and correcting grammar; allow one day for every 15 pages. The amount will vary, of course, with the number and complexity of suggestions and with whether the report is one of several similar reports. The more reports of a type you write, the fewer criticisms you should receive.

    SUGGESTION: Measure the amount of work you can do by type of report, with and without other work. If your firm has word processing equipment, learn how to make corrections yourself. When a terminal is available, making corrections yourself takes no additional time and saves intermediate typing.

11. Getting criticism; allow seven days; getting criticism from others in your organization helps find ambiguities and errors. (Stay away from the draft while others are reading it; you will benefit from greater distance when you are ready to use the criticism.)

    SUGGESTION: Ask critics to return the criticized draft within seven days. Notifying critics at least two weeks in advance will help you get cooperation.

12. Typing rough draft; allow one week per unit of 35 pages or so. Remember to specify that strikeovers are okay and that you want *wide* margins (at least 1 1/4 inches on each side).

    SUGGESTION: Measure actual output under ordinary working conditions, by typist. Measure by number of words, not pages.

13. Revision to improve organization and clarity; allow one week per unit.

    SUGGESTION: Follow the steps outlined in Section 11.3. Measure your output under ordinary working conditions.

14. Writing a first draft; allow up to one week for units (such as chapters) that are descriptive, and up to two weeks each for units that include analysis and recommendations.

15. Preparation of boiler plate appendixes; those usable with no changes can be reproduced immediately. Time for no changes can be reproduced immediately. Time for others depends on kind and amount of changes.
    SUGGESTION: Check time required when you use these appendixes and look for ways to reduce it. Chapter 9 suggests ways to streamline the process.
16. Outline; allow two days when you only need to modify an existing outline, and two weeks if you need to outline from scratch.
    SUGGESTION: Read and use the suggestions in Chapters 7 and 8. Measure the actual amount of time it takes you to do detailed outlines down to the fourth level of importance.
17. Arranging for publicity; contact the publicity department early to arrange your part in any publicity effort. Even when publicity won't be released until later, getting your work on it done early will ease your schedule as a deadline draws near.
18. Analysis; allow one week to several months, depending on type of data and analysis and whether you can repeat patterns from previous reports.
    SUGGESTION: Ask co-workers and supervisors to help you estimate and to suggest aids such as canned computer programs and similar, previous analyses.
19. Data gathering; allow at least one month.
    SUGGESTIONS: As with analysis, ask for help. Look for patterns you can follow, data that already exist. For example, you may need census statistics that already exist in an available, computerized data bank.

Form of Schedule

2.4 Schedules can be in list form (as in Figures 2.1 through 2.3) or in any of a variety of chart forms. On charts it is easier to show what steps *must* be done before other steps. For example, you can prepare a cover anytime—before, during, or after text writing—but you *must* prepare it before you can bind the report. Charts also show what steps can happen along with other steps. For example, during the same time period, you can be writing one chapter, having a second one typed, revising a third, and doing the analysis that will yield tables for a fourth.

2.5 Ideally, the chart for your project should be put together with charts for your other projects and charts for projects being done by your co-workers. The master chart helps prevent conflicts among people who need the same resources. For example, on the same day you cannot be out of town doing interviews and also at your desk writing. On the same day you cannot have the same typist working all day on two different projects. These seem like obvious statements, but often it takes a master chart to point out potential conflict before it happens and when people still can change schedules.

2.6 In business, various techniques use these facts about planning to help individuals and organizations use time and money efficiently. For example, critical path techniques emphasize reduction of time needed to reach a goal. Project evaluation and review technique (PERT) emphasizes the relationship between occurrence time and scheduling. Buffa (1976) and Anderson, Sweeney, and Williams (1978) describe these and other useful techniques.

Shortcuts

2.7 Some steps that save time should be taken by all organizations as a matter of routine procedure. They allow faster work without loss of quality or substance. They also don't increase cost; in fact, they may lower cost. Some steps allow the same quality, but at additional cost. Still other steps trade quality for speed.

Routine Procedures

2.8 Use of word processing equipment speeds up the entire writing process enough that organizations without it should investigate the purchase of equipment. The initial cost is high, but the equipment enables typists to double and often triple output (depending on how much typing is original and how much is revision). The equipment doesn't take vacations or receive a salary or demand benefits, and it won't quit just when you need its experience most. The variety of equipment spans the range from stand-alone units with one input station and one printer to huge systems that link offices across the country. Chapter 4 describes word processing systems in detail and explains how they help organizations save time and money.

2.9 A "house style" for treating citations, bibliographies, tables, headings and subheadings, and so forth speeds up writing, typing, and editing. The more familiar the rules become, the fewer questions project managers and production supervisors need to answer. Sections 11.19 through 11.34 describe the benefits in detail and tell how to prepare a style sheet. Technical editors can do this work for you.

2.10 Boiler plates and "standard" outlines, discussed in detail in Chapters 8 and 9, reduce the time needed to organize a draft and write some sections. Technical writers can do much of this work. (See Sections 8.2 through 8.9 for other uses of standard outlines.) Using the same personnel for certain operations (for example, the same typist for all drafts, the same editor throughout) allows a project to benefit from the greater speed that familiarity can produce. Reserving a specific period of time with typists, editors, proofreaders, reproducers, and binderies will eliminate waiting time, but it also binds you to a schedule with no leeway.

Steps That Maintain Quality but Add Cost

2.11 Technical writers and editors can do some or all of the organizing, outlining, writing, rewriting, and editing. Copy editors can do most of the work described in Sections 13.34 through 13.64. Substantive editors can do much of the work described in Sections 13.2 through 13.33. When organizations have word processing equipment, programmers sometimes can write programs that automatically perform the steps described in Sections 11.11, 13.9, 13.17, 13.47, and 13.63. Paying regular employees overtime wages so they, rather than temporary help, can finish a project allows the project to benefit from their experience. Hiring temporary typists, editors, and proofreaders can help you get work done faster, but unless you can hire people who have had previous experience with your organization, maintaining quality may require you to spend considerable time supervising and checking work.

2.12 Regular use of technical writers and editors may pay for itself over time as staff members learn better writing habits by being exposed to good writing daily and by seeing their own mistakes corrected. The danger is that unless management actively encourages good writing, staff members may view a writing support staff as an excuse to avoid writing entirely. Managers can encourage good writing by:

- □ Letting technical writers and editors hold informal seminars on their work.
- □ Sponsoring in-house courses on technical writing or paying tuition and giving released time to employees who want to take courses offered outside the organization. Shaw (1976) describes a variety of in-house courses.
- □ Encouraging technical writers and editors to consult with the writers with whom they are working. (Knowledge flows both ways, to the benefit of all parties and the organization.)

2.13 Many organizations experiment with free-lance technical editors and writers before hiring them full time. Some use student trainees, from local colleges and universities, who need field experience as part of their training. Still others hire writing teachers as consultants. Muller (1978) describes just one of a variety of consulting arrangements. And some organizations use technical writers and editors from all these sources in addition to full-time staff members. They hire a full-time staff that can handle the ordinary workload and then use help from other sources to cover peak periods or to provide one-to-one help for highly promising staff members whose only handicap is an inability to write.

Steps That Lower Quality

2.14 Among the steps that usually speed up work, but reduce quality are:

- □ Cutting out some steps in revision (Section 11.3 lists the steps).
- □ Asking critics to respond more rapidly.
- □ Hiring temporary editors, typists, and proofreaders, but not supervising them closely.
- □ Eliminating editing and proofreading.
- □ Using mimeograph copying and stapled bindings rather than xerographic copy and perfect binding.

3 | Data Gathering, Record Keeping, and Analysis

3.1 Regardless of length, most documents require some data gathering even if nothing more than a quick look at a file folder. For example, when you are writing a progress report on a project, you will only need to find out how near completion the various parts are and what problems still exist. However, if you were in charge of selecting word processing equipment for your office, you would have to keep records to determine the number, length, and frequency of different kinds of documents; read articles, books, and advertising literature; talk with people in organizations that already have word processing equipment; see demonstrations; and test equipment.

Data Gathering

3.2 This section briefly reviews sources of data that will be used primarily by writers of longer, more formal documents. When yours is one of several reports in a series (other than the first one) or a report somewhat like others done previously in your organization, lists of data sources and requirements for analysis probably already exist. Ask co-workers or a supervisor where to find this information.

Sources of Data

3.3 *Information in libraries.* General information on a topic comes from encyclopedias, basic textbooks, and newspapers. More specialized information comes from advanced textbooks, review articles, monographs, and other people who have worked on a topic. Detailed information comes from previous reports and articles, preprints, convention papers, and so forth.

3.4 Various tools will help you find this information. Card catalogs list books by author, title, and primary and secondary topics. Indexes of articles in newspapers, magazines, and journals will help you find current information. Information services, such as the Institute for Scientific Information (ISI), list sources of information by topic in many areas. Microfiche and microfilm indexes will turn up still more information, as will examination of books and articles listed in bibliographies of previously consulted materials.

3.5 *Newsletters and informal sources.* Newsletters, in-house reports, convention papers, and preprints often report work in progress or recently completed. Sometimes you can find these sources in libraries, but often they are available only from people who are doing research like yours. In scientific reports, this kind of information is particularly important.

3.6 *Primary data.* Sometimes you will need to gather some or all of your own data through observation of demonstrations, requests for bids, interviews, surveys, chemical analysis, records kept over time, and so forth. For example, if you were choosing a retirement program for employees, you would need to examine bids by prospective suppliers, and you might want to survey employees to find out what they want. When your education has not given you the training you need to construct a survey instrument or do a chemical analysis, you will have to learn how or subcontract the job. Much of what you need to learn you can probably find in a library.

Evaluation

3.7 When you evaluate data, ask questions like: Did an interviewee have first-hand information on the topic of interest? For example, an office manager probably has first-hand data on the number, length, and kinds of document typed in an office. Is an author known to be an expert? Not biased in any known way? For example, the authors of *Word Processing* (McCabe and Popham 1977) specialize in office management; they don't work for a company that manufactures word processing equipment. Chances are, then, that their views are unbiased. Still another question is whether unsuspected sources have biased survey data; if so, can you find a way to compensate for the bias? For example, suppose your firm allocates staff to offices on the basis of workload, but the data on workload come only from office managers' estimates. Probably managers would estimate high, "just in case." To correct the bias, the firm might also collect data on actual workload to compare with the estimates. Finally, do several sources of data confirm the same finding? For example, do both published articles and users say that a given kind of equipment is unreliable?

Keeping Records

3.8 The data for some reports and proposals may already exist in organized form, such as in computer files or on PMS (project management system) forms. For example, the proposal for a new computer program might use time and expense estimates that came from PMS forms filled out by the programmers who would design the program. Other PMS forms might list the potential benefits. However, when you will be gathering data over a long period of time or from a variety of sources, try the methods suggested in this section to help you keep data organized and accessible.

Day-to-Day Thoughts and Events

3.9 Use a looseleaf notebook with section dividers to record notes, thoughts, progress, and so forth. Always:

□ Be sure the notebook is durable. For example, chemists need a cover that won't dissolve when chemicals accidentally spatter on it. Frequent travelers need a notebook that will hold up under the battering of life in suitcases and briefcases.
□ Date the entries in each section as if you were keeping a diary.
□ Divide and label the sections so they correspond to major sections in your manuscript. Also include a section for random thoughts. In addition, some writers need a section for administrative details.

Recording thoughts by category imposes organization in a way that will help you when you start to write a draft because you already will have basic information sorted.

3.10 Examples of sections for notebooks are:

- For scientific research: problem, method, results, discussion, conclusions, random thoughts. For details, see Sections 8.10 through 8.15.
- For one of several similar reports, use the major divisions from a prepared outline, plus a section for random thoughts. Chapter 8 gives many examples of possible outlines.
- For a report on word processing equipment, use sections on office needs, demonstrations (subdivided by vendor, when necessary), costs and capabilities, office organization and reorganization, random thoughts, and conclusions and recommendations.

3.11 When you must develop the outline from scratch:

- Make a guess about divisions and then see how they work out.
- Expect, when you begin, to make considerable use of the "random thoughts" section.
- Periodically sort the notes and change the names of categories. You will find fewer and fewer changes necessary as work progresses.

Interview and Survey Notes

3.12 Researchers doing surveys sometimes need an additional section in the notebook for observations about administration of the instrument or behavior of respondents—questions that seem to evoke unusual responses, words that consistently are misunderstood, and so forth. This section is *not* for recording responses; they should be recorded on specially prepared response sheets.

3.13 When you do only a few interviews, one section in a notebook probably will be adequate to record information either in place of or in addition to information on a tape recording of the interview. When you expect to do more than five interviews, get a separate, spiral notebook. Also:

- Make appointments in advance, preferably an hour or so after opening time in the morning or an hour after lunch so your time won't be nibbled away by the questions, mail, and telephone calls that often occur at those times.
- When you intend to record an interview, always let the inter-

viewee know when you make the appointment. A few will object, and you will want to be prepared to take detailed written notes.

▫ Before each interview, write at the top of the page the interviewee's name and job title; the date, time, and place; and your goal for the interview.

▫ Write the date and interviewee's name on a label on the tape, and dictate that information into the microphone so it is recorded just before the interview information. Should the external label fall off, you still will have a way to identify the interview.

3.14 Sometimes a interviewee will refuse to be taped, yet a verbatim transcript is essential. For example, you may be recording the statement of someone who witnessed an accident, and the statement is essential to establish who caused the accident and which insurance company will pay damages. In such cases, arrange to take a court reporter with you.

Taking Notes from Documents

3.15 When you take information from sources other than your own primary data, record accurately both the factual information and complete bibliographic information.

3.16 *Factual information.* Record factual information on either 4 × 6 or 5 × 8 file cards. Keep them in a file box and separate them by category with dividers. Initially use the same categories as in your notebook. Divide further as you begin to see subcategories emerging. Almost always you will end up with more notes than you use, but you will have many fewer than if you took notes randomly. Always look at information in the context of an outline. The context helps you decide how likely it is that you will use the information.

3.17 On each card:

▫ Record one fact (for example, dates, statistical information, definitions, equations), one theoretical statement, or one finding or implication from research.
EXCEPTION: Sometimes you will want a more general note, such as the general theme of a piece of writing, a statement about a general theoretical framework, a brief outline, or a

comment on logic. Again, confine yourself to one note per card.

□ In addition to the information, on each card write the category in which you will file it and a brief key to complete bibliographic data (usually author's name, date, and first few words of title). When the note is specific or is a quotation, add a page number or numbers.

□ *Always* use quotation marks around direct quotations, even when you plan to rewrite them later.

3.18 *Bibliographic data.* Proper documentation requires specific information for each type of document. Detailed information is available in Turabian (1976), University of Chicago Press (1969, Chapter 16), and Mullins (1977, Sections 3.28 through 3.33). Sections 3.19 through 3.23 summarize the details by type of document. To save time later:

□ Record complete bibliographic data the first time you use a document. Waiting until later only forces you to retrace your steps, and sometimes you will find that someone else has checked out the document you need.

□ Record information in your organization's house style (described in Sections 11.20 through 11.24) or in the style that typists will have to use for typing the bibliography. This will save you from making changes later and will help typists to produce a higher quality of work with less supervision. Pay special attention to capital letters, underscoring (italics), and use of quotation marks.

□ Use 3 × 5 file cards (to keep them from getting mixed up with information cards).

3.19 When you use information from a book, write on a card:

□ All authors', editors', or sponsoring institutions' names.

□ The full title, including full subtitles.

□ The series, if any.

□ The volume, when there is more than one.

□ The edition, when not the original.

□ Translator, when you used a version that is not in the original language.

□ The city (and state or state initials, when city is not well known).

□ The publisher's name, often abbreviated.

□ Date of publication (or "forthcoming," when in production, but not yet published; or "unpublished manuscript," when not accepted for publication).

3.20 For chapters in books, record the information in Section 3.19, plus:

- □ The name of the author or authors.
- □ The title and subtitle of the chapter.
- □ Inclusive pages.

3.21 When you use information from an article in a magazine or journal, write on a card:

- □ Name of author.
- □ Title of article, including subtitle.
- □ Name of journal.
- □ Volume number, date, or both.
- □ Issue number, sometimes month or season.
- □ Inclusive pages.

Treat as "in press" (in place of date) articles that have been accepted for publication, but not yet published, and as an "unpublished manuscript" articles that have not been accepted for publication.

3.22 When you cite papers given at meetings, write on a card:

- □ The author's name.
- □ Full title and subtitle.
- □ The words "Paper presented at the meeting of the [formal title of meeting]."
- □ City, month, and year.

3.23 When you cite short, unpublished documents, write on a card:

- □ Author's name.
- □ Full title and subtitle.
- □ Date of the draft.
- □ Author's institution.
- □ Any other identifying information.

3.24 Government documents sometimes offer a bewildering array of identifying data. At minimum, try to find:

- □ The author's name—often an institution, organization, or committee.

□ The full title and subtitle.
□ The technical report number.
□ The city and publisher (often the agency that sponsored the work reported in the document).
□ Month and year.
□ Government Printing House (GPO) order number, National Technical Information Service (NTIS) number, or National Clearinghouse order number.

3.25 File the cards alphabetically, in a divided file box, by author's last name; or, when there is no author, by first significant word in the title. The general rule is alphabetization word by word rather than letter by letter. In addition:

□ Remember that "nothing" precedes "something." Thus, "Smith" would precede "Smiths."
□ Alphabetize corporate authors by first significant word in name.
□ When you have more than one document by an author, arrange cards by date, earliest first. When two or more have the same date, arrange alphabetically by first letter of first word in title that is not *a, an,* or *the.*
□ File single references by an author ahead of works that he or she coauthored with others and of which he or she is the first author.

Findings from Computer Analyses

3.26 Store computer printout in long binders or on racks. When possible, avoid printout. Stacks of printout rapidly eat up office space, the specific printout you need won't always be easy to find, and thumbing through the pages takes time. Instead, access findings by on-line terminal at the time you need them.

Analysis

3.27 You cannot separate writing from thinking. The greater your skill at analysis, the easier and faster writing will become. (Furthermore, your increasing skill will improve your other work.) Analysis always precedes writing and can take any amount of time, from a moment's reflection to months of processing mounds of data. For example, when you write an annual report to your supervisor, in the back of your mind is a raise and perhaps even a promotion. When you plan the report, then, you will want to organize the presentation to give you the best chance at these rewards. You might begin with the statement that you had started the year with six major objectives and had achieved all of them. The rest of the report, divided into six sections (one for each objective), would list the objectives and describe briefly how you had achieved them.

The Basic Principles

3.28 To analyze effectively, you must:

- Know *what* you want to say (for example, I did what I set out to do).
- Know *whom* you are talking to (for example, the boss).
- Know *how* to write for that reader (for example, two pages, in plain language, with topic sentences).
- Know *which* format will enhance the message most effectively (for example, summary statement first; one heading per objective; in each paragraph, a first sentence that specifies the objective achieved).
- Know *when* to present the report (for example, as soon as possible; he or she makes budget decisions next week).

The specific answers vary with the kind, length, and formality of the document, but the basic principles remain the same, and they hold for all forms of communication. Therefore, keep them in mind when you are designing tables and illustrations, wrestling with outlines, polishing sentences, and even when making decisions about style and format.

3.29 For example, Sections 5.23 through 5.25 describe designs of tables that emphasize different aspects of the same data. Chapter 6 describes different forms of illustration in terms of the purposes you might have and the features of design that will emphasize those purposes. Chapter 7 discusses reader, purpose, scope and plan, and different ways to outline the same information. The only difference, as with the discussion of tables, is what aspect you want to emphasize. Chapter 11 describes the nonverbal messages in format and style that you can use to emphasize arguments, and Chapter 12 describes treatments of text that enhance arguments.

A Comparative Analysis

3.30 With these principles in mind, consider the analysis necessary for two documents on the same topic—recommendations for word processing equipment—but with different answers to most of the questions in Section 3.28. The first document, to recommend a policy on purchases, is for a board of managers, who will act on it at their spring meeting. The document will be 50 to 60 pages long and will have four major sections: analysis of the organization's need, cost and capabilities of different vendors, benefits and organizational changes, and policy recommendations. Analysis probably would lead you to decide that to use the document most easily, trustees need the recommendations first; headings and subheadings throughout so they can find topics and subtopics easily; comparative statistics in tables; and a table of contents on the front. Finally, if you send the report a month before the meeting, the trustees will have time to read it.

3.31 The second document, to report evaluation of specific equipment, is for the manager of your division. What he or she wants to know is whether the equipment will meet the division's needs, and if so, how much would it cost and whether you would recommend purchase. Analysis probably would lead you to decide that the best form is a short memo in which the first sentence states your recommendation. The rest of the memo should give information on cost and capability in the context of the recommendation. The reason for this organization is that facts in isolation don't mean much. Eventually, the manager might interpret the facts differently, but you will have helped him or her start thinking by offering a context to start with. Given this analysis, the memo might say something like:

> I recommend purchase of Fribble's model Z because it can provide 500 pages of text on a hard disk in addition to pages stored on floppy disks. Also, it can support four work stations and two printers. Model Z costs $35,000, which is $15,000 more than the Model Y, but the Y only allows access to 80 pages of text at a time—too few for documents the size of ours.

3.32 On both documents, note the need for an unbiased evaluation of data and a persuasive treatment of recommendations (described in Sections 1.9 and 1.10). In the first document, recommendations will come first; the rest of the report will contain data to support the recommendations. In the second example, the entire document is shaped by the writer's decision about what to recommend. The rest of the document contains very little supporting data. Conclusions and recommendations must always be faithful to data; should the manager want details, the writer should be able to supply it. The manager, in turn, should be able either to draw the same conclusion as the writer or to understand the writer's reasons. However, much of the time managers don't ask; they depend on the writer to draw ethically sound, analytically responsible conclusions. Hence, the burden is on writers to base persuasive writing on the most faithful possible interpretation of data.

Sources of Help

3.33 When a document is long, and especially when it draws findings from a large amount of data, you may need additional help with analysis. In such cases:

- Read similar reports, articles, and so forth for ideas.
- Read Chapters 2 through 4 in Lesikar (1974).
- Then read textbooks on the methods used. You may also need to consult with an expert on the method or with a computer programmer who can help you adapt a method to your computer system.
- Before developing a computer program, ask your supervisor or co-workers or a computer consultant about "packaged programs," such as the Statistical Package for the Social Sciences (SPSS), that already exist and that will do the job for you.

4 | Word Processing Systems and Automation in Writing

4.1 Word processing (the term is spelled different ways by different writers) can automate writing just as computers have automated data analysis and business management. Introduced with the Magnetic Tape Selectric Typewriter (MT/ST) in 1964, word processing equipment now ranges from home microcomputer-based and office stand-alone (self-contained) units through large office units and computer-based systems. Among the larger systems are shared-logic, multiterminal word processors that share the intelligence, storage, and power of a central computer; cluster shared-logic systems, in which each cluster is independent; and distributed-logic word processors that appear from the outside to be much like shared-logic systems, but actually distribute intelligence to operating stations (Datapro 1978). To operators the three kinds seem identical, but distributed logic and cluster equipment have a major advantage: a system malfunction won't necessarily stop all word processing.

4.2 McCabe and Popham (1977) describe in interesting, readable, and useful detail the development of the word processing revolution and the change it has caused in office structure and function. They define *word processing* by itself as the "automation of document production [and] the combination of people, procedures, and equipment that transforms ideas into printed communications and helps facilitate the flow of related office work" (McCabe and Popham 1977, p. 32). A *word processing system* combines equipment and personnel in "an environment of job specialization and supervisory controls for the purpose of producing typed documents in a routinized, cost-effective manner" (McCabe and Popham 1977, p. 32). Datapro (1978), another excellent and detailed resource, has a highly useful glossary and criteria for choosing equipment.

4.3 Advertisers provide concrete details to flesh out abstract descriptions. For example:

> Text is typed at a keyboard and is immediately displayed on a video screen. At the same time, it is memorized by the machine. The text then may be modified without retyping it. It can be stored on magnetic diskette and later retrieved for further changes. At any time, drafts of the text can be printed on a typewriter-quality automatic printer. Finally, the document can be modified and then reprinted as many times as desired. A good [word processor] can almost completely eliminate the use of paper, pencil, and typewriter [as tools for writing] (Vector Graphic n.d., p. 1).

What Good Word Processing Equipment Can Do

4.4 McCabe and Popham (1977) give a wealth of information on word processors like Lanier's and Wang's, which are meant primarily for word processing. Warren (1978) describes the variety of processors, including those on microcomputers, available at the end of 1978. Among the word processors available on microcomputers, Vector Graphic's WORD MANAGEMENT SYSTEM is particularly easy to use. Prices on systems like Lanier's start about $11,000. Microcomputer systems start about $7,000. These figures include the printer—at between $2,800 and $4,000, by far the most expensive piece of equipment. (One caution to readers: word processing equipment has been changing very rapidly. The vendors and prices mentioned in this chapter are accurate for 1979 and may not be accurate in later years.)

4.5 This section describes briefly some of the more valuable features of word processing equipment. Not all equipment provides all these features. For example, only a few provide super- and subscripts without human intervention. However:

□ If you are unfamiliar with word processing equipment, treat this section as an introduction to the topic.
□ If you are evaluating word processing equipment for lease or purchase, ask about these features.
□ As you read, keep in mind the kinds of typing your office does; short letters and memos don't require the on-line storage that you need to process long documents effectively. The *functions* you need should be your most important concern. Also read McCabe and Popham (1977) and Datapro (1978).

To get a "feel" for what word processing can do for writers, read the articles by Frankenthaler (1976) and Pournelle (1979). Neither writer had ever worked on a computer before beginning to use word processors.

General Features

4.6 Some general features of some word processing equipment save time by permitting the same action on several documents simultaneously, by permitting the use of indexing, accounting, and other programs, by automating numbering, and by speeding communication between offices.

4.7 *Wild card procedures.* "Wild card" procedures enable systematic change in several documents at once. For example, if you are writing about word processing and accidentally hyphenate the two words in several chapters, you could make a single, wild card change that would affect all chapters. In the following example:
□ "C" means "change."
□ The slashes act as "delimiters"—the first two enclose all and only the first "string," or exact set, of characters and spaces to be changed.
The second and third delimiters enclose all and only the second string—the exact set of characters and spaces that the writer wants to replace the first string.
□ *.WRD means "change all instances of the first string to the second string, in all documents, or files, whose file names have the index code WRD as a suffix":

C/word-process/word process/*.WRD

4.8 *Interface with computer programs.* Some word processors enable document (file) naming systems that make retrieval easier and catalog systems easier to maintain. For example, a book on word processing might logically call its chapters 1.WRD, 2.WRD, 3.WRD, and so forth. To print a single copy of the entire book, then, a typist would only need a single command to call the chapters from storage and print them. For example, something like:

GET,PRINT:1,2,3,4,5,6.WRD

where GET and PRINT are a sequence of commands, separated (delimited) from the statement of what to GET and PRINT (here, the first six chapters of the word processing book).

4.9 Some systems allow nonprinted coding within the text of a document so the writer can use an index program (supplied with the word processor) to scan an entire document, build an index from the coded words and phrases, and then format it. Sections 11.11, 13.9, 13.17, 13.47, and 13.63 describe computer programs, based on string procedures, that can (1) diagnose poor writing and (2) in some cases improve it. Other internal coding systems allow typists and writers to insert notes and reminders to themselves. Still other codes may "call" other segments of text, such as the addresses from a mailing list (to be sequenced with repeated copying of a form letter) or variant paragraphs (again, for form letters). And still others automatically create tables of contents and lists of tables and illustrations, complete with page numbers, from the text. Finally, some systems come with accounting programs that automatically record time spent by document and operator, thus easing the tasks of billing, evaluating workers, and estimating the cost of future work.

4.10 In 1979, manufacturers were just beginning to exploit mergers between data processing and word processing equipment. Hurwitz (1979) describes advantages and disadvantages, specific equipment, and prospects for the future.

4.11 *Automatic numbering of lists.* Most writers know the frustration of discovering one or more additional items that must be inserted in a set of instructions, tables or illustrations (usually at the beginning!).

Some word processors solve this problem simply by allowing the typist to specify the beginnings and ends of lists, or the first and last tables and illustrations in a set. Then, when the processor formats the document for printing, it counts the items and inserts the numbers in sequence.

4.12 *Communication with other offices.* Communicating typewriters can communicate between distant offices, over long-distance telephone lines. The equipment on the receiving end types the copy at a rate of several hundred words per minute. This ability allows a firm with many offices to communicate rapidly and to distribute a workload evenly among several widely separated word processing centers in an organization.

4.13 *Other features.* Some equipment permits "time sharing," so several typists and several printers can work at the same time on the same system. Also, some systems allow on-line storage of 100 or more pages of text—a feature of great importance to typists working on reports and other documents whose single chapters or sections may exceed 30 pages in length. Also important to report writers is the ability to draw graphs on the system and then access them for use as illustrations.

Characteristics of Input

4.14 Formatting can occur either via commands, which the operator enters with text, or by use of command keys as needed. The transcriptionist may type the words on paper or into a CRT (cathode ray tube) paperless terminal for recording on disks, diskettes, cartridge tape, magnetic tape, or magnetic cards. Equipment that uses a CRT, especially in conjunction with command keys rather than written commands entered with text, usually is easier for typists to learn. Computer-based systems, like the Alpha-Micro's TXTFMT and Applied Data Research, Inc.'s ETC, usually have commands. The WORD MANAGEMENT SYSTEM works mostly without commands.

4.15 Some features that make typing easier are:

□ Continuous, or scrolled, text so typists don't have to type a carriage return at the end of each line of typing, and the processor can read an entire document as if it were a single line. (When the processor has to read each typed line individually—much as it would have to read punched computer cards individually—string location and change commands, defined in Section 4.17, can't find phrases typed partly at the end of one line and partly at the beginning of the next.)

- ▢ "Macro" commands that call in previously stored strings of text, such as the open square that precedes the word "macro" in this sentence.
- ▢ Easy tabulation, indenting, and centering.
- ▢ Easy underlining and shift functions (for capitalization).
- ▢ Ability to specify, at the beginning of a document, a page number and running head (top or bottom, left, right, or alternating), spacing, margin width, type density (10 or 12 characters/spaces per inch), right justification (even margins on both sides), boldface, number of lines per printed page, amount of space between paragraphs, format of headings at each level, and so forth.
- ▢ Ability to change these features at will and to specify additional space at specific points in a manuscript, such as above and below headings and quotations.

Corrections

4.16 During typing, the typist can correct errors simply by backspacing and typing the correction over the original. Even though paper will show strikeovers, the storage medium will have recorded the correction. On most CRTs, the correction instantly replaces the original on the screen.

4.17 Corrections of a draft after rewriting are nearly as easy. Editing features in word processing systems allow typists to get a copy of the document from a disk, tape, card, or cassette, and:

- ▢ Replace words, lines, paragraphs, and pages.
- ▢ Move sentences or paragraphs around.
- ▢ Insert words, sentences, and paragraphs.
- ▢ Change the style of headings, tables, and citations.
- ▢ Change the spacing of columns in tables without retyping the data in the columns.
- ▢ In a single operation on a whole document, search for and

change all misspellings and misused words and phrases the writer wants systematically changed. This feature, called a "global" or "string" change, is like the wild card change described in Section 4.8 and is especially useful for tailoring boiler plates (described in Chapter 9) for specific clients.

□ Pull in sections of boiler plate from other documents.
□ Automatically adjust line length, margins, and justification to incorporate the changes.
  NOTE: One great timesaver here—because unedited portions of a document remain the same, proofreaders only have to recheck the edited portions.

Output Format

4.18 When the text is ready for final typing, or printing, the typist issues a command, pushes a button, or puts the text through a "postprocessor" that prepares it for printing. When the word processor uses written commands, the postprocessor strips them away from the "output," or typed, file as it executes them. (This doesn't destroy the commands on the "input," or working, file. The output file is only a form of the text suitable for readers who need words, not bits of binary data.) Some word processors require the postprocessor to inspect the processed text for:

□ "Widows," such as a header at the end of a page or a single last line of a paragraph at the top of a page, and prevent them by forcing the text to begin on a new page earlier than it otherwise would.
□ Automatic nesting of lists and outline forms, with automatic counting and renumbering, so writers can add items without having to renumber all subsequent items.
□ A call for tables and illustrations that would type them on pages with text, with appropriate spacing and lines above and below (specifiable by commands in the input file).
□ Ability also to specify whether table or illustration is to appear all on one page, or whether it may be broken over two pages.
□ Ability to call footnotes for printing at bottoms of pages.
□ Ability to access address lists—useful for form letters and questionnaires.
□ Automatic alphabetizing of reference lists.

□ Ability to "string" together several documents such as chapters of a book.

Miscellaneous

4.19 When the word processor is part of a computer system, the following are desirable features:

□ Easy back-up procedures to protect documents in case the system "crashes" (breaks down).
□ Ability to write programs that will do repetitive jobs automatically.
□ Easy indexing, with ability to specify printed format and to reorganize and change levels of entries. Belnap (1977) describes such a program.
□ An indexed "bank" for bibliographic items with ability to extract and print specified items.
□ Ability to list the input document (text and associated commands) as well as the version processed for print.
□ Protection from momentary fluctuation in electrical power.
□ Ability to hold in memory contents of one disk or tape while waiting for additional contents from another.
□ Library system to keep track of file names and codes for what is in them.
□ Several high-speed upper- and lowercase printers.
□ Several NEC, Diablo, or Qume printers with tractor feed (the "tractor" allows users to print on either regular paper or special computer paper with snap-off sides and continuous feed).

The Nature of Word Processing Systems

Personnel and Office Structure

4.20 Word processing systems radically change traditional personnel requirements and division of labor in offices. The more retyping an office has (in contrast to original typing), even if writers want many and complicated changes, the greater the savings in time and cost of personnel. When word processing is available, private secretaries no longer are a necessity. Typists become technicians, supervised by a word processing supervisor or administrator. For nontyping secretarial duties traditionally performed by the private secretary, several executives may share a single administrative assistant.

4.21 Although many executives resist giving up a private secretary, the traditional secretary with an ordinary typewriter normally produces only about 100 lines of mailable typed copy each day (McCabe and Popham 1977, p. 22). Typists with word processing equipment can produce many times more, with much less human effort, and at much lower cost. To document these facts, in Chapter 6 McCabe and Popham give case studies of different organizations with different word processing needs. The studies would convince even the most traditional executive that having a private secretary no longer makes economic sense.

4.22 When you buy a word processor, look for equipment that has simple, readable instructions and lots of examples. Don't buy without trying the instructions yourself and giving typists a chance to try them. When you install word processing equipment for the first time, prepare in advance for different personnel requirements and organizational structure. McCabe and Popham (1977, Chapter 4) list in detail qualifications for positions and suggest additional readings. Chapter 5 describes the human aspects of word processing. Datapro (1978) gives additional information.

How Words Go In

4.23 Sometimes text enters via optical scanning equipment, described in Section 4.29, which reads typed pages and transfers words directly to memory. The process is expensive, especially when documents haven't been typed on special equipment. However, organizations that are just beginning to use word processors can use optical scanners to put all documents on at once, without waiting until someone can type them on.

4.24 In ordinary, everyday use, words enter the system primarily through dictation to a machine because dictation to a secretary takes up two people's time unnecessarily. And also, handwriting and typing produce drafts much more slowly than dictation does. Mc-

Cabe and Popham (1977, pp. 23–30) describe two different kinds of dictation equipment—discrete media and endless loop.

4.25 *Discrete units.*Individual, discrete dictation equipment has been around for decades. As time passed, the old cylinders and belts gradually gave way to modern magnetic belts, disks, cassettes, and tapes. Some units fit in the user's pocket, others stay on the desk. However, for most organizations of any size, individual units make less sense than centralized systems.

4.26 Centralized, discrete equipment features automatic changers that permit "continuous central recording of dictation without the need for constantly changing the recording medium" (McCabe and Popham 1977, p. 23). Nevertheless, the medium must be removed by hand for transcription. Some systems now operate via telephone lines, even from outside the office and on long distance, so writers no longer need to take the equipment with them. Some systems even have VOR—a feature that activates a recorder when a voice sounds and stops it after more than five seconds of silence so the medium won't have long patches of silence to waste the typist's time. McCabe and Popham describe in detail the various companies and equipment.

4.27 *Endless loop systems.* Endless loop, or tank-type, systems record on tape that is sealed in a tank and loops around endlessly. Because no one needs to remove the medium, the tank can be stored in some little-used corner. These systems can expand as an organization grows; can operate via telephones; can be supervised from a console; and allow supervisors to distribute work to typists and erase completed dictation with the aid of an internal computer. A major advantage over discrete media is that transcriptionists no longer need to wait for the system to eject the medium. They can type along just a short distance behind the writer. When a report or proposal is rushed, then, dictators can have finished drafts almost as soon as they have finished dictating. McCabe and Popham describe a variety of companies and equipment.

Printing

4.28 Most of the time printing occurs on a printer such as the Qume or Diablo or NEC, but some firms also buy high-speed line printers and thermal printers for intermediate drafts.

4.29 A relatively recent development is the ability to go directly from tape or disk to print via a conversion process that reads the typing instructions and translates them for reading by photocomposition equipment. When text is in that form, operators can use a stand-alone, CRT-equipped microcomputer to add printing instructions (boldface, lightface, italics, and so forth). Because the words have transferred directly, there is no possibility of textual errors that did not exist in the typed copy. As a result, when writers proofread, they only need to check the effect of the printing instructions. Optical character recognition (OCR) equipment can accomplish the same result by scanning specially typed pages and transmitting the words and printing instructions directly to memory without "rekeyboarding" (retyping). As a result, even organizations without word processing equipment can go directly from type to print if they wish.

Summary of Advantages

General

4.30 Some of the general advantages are obvious. Typists no longer need correction fluid or paper to produce perfect typing, and the final copy has no blemishes on it. Offices need not be swimming in old drafts. With CRT systems, nothing needs to be put on paper until a typist is satisfied with it, and if old disks are saved there is often no need for file copies of letters (which saves paper, filing, and copying costs). Communicating systems (described in detail by McCabe and Popham 1977, pp. 17–18) allow nearly instant transmission of documents between offices that are separated by hundreds of miles. String changes allow correction of all identical mistakes at the same time.

Special Advantages for Typing Documents

4.31 Special applications of these and other features make word processing systems indispensible for technical writing. String changes allow tailoring of boiler plates. File copying enables typists to build documents from previously stored paragraphs. The result can be a will, a report, an advertising letter, a form, a questionnaire—or anything else a writer wants to create. Editing features allow instant corrections; file copying and editing can combine to yield alternate versions of the same text. Endless loop dictation can enable typists to give drafts back to writers shortly after they have finished dictating.

4.32 When standard outlines (described in Chapter 8) are kept on a word processing system, typists can modify them for writers to use as checklists or as models for prospective clients. Bibliographic items can be collected and stored for quick, easy printing when the writing is done. Forms for tables can be called from storage when data are ready for entry. Some systems even provide programs for plotting and printing graphs. And some systems, especially those on large computer systems, provide cross-referencing, indexing, and automatic numbering of chapters, paragraphs, and so forth.

II. ORGANIZING AND STANDARDIZING INFORMATION

5 | Tables: Principles, Formats, and Design

5.1 Text is only one way to tell others about a fact or idea. Tables, equations, graphs, and other illustrations can communicate some kinds of information better and more clearly and briefly than text can, and some information can be presented only in tables and illustrations. This chapter discusses the preparation, use, and design of tables. Chapter 6 discusses the same aspects of illustrations, especially charts and graphs. Both tables and illustrations are discussed before writing because many reseachers begin a document by constructing tables and illustrations from which they subsequently write the text. In general, the longer the document the more likely the need for tables and illustrations. Writers who don't use tables and illustrations can skip Chapters 5 and 6 and go on to Chapter 7.

5.2 In general, use tables instead of text when:

- They make a point more clearly than you can make it in text alone.
- The information in them is not duplicated in the text or in other tables, equations, or illustrations.
- In the text you want to discuss the information and perhaps draw conclusions.
- Writing the information in text would take at least three times as much page space (this criterion is especially important in documents being prepared for publication).

Do not use them solely to impress readers.

Definitions and General Principles

Definition

5.3 Tables are systematic arrays of numbers or words that display values in rows and columns. Use a table when:

- You have no fewer than 9 entries (and preferably 16 or more), and relationships in the data will be clearer in a table than in text.
- Its use will reduce the amount of discussion you would otherwise need in text. For example, when data in a table show a trend clearly, the text only needs to point out the trend; the writer doesn't need to mention each supporting figure.

In instructions, writers can use tables to summarize descriptive information such as error messages or codes. The systematic presentation helps all readers, and the tables can be taken out and used separately by experienced personnel who no longer need a full set of instructions.

General Principles

5.4 The general principles are:

- Arrange analytic tables so readers can see comparisons and test inferences easily. For example, when you want to compare the information in two columns, plan the table so that the columns are next to each other.
- Make the general topic of the table clear in the title, the column and boxheads, and the row stubs (defined in Sections 5:8 through 5.11). Use notes to give sources and explain abbreviations. Readers should depend on the text only for explanations and interpretations.
- Don't mix different kinds of information in the same column.
- Construct in similar format tables that use similar data, analyses, and descriptions. For example, when you use the format in Table 5.3 for a correlation analysis, use that format for all similar correlation analyses in the same manuscript.
- Use the same terms in headings and row stubs. For example, don't use "passenger cars" in one table and "coaches" in another as headings for columns that give information on train

cars for passengers. Don't use "education" in one table and "grades completed" in another as row stubs that label data on how much education people have completed.

□ For information on presentation of statistical information, such as analysis of variance and error mean squares, consult Linton's *Simplified Style Manual* (1972, pp. 104-6) for different ways to present them.

Parts of a Table

5.5 *Table number*. The table number, shown at the top of Figure 5.1, permits easy identification and reference. When a document contains very few tables and figures, sometimes they are not numbered. In general, however:

□ Number tables separately from illustrations (which are defined in Section 6.2 and discussed in detail in Chapter 6), and list the two categories separately in the front matter.

□ Use sequential arabic numerals (1, 2, 3, and so on) throughout a document.

□ When a document has several chapters, use sequential numbers preceded by the chapter number and a decimal point. For example, the tables in this chapter are numbered 5.1, 5.2, and so forth.

□ In text, refer to tables by number and not by title.

Style for capitalization and placement of number and title can vary. The examples in this chapter show a variety of styles, or designs, for number, title, and other aspects of style; for discussion of style, see Sections 5.28 through 5.45.

5.6 *Table title*. The title should indicate clearly and briefly the topic of the table. For example, for Table 5.1, "Trends in Transportation" would be too telegraphic a title. In contrast, "Number of Passengers Who Used Trolleys, Trains, Subways, and Buses, in the North, South, East, and Far West, from 1900-1919, 1920-1945, 1946-1955, 1956-1965, 1966-1980, and 1981-2000" would be too detailed. In general:

□ Omit from the title information that is contained in row stubs, column heads, and spanner heads (defined in Sections 5.8 through 5.11).

TABLE 5.1

TITLE OF TABLE TO SHOW PARTS OF A TABLE

| Stubhead | Example of Boxhead[1] | | |
	Cost in Dollars	Column Head	Percentages
Spanner Head (Goes <u>Below</u> Column Heads)[1]			
Row stub	$ 10	4	1.0%
Row stub	110	100	15.3
Subordinate stub	1250	64	112.2
Second subordinate	1540	. . .	14.6
Row stub	3	1.2	.1
Second Spanner Head			
Row stub	$ 1567	0	2.6%
Subordinate stub	12	. . .	27.9
Subordinate stub	278	1765	281.0
Row stub	1567	0	0.0

Source: Mullins (1980, p.6).

Notes: General notes apply to the entire table.

[1]Specific notes apply only to the designated entries. Subordinate stubs and spanners are not present in every table.

FIGURE 5.1.   Illustration of parts of a table

In Table 5.1, the spanner heads give the specific dates, the column heads specify the geographic areas, and the row stubs list the types of transportation.

5.7 *Body*. The body is the entries in a table. The entries go in *cells* formed by the intersection of rows and columns. Each entry describes a relationship between the row and the column that intersected to form the cell that contains the entry. Construct the body according to the following general principles:

□ Use as few entries as possible without eliminating vital information.

- Within each table, use the same rules for retaining decimals and for rounding.
- Arrange entries so that the most important comparisons are between adjacent numbers.
- To prevent confusion of percentages and numbers, place a percent sign after the first number in a column of percentages

TABLE 5.1 *Number of Users of Mass Transportation in Four Geographic Areas, Between 1900 and 2000*

Kind of Transp.	North	South	Midwest	Far West
Between 1900 and 1919				
Trolleys				
Trains				
Subways				
Buses				
Between 1920 and 1945				
Trolleys				
Trains				
Subways				
Buses				
Between 1946 and 1955				
. . . .				
. . . .				
Between 1956 and 1965				
. . . .				
. . . .				
Between 1966 and 1980				
. . . .				
. . . .				
Between 1981 and 2000				
. . . .				
. . . .				

that add up to 100 percent. Also use "percentage" in the column heading.

▫ When a column head does not apply to an item in a row stub, leave the cell (intersection) blank.

▫ Use three or more dots (leaders) when you have no data for a given cell. When the quantity in a cell is zero, enter "0." For more detail, see Section 14.20.

▫ When rounding prevents the sum of percentages in an additive column from totaling 100 percent, say so in a footnote.

▫ Use as few horizontal lines as possible.

▫ Don't use vertical lines; instead, use variable spacing to separate and group columns. See Sections 5.34 through 5.38 for help.

▫ Don't use intersecting lines to connect items in different columns.

5.8 *Stub.* Stubs, or names of rows, are in the far left column. The names should be as short as clarity will permit. Within each table, they should also be grammatically parallel and conceptually equivalent. For example, in Table 5.1 use "trains" and "buses," not "trains" and "local commuting." Abbreviations are often useful; for example, f = female and m = male, or N, S, E, W for North, South, East, and West. When you use the same abbreviations in several tables:

▫ Use an explanatory footnote in the first table.

▫ Don't repeat the note in later tables. When several sections or chapters have intervened, add to the later tables a note that refers readers to the table that contains the explanation.

5.9 *Boxhead, column head, and stubhead.* A boxhead usually describes a group of two or more columns of the same kind, but it can also be the name of a single column. For example, in Table 5.2, if the writer were to divide the column head "Far West" into "California" and "All Other States," then all four geographic areas would become boxheads because they are at the same level of importance. Column head, a more specific term, describes what is in a column. A stubhead, which is a specific column head, describes the column of row stubs. Figure 5.1 shows examples of all three. The basic principles are:

▫ Make boxheads grammatically parallel and conceptually equivalent to each other, following the guidelines in Section 5.8. The same principle holds for column heads and stubheads. For example, in Table 5.1, the column heads are all geographic areas.

□ When you use abbreviations, add them to the table in a note, following the instructions in Section 5.8.

□ Read Sections 5.19 through 5.25 for ideas on how to use boxheads to construct efficient, effective tables that (1) avoid repeating words in column heads and (2) parallel the outline for the accompanying text.

5.10 *Columns and stub columns.* Columns are vertical collections of entries. The stub column is simply the column of row stubs, or of row stubs and their subcategories. As with boxheads and column heads, stubs and substubs can prevent repetition and reflect divisions and subdivisions in an outline. In general:

□ Omit columns that readers could calculate from other columns.

□ When stubs have substubs, indent the subcategories at least one space from the margin to distinguish them from the row stub they subdivide. Make the subcategories syntactically and conceptually equivalent, as explained in Section 5.8.

□ Follow the instructions in Sections 5.16 through 5.18 and Sections 5.23 through 5.25 for ideas on how to use stubs and substubs to construct tables that parallel the outline for text.

5.11 *Spanner head.* By spanning the width of a table, spanner heads permit writers to divide tables into sections or to group several batches of data that have the same column heads. Tables 5.1 and 5.2 use six and four spanners, respectively. In books, designers often delete the lines around spanners and use italics to display them. For example, see Table 5.2 (in type, underlining is the substitute for italic). For more information on style, see Sections 5.39 through 5.45.

5.12 *Notes.* Tables may have three types of note: source, general, and specific. Figure 5.1 shows examples of all three. The purposes are these:

□ Source notes show the sources of all data that do not originate in the research being reported.

□ General notes give information that pertains to the entire table. For example, you might want to report the exact question used

TABLE 5.2 *Number of Users of Various Forms of Mass Transportation in Four Geographic Areas, Between 1900 and 2000*

Years	North	South	Midwest	Far West
Trolleys				
1900–1919				
1920–1945				
1946–1955				
1956–1965				
1966–1980				
1981–2000				
Trains				
1900–1919				
1920–1945				
1946–1955				
1956–1965				
1966–1980				
1981–2000				
Subways				
· · · ·				
· · · ·				
Buses				
· · · ·				
· · · ·				

SOURCE: Mullins (1980, p. 12).

NOTE: This table shows a different style of spanner and a style for the table number and note (all caps, second lines indented) that makes both stand out on a page.

[1] Type specific notes last; indent turnover lines so first letter in each subsequent line begins exactly under first letter in first word in first line.

to elicit certain data, or to describe how you counted passengers on buses.

□ Specific notes explain specific entries.

Figure 5.1 shows numeric superscripts for specific notes, but some styles require superscript letters, especially when the cells of the table contain numbers, and some scientific styles require that writers designate notes of statistical significance with one or more asterisks. Chemists, whose tables often contain both numbers and letters, often use a sequence of asterisks, daggers, double daggers, section marks, and so forth.

Formats

Common Formats for Tables

5.13 Formats for cross-tabulation, analysis of variance, regression, and other types of table are shown in many textbooks on methodology and statistics and in some style manuals. Tables 5.1 and 5.2 show ways to summarize statistics. Tables 5.3 and 5.4 show two ways to present correlation analyses. Zeisel's *Say It With Figures*

TABLE 5.3 *Correlations Between [Independent Variables] and X, Y, and Z (Two Measures Each)*

	X		Y		Z	
	A1	A2	A1	A2	A1	A2
Variable	2	2	3	3	2	2
Measure	2	2	3	3	2	2
Measure	2	2	3	3	2	2
Variable	2	2	3	3	2	2
Measure	2	2	3	3	2	2
Measure	2	2	3	3	2	2
Variable	2	2	3	3	2	2
Measure	2	2	3	3	2	2
Measure	2	2	3	3	2	2
Variable	2	2	3	3	2	2
Measure	2	2	3	3	2	2
Measure	2	2	3	3	2	2
Variable	2	2	3	3	2	2
Measure	2	2	3	3	2	2
Measure	2	2	3	3	2	2

TABLE 5.4 *Associations Between [Independent Variables] and Dependent Variables 1 and 2 (Two Measures Each)*

	Dependent Variable 1			Dependent Variable 2		
		Coefficients			Coefficients	
	Corr.	Unst.	Stnd.	Corr.	Unst.	Stnd.
Variable	2	2	3	3	2	2
Measure	2	2	3	3	2	2
Measure	2	2	3	3	2	2
Variable	2	2	3	3	2	2
Measure	2	2	3	3	2	2
Measure	2	2	3	3	2	2
Variable	2	2	3	3	2	?
Measure	2	2	3	3	2	2
Measure	2	2	3	3	2	2
Variable	2	2	3	3	2	2
Measure	2	2	3	3	2	2
Measure	2	2	3	3	2	2
Variable	2	2	3	3	2	2
Measure	2	2	3	3	2	2
Measure	2	2	3	3	2	2

(1968, Chapter 9) shows many ways to present cross-tabulations. Davis and Jacobs's "Tabular Presentation," in the *International Encyclopedia of the Social Sciences* (1968) shows many ways to arrange tables of percentages. Linton's (1972) *Simplified Style Manual* and the APA *Publication Manual* (1974) show examples of tables that social and behavioral scientists often use.

5.14 When you have trouble finding a tabular format for a batch of numbers, and textbooks and style manuals give no help, you might:

□ Consult articles, books, and reports on topics similar to yours, and ask co-workers for aid. People who have had similar problems and have used similar data have often solved similar problems in constructing their tables.

□ Set up formats as soon as possible after you begin gathering data. Knowing exactly what statistics you need saves you from gathering unnecessary data. Also, properly prepared tables give you a head start on writing.

Condensing Tabular Data

5.15 Both clarity and efficiency dictate combining and condensing tabular data as much as possible. The reasons are:

□ Readers can make comparisons more easily when all the data are in the same table.

□ Combining tables saves space, so typing, typesetting, and reproduction cost less.

□ Because well-designed tables display relationships all at once, so many readers can grasp an argument more quickly from tables than they could from text.

□ Well-designed tables save work time.

5.16 *Vertical combination.* Spanners allow writers to join batches of information that have equal, or *coordinate*, relationships and similar or nearly identical column heads. (Section 7.14 explains coordinate and subordinate relationships.) For example, Tables 5.1 and 5.2 use spanners to identify and separate batches of information that are equally important.

5.17 Similarly, substubs can identify and separate information that subdivides, or is *subordinate to*, a row stub. For example, suppose the researcher discovered that from 1956 on, diesel-powered buses carried far more passengers than buses that used gasoline. She does not need a new table to show that information.[1] Instead, in the bottom three panels of Table 5.1, she can simply add subcategories to the row stub *Buses* in this fashion:

---

[1] Trying to avoid the allegedly sexist male pronouns is one of the modern writer's plagues. By alternating use of examples (like this one) that involve males and females, this book demonstrates one good way to avoid sexist pronouns without resorting to the awkward he/she, him/her, and so forth. This is one of several techniques recommended by the McGraw-Hill Book Company (n.d.).

□ Buses
  Diesel-powered
  Gasoline-powered

5.18 It is acceptable to have:

□ Substubs for some rows but not others.
□ Substubs for *the same row stub* in some panels but not others.
□ Data in some of the cells but not others.

For example, both kinds of bus might have been popular in three geographic areas, but not the fourth. In that case writers simply leave blank the cell for the kind of bus that was not used in that area. For the proper way to treat the cell, see Section 5.7.

5.19 *Horizontal combination.* Information also can be combined horizontally, with boxheads, when the row stubs are the same or when the only difference is that some are omitted. For example, Table 5.3 has several independent variables, listed as row stubs, and several measures of each variable, listed as substubs. In addition, the dependent variables (treated as boxheads) have two measures each (treated as column heads). Table 5.4 shows a similar format that displays, for each of two or more dependent variables, the correlations, unstandardized coefficient, and standardized coefficients.

5.20 If the designer of Table 5.2 had wanted to subdivide the column head "Far West" to show data on California in contrast to all other states in the Far West, he could simply have treated the geographic areas as boxheads and then added column heads beneath the category "Far West," in this manner:

Far West	
California	*Other States*

5.21 In the same table, it is acceptable to:

□ Divide some boxheads but not others.
□ Have data under a boxhead or column head in some panels but not others.

For example, in all parts of Table 5.2, the time periods from 1900 through 1955 might have no data for one or the other kind of bus. Or one kind of transportation might be unknown in one or more geographic areas. In such cases, simply leave the cells blank.

5.22 Sometimes a little imagination helps researchers improve the format of tables. For example, Tables 5.5 through 5.8 might reflect

TABLE 5.5 *Athletic Subtypes: Rank Order of Other Subtypes*

Basketball	Football	Ice Hockey
1	2	3
1	3	2
2	1	3
2	3	1
3	1	2
3	2	1

TABLE 5.6 *Basketball Subtypes: Rank Order of Other Subtypes*

Basketball	Football	Ice Hockey
1	2	3
1	3	2
2	1	3
2	3	1
3	1	2
3	2	1

TABLE 5.7 *Football Subtypes: Rank Order of Other Subtypes*

Basketball	Football	Ice Hockey
1	2	3
1	3	2
2	1	3
2	3	1
3	1	2
3	2	1

TABLE 5.8 *Ice Hockey Subtypes: Rank Order of Other Subtypes*

Basketball	Football	Ice Hockey
1	2	2
1	2	3
2	1	3
2	3	1
3	1	2
3	2	1

someone's first thoughts about how to present data on athletic subtypes, but readers would have to flip from table to table to compare the data. Combining the information horizontally, as in Table 5.9, makes comparison much easier, takes up less space on pages, and saves on typing, proofreading, and reproduction costs. The note to the table explains the abbreviations in simple, readable fashion.

The Relationship Between Tables and Text

Parallel Organization

5.23 Organize tabular data so the format of tables parallels the outline for text. For example, in Outline 7.4 (Section 7.18, Chapter 7), periods of time (for example, 1900 through 1919) make up topics

TABLE 5.9 *Rank Order of Subtypes by Each Subtype*

Athletic			Basketball			Football			Ice Hockey		
B	F	I	B	F	I	B	F	I	B	F	I
1	2	3	1	2	3	1	2	3	1	2	2
1	3	2	1	3	2	1	3	2	1	2	3
2	1	3	2	1	3	2	1	3	2	1	3
2	3	1	2	3	1	2	3	1	2	3	1
3	1	2	3	1	2	3	1	2	3	1	2
3	2	1	3	2	1	3	2	1	3	2	1

NOTE: B=basketball, F=football, I=ice hockey

at the first level of importance. (Section 7.12 explains levels of importance.) Geographic regions are at the second level, and types of transportation are at the third level. If the writer had added information on diesel- and gasoline-powered buses, it would have been at the fourth level of importance, and the table would have included substubs to divide "buses." Therefore, in Table 5.1, the writer uses time periods as spanners to group the data on a given period in the same panel. Reading down columns allows readers to see patterns in the same region over time. Reading across rows allows readers to see patterns in use of a given kind of transportation across regions.

5.24 In contrast, readers would have a relatively hard time tracing patterns in use of a kind of transportation over time, either generally or by region. For those purposes, Table 5.2, which parallels Outline 7.7 and puts all information on a kind of transportation in one horizontal panel, would be more satisfactory. In that case, if the writer had also wanted to subdivide geographic area, he or she would have expressed it in the outline as a subdivision, at the second level of importance, of topic IV. In the table, he would treat "Far West" as a boxhead and add column heads following the procedure described in Section 5.20.

5.25 This kind of planning ahead is much easier for writers who are using standard outlines (explained in Chapter 8). When you are not using a standard outline, follow these steps:

1. Think about the emphasis you want. For example, the designer of Table 5.1 wanted to show trends over time, so she used time periods as spanners.
2. Make an educated guess at format and try it. You may have to try more than one before you find something suitable.
3. When you prepare your outline, follow the pattern in the tables. When that pattern doesn't work, redesign the table so the text and tables parallel and support each other. If you don't, readers will have a hard time following your argument even though they probably won't be able to say why.

Identical Terms

5.26 Choose carefully the terms used in row stubs and column heads. Also:

□ Be sure they describe phenomena accurately, or at least (when shortened or abbreviated) will unfailingly call to the reader's mind the meaning you intended.

For example, when you have several tables that report data on the variable "job status," use that term in *all* tables and text; don't use, say, "occupational status" for variety. If one variable were "ratio of doctors to women in the population of an area," and you had no other variable that was a ratio of doctors to some other group in the population, as an abbreviation you might use "M.D. ratio" or "M.D. ratio to women," but certainly not "physician density." If you had another variable that included the ratio of doctors, you would have to use the longer abbreviation. Readers follow an argument much more easily when writers take care to use the same terms every time, in both text and tables. (Contrary to popular belief, readers don't get bored—only the writer.) When abbreviations are necessary:

□ As closely as possible, use words from the full term, in the same order (but take care not to create unintelligible strings of noun modifiers; for help see Section 13.45).

Using the same terms is more than a tremendously powerful non-verbal way of building support for an argument; it also saves the time of thinking up ways to vary prose, and it usually shortens text, which in turn reduces the cost of typing, proofreading, and repro-duction.

5.27 When you are using word processing equipment with string, or global, search capabilities (defined in Section 4.17), you can easily check the text and tables for variations you might have used, and change them. (Chapter 4 describes in detail the use of word processing systems.)

How to Create Good Designs for Tables

5.28 Good designs begin with deciding what message you want a table to convey. For example, when you want to compare two columns of figures, design the table with those columns next to each other. When tables will be typed on pages with text, use a design that will make the tables stand out from the text (see Section 5.32).

Sections 5.29 through 5.45 discuss just a few of the more important, yet easy, ways to enhance a message through careful use of design and style. Four basic principles govern choices about design and style. The principles can be summarized in these four words:

- □ Emphasis.
- □ Simplicity.
- □ Consistency.
- □ Distinctiveness.

Sections 11.19 through 11.35 explain these principles in detail.

Physical Relation of Tables to Text

5.29 When you are writing a manuscript for possible publication or for an organization that forbids tables on pages with text:

- □ Place each table on a separate piece of paper.
- □ Check style requirement of the publisher to find out *where* in the text to put the pages and whether to assign page numbers. Possibilities are immediately after the page on which you discuss each table, or all together at the end of the manuscript; and with or without typed page numbers.
- □ Type no bars or lines (also called rules) across the page either above the title or below the notes.
- □ Use *no* vertical bars.

5.30 When you have a choice about whether to type tables onto pages of text:

- □ Type onto text pages the tables that take up less than three-quarters of a sheet of paper.
- □ Begin each table as close as possible to the first mention of it and still get the entire table typed on the same page. You may insert it either just before or just after the first mention in text.
- □ Type on a separate page tables that are longer than three-quarters of a page. Some tables may even require several pages.

Occasionally an organization's style or printing requirements will demand that you type *all* tables into the text, regardless of length.

5.31 When the document has been typed on word processing equipment, ask whether it can "call" tables into the text at the places where you want them. When that convenience is available, typists can type tables separately and still provide finished drafts that show a variety of placements in the text.

5.32 When typing tables onto pages with text, design pages to make the tables stand out. Two simple techniques are:

□ Ask typists to leave an extra line or two of space between the last line of text before the table and the first line of text after the table.

□ Into that space draw or type one or two closely set horizontal lines, exactly the width of the table. Put these lines above and below the table.

□ When the organization for which you are writing does not have conflicting requirements, choose a style for table number and title that will make the number stand out. For help, see Sections 5.40 and 5.41.

CAUTION: In the same document, use the same style for all tables—those in text and those on separate pages.

Space and Lines Within Tables

5.33 Tables have three sections—the number and title, the body, and the notes. To emphasize these sections, in general:

□ After the title, leave a space followed by one or two closely set horizontal lines, followed by another space, before beginning the body.

□ After the body, leave a space followed by one bar, followed by another space, before beginning the notes.

5.34 *Vertical grouping within the body.* When you want to group categories vertically or improve the readability of a table with more than six row stubs:

□ Vary the spacing.

For example, in Table 5.2 there are double spaces between each spanner and its associated row stubs. Between the last stub in each set and the next spanner, however, there are triple spaces. The alternation of double-spacing and triple-spacing gives visual emphasis to the grouping of each variable with its measures.

5.35 When a table has more than six row stubs and no substubs to break up the spacing:

□ Every fourth or fifth row, skip a space. When the table is already double-spaced, skip an additional space.

Especially when columns are far apart, the additional space groups the row stubs and the entries in batches small enough so that the reader's eye is less likely to slip up or down when reading across the rows.

CAUTION: Don't use leaders (a row of dots from the end of each row stub to the entry in the first cell) or lines or hand-drawn brackets to accomplish this effect. They only clutter the page. When the material is for publication, variable spacing usually is the only acceptable treatment.

5.36 *Variable horizontal spacing.* When you want to emphasize groups and subgroups of columns:

□ Vary the horizontal spacing. In general, the minimum allowed between columns is three spaces—when columns are closer than three spaces, readers can't tell where one column stops and another starts.

□ Leave the largest amount of space between categories of column. For example, in Table 5.4 the largest amount of space is between columns 3 (standardized coefficients for dependent variable 1) and column 4 (correlations, dependent variable 2).

□ Leave the next largest amount of space between subcategories. For example, in Table 5.4 the next largest amounts of space are between columns 1 and 2, and columns 4 and 5 (to separate the correlations from the coefficients).

□ Leave the smallest amount of space between columns in the same subcategory. For example, in Table 5.4 the smallest amount of space is between the columns of coefficients—columns 2 and 3, and 5 and 6.

5.37 To determine how many spaces to leave where:

□ Count the number of horizontal spaces required by the longest row stub and the longest entry in each column.

□ Total those numbers and subtract from the total number of spaces in the width of the table.

For example, in elite type, which allows 12 spaces per inch of type, a table that is six inches wide has 72 horizontal spaces. If the longest row stubs and entries totaled 42 spaces, you would have 30 spaces to spread out between columns. Most of the time a typist will do the counting and spacing (and, when the document is on word processing equipment, even may be able to offer several alternatives), but you need to know enough about the process to be able to explain exactly what you want and why.

5.38 On occasion, when you are not preparing tables for publication, you may find useful one or two (closely drawn) vertical lines. In general:

□ Exhaust all the possibilities with space before resorting to lines. Space is simpler, and if the table is to be printed, space is cheaper.
□ Make only one division—usually in the center of the body, to divide left from right.
□ When you have more divisions, use identical lines to divide a table into equal parts.
□ When you are dividing columns into sections and subsections, use closely drawn double lines between equal sections and single lines between subsections.

Editorial Style

5.39 Editorial style has nothing to do with writing style. Instead, the focus is on capitalization, placement on page (centered or flush left), underlining, and so forth. In each section below, the details to watch for are listed first, followed by recommendations to follow when you are not required to adhere to a specific style.

□ As with design, make choices on the basis of emphasis, simplicity, consistency, and distinctiveness. For more detail, see Sections 14.19 through 14.22.

Table Number and Title

5.40 *Details to check.* Styles vary widely in treatment of number and title. Some possible variations are:

□ Number can be arabic (more common) or roman; in appendixes tables may be assigned letters (A.2, A.2) or numbers followed by prime signs (1', 2'). The number may stand by itself or be preceded by the word *table,* which may be completely capitalized or only initially capitalized. The number may be centered on its own line above the title, or flush left with the title following on the same line.

□ The title may be centered beneath the number, with subsequent lines also centered but shorter, with all lines of the title forming an inverted pyramid (this pattern is required by the American Psychological Association's style). Tables 5.1, 5.2, and 5.5 show other varieties of placement.

□ Capitalization and underlining also can vary, as shown in Figures 5.1 and Tables 5.1 and 5.5.

□ Bar above body and below title occasionally is absent.

5.41 *Recommendations.* In the absence of requirements:

□ Capitalize TABLE completely, and the title with initial caps only, to make the table number easy to find on pages of text.

□ For the same reason, put numbers and titles on the same line and indent subsequent lines, following the style in Table 5.2.

Body of Table

5.42 *Details to check.* In the row stubs, column heads, and boxheads:

□ Capitalization may vary. On row stubs and substubs, most styles require sentence capitalization—capitalization only of the first word and any proper nouns. In contrast, for column and boxheads some styles require initial caps on all words except a, *an,* and *the,* and prepositions up to five letters long. The titles of Tables 5.1 and 5.2 follow this style.

□ Indentation of second lines of column headings can vary. Some styles require that subsequent, or "turnover," lines be centered below the first. Others require that all words in a heading be placed flush with the left margin of the column.

5.43 *Recommendations.* In the absence of requirements:

□ Initial caps only, following the rule in Section 13.48, is simplest and least likely to produce typing errors.

□ Center turnover lines of column heads; they look more attractive that way.
□ Indent turnover lines of row stubs one space from the left margin.
□ Indent substubs two spaces and turnover lines an additional space.

Notes

5.44 *Details to check.* Figure 5.1 shows a fairly conventional treatment of notes. Some possible variations are:

□ Capitalization and indentation; Figure 5.1 and Table 5.2 show two different treatments.
□ Order of source, general, and specific notes; some styles put the source note at the bottom, general in the middle, and specific on the top.

5.45 *Recommendations.* Treatment of notes should match treatment of the number and title. If you choose to display TABLE in all caps and indent turnover lines, do the same in the notes with the words SOURCE and NOTES and turnover lines. In the absence of requirements to the contrary, use:

□ All caps on SOURCE and NOTE, and indented turnover lines, following the treatment in Table 5.2.
□ The order shown in Figure 5.1—source, general, and specific notes.

6 | Illustrations: Principles, Kinds, Uses, and Design

6.1 Like tables, illustrations can be more effective than words. In general, use illustrations instead of text when they meet the criteria listed in Section 5.2.

Definitions and General Principles

Definitions

6.2 Illustrations can be line drawings (like path models), paintings, photographs, charts, graphs, diagrams, and maps. They can be line copy (all black and white, with no shading) or continuous-tone (sometimes called halftone) copy, such as wash drawings and photographs, that contain shading. They can be reproduced by letterpress (a fairly restrictive process used in scholarly and trade books) or offset methods. (Fine quality reproduction of paintings in art books uses still a third process—gravure.)

General Principles

6.3 Some of the information on illustrations comes from *A Manual of Style* (1969, Chapter 11), MacGregor's fine articles in *Scholarly Publishing* (1977a,b,c, 1978), and Tukey (1972). For more help see Lesikar (1974, Chapter 7) and Bostick (1979).

6.4 Different kinds of illustration serve different purposes. Each kind has advantages and disadvantages, and no single form can solve all problems. In general, however:

▢ Use charts, graphs, and diagrams to display trends or magnitudes of relationships in data, clarify complex ideas, and show how things work.

▢ Use photographs to present scientific proof or records, show actual color or tone or texture, add aesthetic appeal, or create a mood.

▢ Use drawings or paintings instead of photographs when you want to control the viewer's perception by showing only essential detail. Both can highlight important points, relationships, differences, and changes by changing scale, contrast, and color. Both can simplify shapes, accent details, and show directions and order of sequences, as well as elicit subliminal or psychological responses.

6.5 Good illustrations meet these criteria:

▢ They are relevant, not merely faddish.

▢ They conform to the requirements of emphasis, consistency, simplicity and distinctiveness, as described in Section 11.19.

▢ They add information; duplication should occur only when absolutely necessary to reinforce a crucial idea.

▢ They give information on only one topic.

▢ They are easy to understand.

▢ No other form of illustration would express the topic better.

▢ Reduction (for example, for publication) will not cost important detail.

▢ In the case of drawings, charts, graphs, and diagrams, the artwork is of high quality.

▢ In the case of photographs, all have consistent lighting, background, scale, and so forth.

Kinds and Uses of Charts and Graphs

6.6 Charts and graphs, commonly used in reports and proposals, come in a variety of identifiable types, each of which is better suited for some purposes than others.

Arithmetic Line and Curve Charts

6.7 *General principles.* When you use arithmetic charts, plot time and any other independent variable (variables that change regularly) along the horizontal axis. Plot the dependent variable on the vertical axis. Figures 6.1 through 6.5 show examples. In general, use arithmetic line or curve charts:

- □ To show tendencies or movements, not actual amounts.
- □ To show long series of data.
- □ To compare several series.
- □ To interpolate or extrapolate.

6.8 *Do not use* arithmetic charts:

- □ To emphasize rate of change (use a semilogarithmic chart).
- □ To compare relative size or difference between elements (use a bar or column chart).

6.9 *Specific uses.* Arithmetic charts usually show only Quadrant IV of a graph, but when you have *positive and negative values,* use a chart like Figure 6.1, which includes Quadrants I and IV. The income figures might take a negative value if bad weather during one or more years had forced a fruit-producing state to buy fruit grown outside the state. Not only would the state lose the income it normally received from export; in addition, it would have to spend money on imports.

6.10 To compare a trend with an index or other base measure, use a chart with a *special referent line* like the one in Figure 6.2, which shows the change in the cost of fruit between 1970 and 1995, with reference to the cost in 1980.

6.11 To emphasize a trend, use a *surface or silhouette* chart like Figure 6.3, which shows the decline in income from sales of wheat between 1970 and 1995.

6.12 When you want to compare the trend of a whole with the trend of its parts, use a *multiple surface, or band,* chart like Figure 6.4—total sales and relative popularity of different fruits between 1970 and 1995. The whole is not simply an arithmetic line chart filled in, as is the case with Figure 6.3. Instead, the width of each

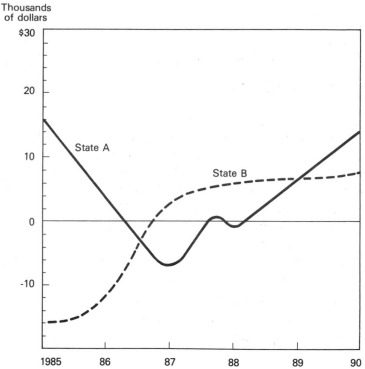

Thousands
of dollars

FIGURE 6.1   Arithmetic Curve Chart: Income from the Sale of Fruit in Two
States, 1985–1990

band has a unique value, and the top line is the total of all values. For example, Figure 6.4 shows that the sale of apples yielded more income than any other kind of fruit; the sale of grapes provided the next largest amount; and the sale of bananas, the least. When you design a multiple surface chart:

□ Place the curve with the least movement next to the horizontal axis, the second smoothest curve next, and so forth.

□ CAUTION: Do not use more than five curves, and do not use this form when the curves move erratically. (Instead, use a divided bar or grouped bar chart, or a simple arithmetic chart; MacGregor, 1977a, p. 153.)

6.13 When you only want to show the trend of the parts of a whole, use a *100% surface chart* like Figure 6.5, which shows the relative contribution of bananas, grapes, apples, and all other fruit to total income from the sale of fruit between 1975 and 2000.

Oval Plots

6.14 Use *oval plots* for trends that are cyclical, such as annual temperature figures. For example, Figure 6.6 compares the monthly temperature cycles of four Arizona airports with the cycles of seven east-coast airports. In comparison to linear plots, the oval plot is a more compact way to present data. Tukey (1972) contains many other kinds of graph that statistically sophisticated readers might find useful.

Column and Bar Charts

6.15 *General principles.* Column charts and bar charts are popular because they are simple, adaptable, and readily understood by lay audiences. In some cases they can interchange with arithmetic line charts. In general:

□ Use column and bar charts to compare magnitude or size; never use squares, cubes, circles, or spheres as a substitute.

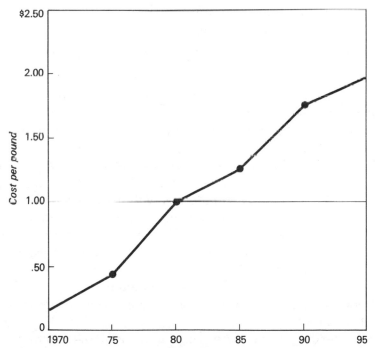

FIGURE 6.2 Chart with Special Referent Line: Change in Cost of Fruit, 1970–1995, with Reference to Cost in 1980

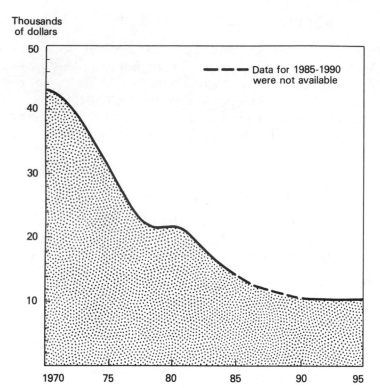

Figure 6.3   Surface Chart: Decline in Income from Wheat, 1970–1990

- Use column charts to emphasize differences in one item at *different* points in time.
- *Do not use* column charts to show trends (use an arithmetic line chart like the one in Figure 6.1).
- Use bar charts to stress the difference between items at a *single* point in time. When possible, place the longest bar at the bottom.
- Line up ends of bars and columns with the axis.
- When one bar or column is much longer than the others, break it, but also break the corresponding axis and display the actual value in the broken segment. Figure 6.15 shows an example.
- Make all bars and columns of equal thickness and either wider or narrower than the spaces between them.
- When you have many bars or columns, eliminate the spaces between them.
- For other principles of design, see Sections 6.42 through 6.49.

Other than the vertical versus horizontal orientation, the basic difference between the two kinds of chart is in the ability to display the effects of time.

6.16 *Specific uses for column charts.* When you want to compare independent series of data over time, use a *grouped column chart*. For example, Figure 6.7 compares income from sales of apples, bananas, and grapes at four points in time. As a rule:

☐ In each group, use no more than three subcolumns.

6.17 When you want to compare totals and sums of totals over a period of time, use a *subdivided column chart*. For example, Figure 6.8 shows total sales of fruit and what kinds of fruit contributed how much to the totals.
CAUTION: Because the upper segments lack a common base line, they are hard to compare.

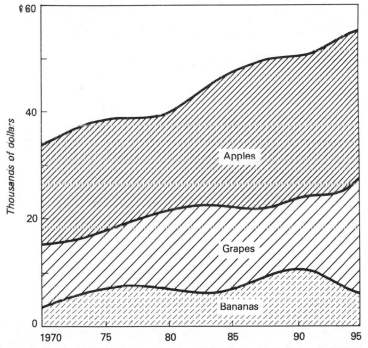

Figure 6.4 Multiple Surface Chart: Total Sales and Relative Popularity of Different Fruits, 1970–1995

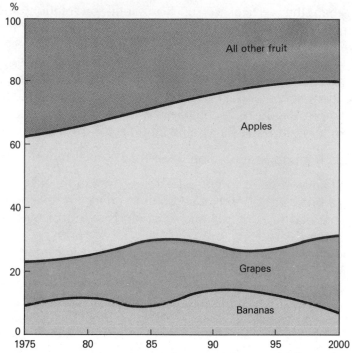

FIGURE 6.5 100% surface chart: Relative contribution of different fruits to income from sale of fruit, 1975–2000

6.18 When you want to show positive and negative values over a period of time, use a *deviation column chart*. For example, Figure 6.9 shows differences in income from apples during a period when crop failure in some years forced importing rather than exporting. Note that like Figure 6.1, this kind of chart also uses Quadrants I and IV.

6.19 When you want to compare parts of a whole at *one* point in time, use a *100% column chart*. For example, Figure 6.10 shows total income in three states from sales of fruit in 1980. (See also pie charts, Section 6.27.) The general rules are:

▫ Keep the portion of greatest interest next to the base line.
▫ To make comparison easier, draw lines between the sections.
▫ In the title, state the point in time.
▫ *Do not* use a 100% column chart for a time series.

6.20 *Specific uses of bar charts.* When you want to compare aspects of several items at the same time, use a *grouped bar chart.* For example, Figure 6.11 allows readers to compare figures for income from the sale of fruit by three states in 1980.

6.21 However, when you want to compare totals and sums of totals at the same time, use a *subdivided bar chart.* For example, Figure 6.12 shows figures for three states, for 1983, for the sale of apples and bananas and the contribution these sales made to the total sales of fruit in those states.

6.22 When you want to compare the parts of a whole, use a *100%*

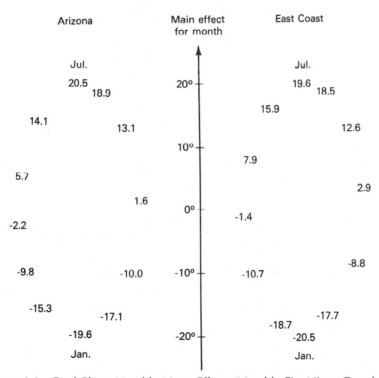

Figure 6.6 Oval Plots: Monthly Mean Effects (Monthly Fits Minus Grand Fits) for Four Arizona Airports and Seven East-Coast Airports (Unit 1 F). January was the lowest and July was the highest in both cases. Reprinted by permission from STATISTICAL PAPERS IN HONOR OF GEORGE W. SNEDECOR edited by T. A. Bancroft (c) 1972 by The Iowa State University Press, Ames, Iowa 50010. Labels added and unit changed from .1 to 1 F.

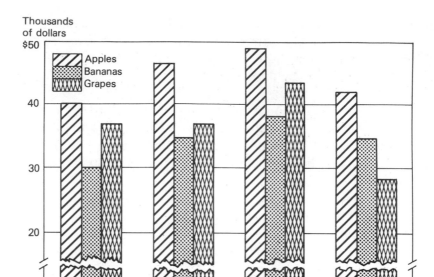

FIGURE 6.7 GROUPED COLUMN CHART: Sales of Apples, Bananas, and Grapes in 1975, 1980, 1985, and 1990

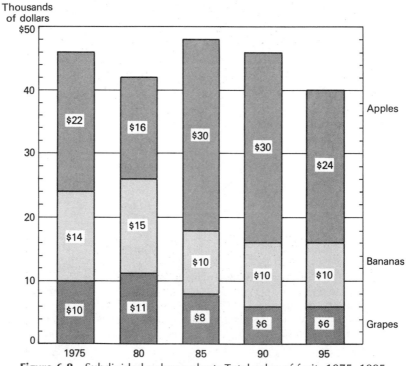

Figure 6.8 Subdivided column chart: Total sales of fruit, 1975–1995

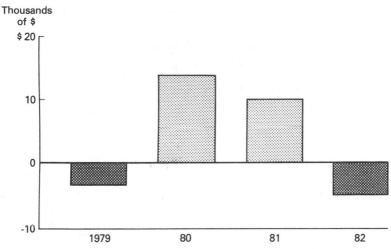

6.9 DEVIATION COLUMN CHART: INCOME FROM SALE OF APPLES
IN 1979–1982

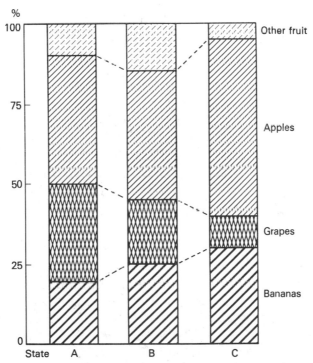

6.10 100% Column Chart: Total Income from Sales of Fruit
in Three States in 1980

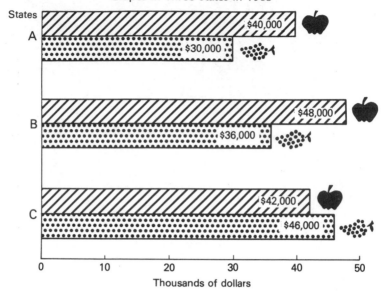

FIGURE 6.11 Grouped Bar Chart: Income from Sale of Apples and Grapes in Three States in 1983

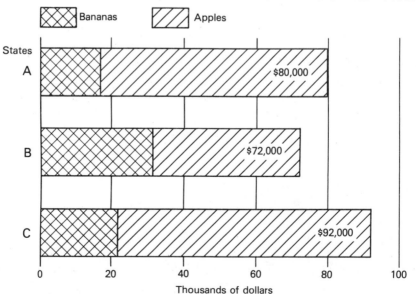

6.12 SUBDIVIDED BAR CHART:
INCOME FROM SALES OF APPLES AND BANANAS IN THREE STATES IN 1983

bar chart. For example, Figure 6.13 shows the contributions of individual fruits to the total sales of fruit by five towns in 1985; it also allows readers to compare the relative contribution of different fruits in different towns.

6.23 When you want to compare two different types of data, use a *paired bar chart.* For example, Figure 6.14 shows the total income from fruit relative to the total number of workers hired to harvest it.

6.24 When you want to show positive and negative values at one time, use a *deviation bar chart.* For example, Figure 6.15 shows the percentage change in income to five states, between 1980 and 1981, from the sale of apples. The states to the right of the midline sold more apples in 1981 than in 1980, and the states to the left sold less. Note that this kind of chart uses Quadrants I and II. Remember:

▢ When possible, arrange the bars in descending order.

FIGURE 6.13 100% bar chart: Comparative sales of fruit by five towns in 1985

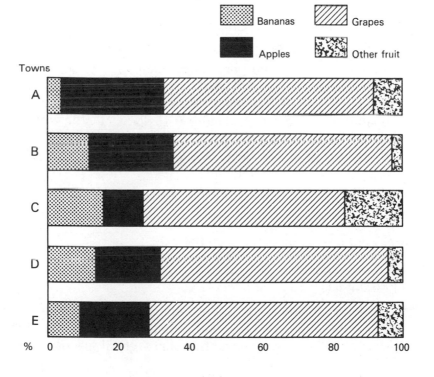

Figure 6.14 Paired Bar Chart: Total Income from Fruit Relative to Number of Workers Hired in 1985

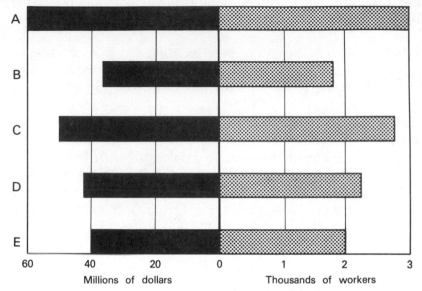

Semilogarithmic Charts

6.25 *Description and use.* Semilogarithmic charts show rates of change as proportional and percentage relationships. Because they show both relative change and absolute amounts, they allow writers to make comparisons even when dealing with relatively large and small quantities. For example, Figure 6.16 shows that even though state A has been producing fewer apples than state B, apple production in state A has been increasing much more rapidly. In general, use semilogarithmic charts:

□ When quantities differ greatly.
□ When the variables are expressed in different units.

6.26 *Do not use* semilogarithmic charts to:

□ Compare amounts.
□ Illustrate data for lay audiences.

6.27 The basic difference between arithmetic and semilogarithmic charts is that in arithmetic line charts, equal spaces represent equal *amounts* of change; in semilogarithmic charts, equal spaces represent equal *rates* of change. To see the difference, compare Figure 6.16 with Figure 6.17. Both show the same information, but Figure 6.17 is an arithmetic chart. In Figure 6.17, the line for state B seems to be growing much faster that the line for state A. However, the difference is due only to the fact that the line for state B represents much larger amounts. A semilogarithmic chart like Figure 6.16 shows that in state A, production is increasing at a much faster rate.

6.28 *Preparation.* A logarithm is "the power to which 10 must be raised to produce a given number" (MacGregor 1977, p. 159). So, in the equation

$$10^2 = 100$$

2 is the logarithm and 100 is the antilog. On the chart:

□ Place the logarithmic divisions on the vertical axis.
□ Place the arithmetic divisions on the horizontal axis. (On *full*

6.15
DEVIATION BAR CHART: PERCENTAGE CHANGE IN INCOME
FROM SALE OF APPLES, 1980–1981

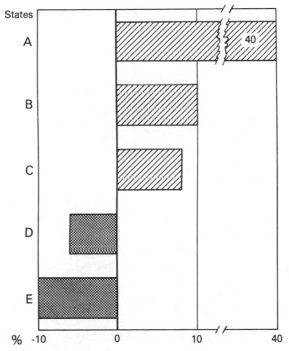

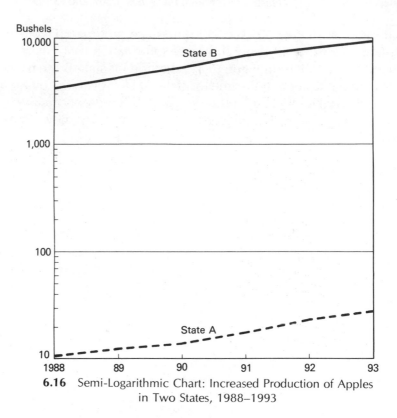

6.16 Semi-Logarithmic Chart: Increased Production of Apples in Two States, 1988–1993

logarithmic charts, both axes are divided logarithmically.)

□ To save time, buy commercial semilog paper.

Pie Charts

6.29 Like 100% column charts, pie charts show relations of parts in a whole, but pie charts are less satisfactory because the areas are hard to compare accurately. A 100% bar or column chart and a simple bar chart can show the same data and are just as successful with lay audiences. The general principles are:

□ *Do not use* pie charts to compare parts of two or more wholes (use 100% column charts).
□ When possible, arrange sectors according to size, the largest at

the central point of the upper half of the circle and continuing clockwise with progressively smaller portions.

□ Make no sector less than five percent (18 degrees).

□ Use no more than five sectors.

□ You may separate one—but only one—sector for emphasis.

□ Put labels outside the circle; don't use leader lines, arrows, or keys.

Figure 6.18 shows an example—income from the sale of fruit by states in 1983.

Frequency Distribution Charts

6.30 *General use.* When you want to plot discontinuous variables (such as number of people), which have a limited number of values, against continuous variables (such as age or weight or salary), which have an infinite number of possible values, you should:

6.17 Arithmetic chart: Increased production of apples in two states, 1988–1993

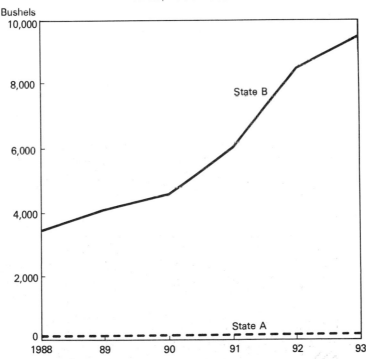

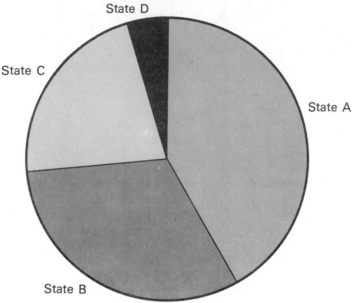

6.18. PIE CHART:
Income from Sale of Fruit, by States, 1983

- Use a frequency distribution chart to show the distribution of the variables.
- Place the continuous variables on the X axis.

The three kinds of frequency distribution chart are the histogram, polygon, and smoothed curve. Parts A, B and C respectively (in Figure 6.19) show how the three kinds display the same data on the average annual production of apples, by counties, in thousands of bushels.

CAUTION: When using polygons and smoothed curves, don't leave a gap at the sides (unless you are also showing the histogram), and don't extend the curves (because the points represent absolute numbers, not trends or percentages). Simply stop at the appropriate fixed points inside the vertical axes. Parts B and C display gaps only because moving the vertical axes made Parts B and C smaller and made the whole of Figure 6.19 look unbalanced.

6.31 *Age and sex pyramids.* Age and sex pyramids are a special kind of frequency distribution chart. When you use them to compare data on two groups:

- Plot age on the vertical axis.

Part A: Histogram

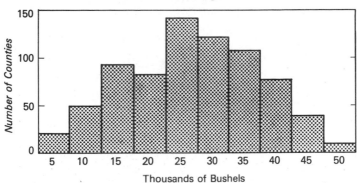

Part B: Polygon

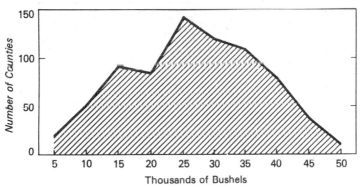

Part C: Smoothed Curve

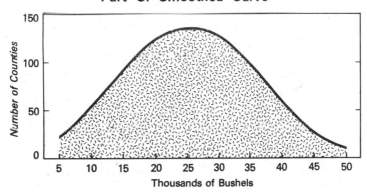

Figure 6.19. Frequency distribution charts: Average annual production of apples by counties, 1988-1992. (Gap at sides in Parts B and C is solely to make their overall size match the size of Part A. See discussion in Section 6.30.)

□ Plot number of men and women on the horizontal axis.

□ Be sure the figure indicates which side represents which sex.

For example, Figure 6.20 shows the distribution of Company A's employees, by age and sex, in 1980.

Pictorial Charts

6.32 Pictorial symbols, like apples or oranges to represent fruit, can help make abstract ideas easier to understand. The symbols appeal to readers and audiences at lectures, and they express ideas in a nearly universal language. The general rules are:

□ Use symbols either to represent specific numbers (for example, each picture of an apple could represent 10 apples) or, with a conventional chart, to identify and emphasize. For example, Figure 6.11 shows apples and grapes beside the bars. Figure 6.20 uses stick figures, with the woman in a skirt, to show which side of the pyramid represents which sex.

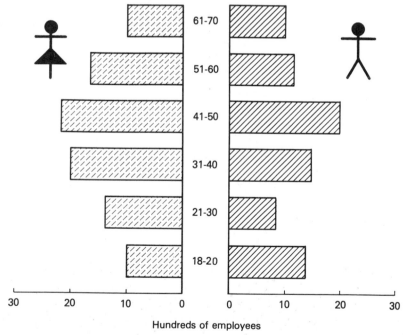

FIGURE 6.20. Age and Sex Pyramid: Distribution of Company A's Employees by Age and Sex, 1980

□ Choose symbols that have a strong association with an idea.

□ Avoid dated or regional symbols.

□ Avoid symbols that the audience might mix up. For example, apples, oranges, and grapefruit all are round and easy to confuse.

□ Design symbols clearly and simply, with as little detail as possible, so they reduce or enlarge clearly and remain easily identifiable. Readers and other audiences shouldn't have to rely on labels.

6.33 When you use symbols as counting units:

□ Keep about the same size units that have the same value. For example, in Figure 6.11 the apples and the bunches of grapes have about the same vertical and horizontal dimensions.

□ Space the symbols evenly so they line up neatly in vertical columns. Of the two examples below, [2] is better than [1].

[1]
$ $ $ $ $
%   %   %   %   %

[2]
$ $ $ $ $
%   %   %   %   %

□ *Never* compare the *size* of symbols. It is almost impossible to draw or to compare visually symbols that have different volumes. Instead, change the number of symbols. For example, don't use a big apple and a little one; use two (or three or four) apples and one apple, all the same size.

Design

General Considerations

6.34 When you plan the design of charts and graphs:

□ Consider the medium. Print, television, 35-millimeter slides, overhead projections, and so forth have different requirements. Furthermore, different publishers have different requirements. The limitations affect size and shape of illustrations, size and number of words you may include, width of lines, tone patterns, and so on.

□ Decide what you want a graph or chart to stress—trend, mag-

nitude, or rate of change—and then choose the type of graphic.
□ Find out what reader or audience you are preparing for. How large is it? How well educated?
□ Consider whether the illustration is to stand alone or be part of a group. Those in a series should be prepared in the same size so all words, lines, and other elements will be of uniform size in the final publication or projection. In addition, plan for consistent color, style, and general appearance.

6.35 Use a rectangular, coordinate surface to show how change in one amount relates to change in other amounts. Usually the illustration is in Quadrant I, although, as shown in Figures 6.1, 6.9, and 6.15, some charts require other quadrants. The examples in this section come from illustrations in the earlier part of the chapter.

Number and Title

6.36 The title must tell what, where, and when, and should be as short as possible without being telegraphic. The general principles are:

□ Use the largest size of lettering in the title.
□ Unless the style requires otherwise, center the title at the top or the bottom of the grid.
□ Make sure the style of the title will be consistent with the style for the titles of tables and with other aspects of style throughout a document.

The titles, or captions, of illustrations in this chapter show a variety of ways to treat the title. (This is normally *very* poor practice in a document; it is done here only to show the variety of styles without lengthening the book). Among the features that can vary are capitalization, punctuation, use of the word *figure* (or *chart, graph,* or *illustration*) before the number, and placement above or below the illustration.

Axes, Grid Lines, and Curve Lines

6.37 Relative to each other:

□ Make grid lines less important than axis lines and curve lines. Indicate major divisions with small ticks and minor divisions with smaller ticks inside the scale line. For example, see Figure 6.1. Figure 6.2 shows a grid line used to indicate an index. Sometimes, as in Figures 6.3 and 6.4, designers omit grid lines entirely and use only the ticks.

CAUTION: People have significantly less trouble reading graphs that include completely ruled grid lines (Bostick 1979, pp. 32–33).

□ When words or bars cross a grid line, break the grid line.

□ Make axis lines more important than grid lines and less important than curve lines. Figures 6.2 through 6.4 show examples. Sometimes designers omit the Y axis and use, instead, horizontal grid lines that span the illustration and are exactly as wide as the X axis.

□ Make curve lines stand out; when two or more cross, interrupt one of the lines, as in Figure 6.1.

□ On a very steep curve, usually it is best to round off the point. Figures 6.1 and 6.2 show examples.

□ In published material, show the points in a shape, such as a circle, triangle, or square, that has the same width as the curve line. Figure 6.2 shows an example.

6.38 When displaying more than one curve line, treat each line distinctly but in a manner equal to the others. In general:

□ Make each curve line about two times wider than the X and Y axes. The weight depends on the number of curves; the fewer the curves, the wider each can be.

□ Distinguish the curves by color or pattern (for example, dots, dashes), but not width. When one curve is wider, it seems more important.

□ Distinguish points on different curves with different shapes, such as triangles and circles, and not with different sizes of the same shape (for example, larger and smaller circles).

Amount and Time Scales

6.39 *Amount scales.* On all arithmetic line, column bar, and frequency charts:

□ Always start the amount scale at zero. Not doing so presents a visual distortion of the truth.

□ Always write in the zero.
□ When you don't need a large part of the grid, break the grid line, but retain the zero base line. Make the division obvious, and don't use this device unnecessarily. Figure 6.7 shows an example.

On a semilogarithmic chart and on arithmetic charts based on an index, it is not necessary to start at a zero base line. Start semilog charts at any convenient value.

6.40 When you need to use two amount scales, as in Figure 6.21:

□ Label each scale and its corresponding curve clearly.
□ Optional: use color coding to prevent confusion. For more information on use of color, see Section 6.56.

6.41 *Time scales.* When data for a certain time period are missing:

□ Keep the time divisions equal; don't break the chart.

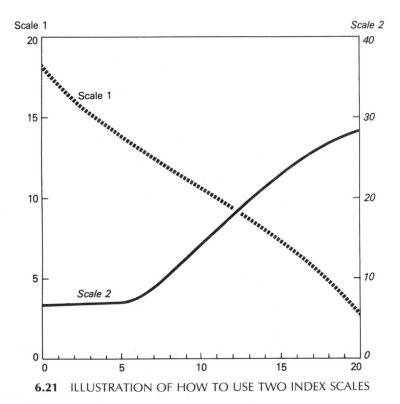

6.21 ILLUSTRATION OF HOW TO USE TWO INDEX SCALES

□ Use dotted lines to connect curves over the periods for which data are missing.

For example, Figure 6.3 shows that data were not available for the period 1985-1990.

Scale Legends and Figures

6.42 In scale legends:

□ Use smaller letters than you use for the title.
□ Make legends concise; when necessary, include the unit of measurement.
□ When possible, label the amount scale horizontally, directly over numbers in the amount scale, as in Figure 6.1. When the title is too long, use italic letters, parallel to the axis. For example, see Figure 6.4. (In print, the availability of small type sizes may make vertical lettering unnecessary.)

6.43 On the scales of charts and graphs:

□ Consider placing figures at only every second or fourth grid ruling. For example, see Figure 6.4.
□ Use as few zeros as possible.
□ State the number of units in the scale legend.
□ Use standard intervals—10, 20, 30; 5, 10, 15—in the scale.

6.44 On some bar and column charts, you may be able to omit the scale and put actual amounts in the bars or columns, as in Figures 6.8 and 6.11. However, to prevent an illusion of greater length than you intend:

□ Don't place the numbers beyond the ends of the bars or columns.

6.45 With a divided bar chart, place the label for each division either above or below the first bar. With divided columns, place labels to the right or left. In either case, you may be forced to use a key, as in 6.12, to avoid crowding the illustration.

Legends and Keys

6.46 *Legends.* When you label a curve:

□ Place the curve legend horizontally and not slanted. For example, see Figure 6.1.

□ When possible, avoid leader lines and arrows.
□ Don't draw boxes around labels.
□ When words cross a grid line, interrupt the grid line.

6.47 *Keys.* Avoid use of a key whenever possible. Instead, label curves, bars, and columns directly, as in Figure 6.5. However, when you have to use a key:

□ Place it where it will balance other elements. For example, see Figure 6.3.

Tones

6.48 On surface, bar, column, frequency distribution, and pie charts, use black and white tone patterns to make individual units easy to identify. The general rules are:

□ Give all bars and columns a tone.
□ Don't use white for all or any part of a bar or column.
□ For tone, use the seven commercially available patterns (10 percent through 70 percent gray) plus all white and all gray.
□ *Never* place adjacent tones, such as white and 10 percent gray, or 40 percent and 50 percent gray, side by side, even if the bar or column or other shaded area is unique. Instead, keep a contrast of at least 30 percent between adjacent bars.
□ Make either the smallest or the most important bar the darkest, and make it contrast strongly with adjacent tones.
□ Avoid optical illusions by keeping all striped patterns at a 45-degree angle to the base line, and running from left to right. For example, see Figure 6.13 and Figure 6.19, Part B.

6.49 When you are preparing illustrations for publication:

□ Use a tone pattern that reduces well. For example, you could achieve a 20 percent gray value with a pattern that had either 27.5 or 60 lines per inch, but on reduction, the dots on the latter would run together in a dirty smudge.
□ Don't choose varied, or "pretty," patterns of dots, even when the patterns repeat.
□ Unless you know the techniques of design and tone, seek the help of an expert.

Source

6.50 Place acknowledgment of a source at the lower left corner of a chart. Use the smallest letter size and follow a style of citation that is consistent with the rest of the manuscript. For example, see the acknowledgment on Figure 6.11. (The acknowledgment on Figure 6.6 is inconsistent with that on 6.11 because The Iowa State University Press, which granted permission for use of Figure 6.6, requested a different form.)

Artwork

6.51 Above all, make artwork legible—easy to read and interpret. Never sacrifice legibility for beauty. When you manage to achieve both, consider it a bonus.

6.52 *Words.* Lowercase letters are easier to read than uppercase. Especially when a title contains more than five words, choose lowercase letters with initial uppercase. Number of words and size of letters depend on viewing distance. For information on how to make choices, consult a drafting professional. In general:

- □ Choose legible letter styles, preferably without *serif* (a short, light line that projects from the top or bottom of a main stroke of a letter). Styles marked "Gothic" or "sans serif" meet this criterion.
- □ Try not to mix styles.
- □ Don't use exceptionally bold or thin letters.

The problem with serifs and thin strokes is that often they get lost on projection or reduction. The best styles are Helvetica Medium, Grotesque 216, Futura Medium, Franklin Gothic, Folio Medium, and Univers. Univers probably is the most useful because it contains many different letter weights and widths, plus italics.

6.53 Between letters of a word, use "optical" rather than even spacing, with parallel strokes (for example, I, L, M, N) farther apart and round letters closer. Overlap L's and T's (LT), and V's and T's with A's (VA, TA). Also:

- □ Between words, leave the same amount of space you would need to insert a lowercase "n" into the space.

- Between sentences, leave the amount of space you would need to insert two "n's" in the space.
- Between lines leave an amount of space equal to the height of two and one-half or three "n's."

6.54 *Lines.* To determine the weight, or thickness, of rules and lines:

- Determine the minimum height of the letters (this depends on the display medium; for help, consult an artist or drafting professional).
- Make minor scale lines half the width of the lowercase l.
- Make the X and Y axes one "l" wide.
- Make curve lines two to three "l's" wide.

6.55 *Shape and arrangement of objects and space.* The basic principles of design are:

- Simplicity; in each graph present only one idea. Use a style that is easy to read and understand.
- Emphasis; use size or color or shape to make one element the center of attention. In a graph, for example, the important elements are the title and the curve lines, so the title should have the largest letters and the curves the widest lines.
- Unity; make each element function as part of a whole and not as a separate element. Achieve this effect by grouping elements or by creating obvious similarities of line or shape or color.
- Balance; arrange elements to balance each other. Often, as in Figure 6.3, you can use a key to balance a graph.

6.56 *Color.* Color is expensive and takes longer to prepare than black and white. In general, use color to add information, make objects recognizable, direct attention, create emphasis, or differentiate. Also:

- Use contrasting hues (for example, red versus green) as well as contrasting tone or value (discussed in Sections 6.48 and 6.49).
- *Never* place white letters on light backgrounds or dark letters on dark tones. Examples of good combinations are:

Letters	*Background*
Black	Yellow or white
Dark green or blue	White
White	Dark blue

□ Let the most important element have the most important color and the greatest tone contrast with the background.

□ *Never* place complementary colors (such as red and green or blue and orange) side by side. They appear to vibrate and will annoy readers.

□ On maps and on graphics where colors represent different numbers of items, try to graduate tone value as the number of cases increases. For example, 1–5 cases might be white; 6–10 cases, yellow; 11-20, orange. This graduation will not be possible when adjacent values would have similar tones.

□ Avoid creating large areas of white.

7 Organization and Outlines

7.1 Organization begins with your thoughts about how to present a topic. On short documents, a few notes on a pad may provide all the organization you need. On longer documents, a research notebook (described in Sections 3.9 through 3.11) will help you to organize. As you work on the topic, record the ideas in the notebook. As you begin to see how the ideas fit together, write down your insights. From time to time, divide and subdivide the catetories to reflect your changing ideas about organization. Expect your thoughts about organization to change frequently, even in the middle of a draft. The reason is that organizing, writing, and thinking are much like a game of strategy in which you are playing both parts. Your old writing and organization interact with your new thoughts in a dynamic, creative process that takes on a life of its own and often continues until you have finished the document. Sometimes the process stops only because you have reached a deadline.

7.2 Outlines provide a plan for writing and an internal order, or framework, for a document. Because writing and thinking interact, the outline you use as a plan for writing often is not the outline that reflects the finished form of the document. However, when an employer requires you to follow a "standard outline" (discussed in

Chapter 8), chances are you will start and finish with nearly the same outline. Furthermore, your document will closely resemble documents on similar topics by other writers in your organization. The principles of organizing and outlining apply to documents of all lengths and all degrees of importance. In general, however, writers' problems with these tasks increase as the length of the document increases. Therefore, the examples in this chapter are based primarily on longer documents. For more help with organization, see Tichy (1966, Chapters 5 and 6) and Lesikar (1974, Chapters 2 through 4).

Developing a Sense of Organization

Overview of Topic

7.3 When you have trouble organizing your thoughts, get help from others. Knowing how other people have organized similar data helps you to decide whether your topic is similar or different, and also helps you to identify differences. Specifically:

□ Talk to your supervisor and to co-workers who have written about similar topics. Ask specifically for copies of the outlines and boiler plates they used. (Chapter 9 describes boiler plates in detail.)

□ Find and alter for your own use promising organizational patterns in articles, textbooks, abstract indexes, field reports, lectures, *Reader's Guide*, and so forth.

□ As you progress, try to develop specific ideas about the major sections of the document.

For example, if you were doing research for someone who wanted to advertise a new natural food and had been observing buyers in a grocery store, you might have noticed that people who buy honey but not sugar also buy bread made with unbleached flour. Eventually you might discover that these people buy natural foods because they believe that refined products, bolstered with additives, are not good for them. Therefore, you could recommend placing advertisements of the new food next to displays of currently popular natural foods. For examples of analyses that precede other kinds of document, see Sections 3.1 and 3.30 through 3.32.

Limiting a Topic

7.4 *Reader.* For whom are you writing? Foundation officials? College-educated people? Specialists in urban transportation? Government administrators? Business people? Women who need birth control information?

   □ Be as specific as possible. Think of someone you know who fits the characteristics and keep that person in mind when you write. Many writers find it helpful to write as if they were talking to that person.

The intended reader limits the kind of outline you use, the number of pages you devote to various topics, the sentence patterns you use, and even the words you choose. For example, if you were writing for government administrators and most business people, you would put conclusions and recommendations *at the front* of the report because that is all most such readers might take time to read. If you were reporting scientific findings to other scientists, you would probably place your conclusions at the end. If you were writing a proposal for funds to do research, you would have to specify in detail *how* you intended to do the research. You would also have to state what you expected to find, but not in the detail required by a scholarly article. Sections 11.5 through 11.12 describe in detail how the expected reader affects choice of language.

7.5 *Purpose.* Purpose also limits a topic. For example, a research proposal to study birth control pills would emphasize the need for research, likely methods, possible results, and benefits. Scientists writing a report of research on birth control pills would devote relatively little time to the need and the method of research; in contrast, at least half of the report probably would be devoted to discussion of results, conclusions, and benefits of the research. Still a third document, a pamphlet on how to use birth control pills, would devote little, if any, space to the preceding research. Instead, the writer would concentrate on giving clear instructions for use, cautions against misuse, and specific warnings of possible dangers. For another example of two different documents on the same general topic, see Sections 3.30 through 3.32.

7.6 If you were writing instructions on how to use a computer program, you wouldn't discuss the development of the program at all, and you would discuss benefits only enough so that potential users knew when to use the program and for what purposes. You probably would devote the rest of the document to "playscripts" that described procedures (Matthies 1963) and task outlines (Matthies 1977) that listed the details of individual tasks.

7.7 *Scope.* Defining scope requires progressive refinement of the topic. For example:

[Ex. 7.1]   Transportation
Mass transportation
Mass transportation in small cities
Mass transportation in Smallcity
Smallcity's need for federal funds to help buy buses for the city bus system
A proposal by Smallcity to the Urban Mass Transportation Administration for funds to buy new buses for the city bus system

[Ex. 7.2]   Social psychology and political behavior
Social psychology and voting patterns
Social psychology and women's voting patterns
Social psychological variables and voting patterns of women in national elections
The effect of affection for parents on women's voting patterns in national elections
The effect of affection for parents on women's voting patterns in the national election of 1976

Narrow the scope of the topic as soon as possible, long before you begin writing, because knowing what you have excluded helps you to decide what notes to take, what questions you need to include in a questionnaire, and so forth. Sections 3.27 through 3.33 and 12.21 through 12.23 give more help with narrowing scope.

7.8 *Plan.* Decide how you plan to present information on the topic. For example, for Smallcity's proposal you might plan to present background information on the city first, information on its present transportation resources second, alternatives it might choose if it could get funding for more buses, and finally a detailed plan for the alternative you would recommend. In contrast, the plan for research on voting behavior might call for discussion of (1) why the topic is important, (2) the method for finding information, (3) the results of research, and (4) questions for future researchers.

7.9 *Topic sentence, or theme.* Writing a topic sentence, preferably in fewer than 50 words, helps you to summarize your decisions about reader, purpose, scope, and plan. Be as specific as possible. For example:

> Smallcity is requesting funds to buy 10 new Mercedes-Benz diesel buses so it can maintain present bus routes and add new routes to two heavily populated subdivisions.
>
> Women who had had good relationships with their parents voted for liberal candidates in the 1976 election.

7.10 To help keep the limits of the topic in mind, post above your desk a 4 × 6 card that lists briefly the reader, purpose, scope, plan, and topic sentence. When you have no fixed place, tape the card inside the front of the research notebook. The card might look something like this:

---

1. *Reader*: Federal administrators with college business degrees and knowledge of transportation.
2. *Purpose*: To get $150,000 for purchase of 10 buses.
3. *Scope*: To maintain Smallcity's present routes and add two new ones.
4. *Plan*: Background, present bus system, alternatives, and recommendations, in this order.
5. Smallcity is requesting funds to buy 10 new Mercedes-Benz deisel buses so it can maintain present routes and add new routes to two heavily populated subdivisions.

General Principles of Outlining

7.11 For many writers (but not all, see Chapter 10), the next step is a formal outline. When you have trouble outlining, read this section carefully. Reviewing the mechanics and principles of organizational categories often shows why you are having trouble.

Mechanics

7.12 *Levels of importance.* Outlines divide and subdivide ideas. As Outlines 7.1 and 7.2 show (see Sections 7.14 and 7.15), the most important ideas—those at the first level of importance—usually are indicated by roman numerals. Breaking down ideas at the first level yields ideas at the second level, which usually are preceded by capital letters. Ideas at the third, fourth, fifth, and sixth levels are preceded, respectively, by arabic numerals, lowercase letters, arabic numerals in parentheses, and lowercase letters in parentheses. Section 15.12 (Chapter 15) shows examples at all levels.

7.13 *Ideas need company.* Don't divide an idea at any level unless you will have at least two subideas that are aspects of the idea you divided. When you have a *I* or *1*, you must also have at least a *II* or *2*. When you have an *A*, you must also have at least a *B*. For example, because Section *VI.A.* lists subcategory *1*, it must also have *VI.A.2*. For any given manuscript, you may have *only one* idea that has no equally important partner, and that idea (reflected in the title) is *the subject* of your manuscript. Every other idea either divides or subdivides the subject of the manuscript and must, therefore, have at least one partner at its level in its category. Therefore:

- When dividing an idea won't produce at least two subcategories, don't divide it.
- Remember that division must occur *within* categories. In Outline 7.1, both *IV.A.1* and *VI.D.2* are ideas at the third level of importance, but they do not divide the same idea at the second level; instead, one is a subcategory of A and the other is a subcategory of D.

Trouble with dividing and subdividing usually means that your thinking isn't clear.

7.14 *Coordinate and subordinate ideas.* Outlines show which ideas are equally important (coordinate ideas) and which are subideas, or subcategories (subordinate ideas) of other ideas. For example, consider Outline 7.1, which is for the first chapter in a four-chapter report. The purpose of the chapter is to describe an area and its resources, and thus provide the basis for later chapters that analyze problems and recommend change. (The topic sentence for the whole report is Item 5 in Section 7.10.) In Outline 7.1, information on geographical area, characteristics of the population, and major institutions (roman numerals I, II, and III, respectively) are equally important features that describe Smallcity, and they are subcategories only of the whole chapter. In Section *II*, growth trends, important subgroups of the population, and income levels (*II.A–C*, respectively) are coordinate topics in relation to each other, but all are subordinate to *characteristics of the general population*. Similarly, the four important subgroups (*II.B.1–4*) have a coordinate relation to each other but a subordinate relation to both *important subgroups* and *characteristics of the general population*.

[*Outl. 7.1*] CHAPTER 1: DESCRIPTION OF SMALLCITY

    I. The geographical area
       A. Description of the general location
          1. Adjacent bodies of water, mountains, state borders, and so forth
          2. Large cities and towns in the general area
          3. Features that mark or divide the area (rivers, railroads, bridges and drawbridges, trolley tracks, and so forth)
       B. Smallcity's boundaries, including land outside the city limits that would be affected if bus service were to be expanded)

    II. Characteristics of the general population
       A. Overall growth trends in Smallcity and the surrounding county
          1. Past growth (1950–1979)
          2. Size in 1980
          3. Projected growth in 1985, 1990, and 2000
          4. Comparisons of growth
             a. With other, comparable cities in the general geographic region
             b. With growth in the state
       B. Important subgroups in the population
          1. Elderly people
          2. Handicapped people
          3. Poor people
          4. People living in dormitories, convalescent centers, hospitals, or other group arrangements

C. Average annual income
1. Overall
2. By subgroups in the population
3. Relative to average(s) for the state

III. Major institutions and other traffic generators with addresses, amount of traffic, and peak traffic periods)
A. Medical facilities
1. Hospitals
2. Health centers and clinics
3. Convalescent centers
4. Doctors' offices
B. Governmental offices
1. City hall
2. County courthouse
3. City and county offices in other locations
C. Educational facilities
1. High schools
2. Junior high schools
3. Elementary schools
4. Preschools and day care centers
5. Vocational and industrial training schools
6. Centers for special education
7. Parochial schools
D. Human services
1. Family and children's service
2. YMCA, YWCA
3. Boys' and girls' clubs
4. Mental health clinics
5. Senior citizens' centers
6. Industries operated by disabled people
E. Locations of industry, commerce, and housing
1. Major employers and number of employees
2. Commercial centers (squares, malls, and the like) and department stores
3. Total number of existing residential units by geographic area (for condominiums and apartments, give addresses, number of units, and whether subsidized)
4. Plans for future development of industrial, commercial, and housing areas (for housing, specify type and total number of units in each area)

IV. Economy and development

    A. Employment
      1. Total work force
      2. Breakdown by census categories of worker
      3. Unemployment rate (and causes, if important)
    B. Financing of the local government (for example, by income tax, property taxes, revenue sharing, or other sources of income)

V. Planning for the future
    A. General responsibility (e.g., regional commissions, consultants)
    B. Responsibility for transportation planning

VI. Transportation resources
    A. Intercity buses
      1. Names of companies
      2. Location of stopping and pickup points
      3. Cities served directly and indirectly
    B. School buses (available for all children in all grades in all schools?)
    C. Taxi service (ownership, number of cabs, geographic area served, and rate structure)
    D. Automobiles
      1. Total number of automobiles
      2. Percentage of population (or family units) that own automobiles
      3. Parking facilities
        a. For shopping
        b. For major employers
        c. For hospitals, clinics, and other health facilities
    E. Railroad passenger service
      1. Provided by whom and how often
      2. Location of stations
      3. Amount of parking at each station
    F. Airplanes
      1. Name and location of airport
      2. Kind of plane served
      3. Parking facilities available
    G. Transportation by human service agencies
      1. Description of vehicles and who owns them
      2. Description of service and who provides it
    H. Other relevant kinds of transportation other than local buses

7.15 *Topic, sentence, and mixed outlines.* Use different kinds of outline for different purposes. Outline 7.1 is a topic outline because it contains no complete sentences. Outline 7.2 is a sentence outline because it contains no incomplete sentences. Outline 7.3 is a mixed outline because it contains both sentences and topics.

[*Outl. 7.2*] I. Groups of census tracts form social areas based on similar economic status, urbanization, and segregation patterns; do they also have distinctive patterns of interaction?

    A. Social area analysis is flawed because it (1) treats census tracts as independent units, (2) does not deal with other census tracts as the environment, and (3) does not deal with interaction between the residents of census tracts.

    B. Human ecology is an appropriate theory for research on urban social structure, but it includes no appropriate method.

    C. An appropriate method, such as block modeling, would specify the presence or absence of a relationship between any two units and measure several types of relationship between units; the results would show similarities and differences in the patterns of relationship.

II. Using data on census tracts in Largecity in 1970, I do both a social area analysis of demographic characteristics and a block model of patterns of interaction.

    A. Largecity fits the research objectives because (1) it has a large number of census tracts, (2) the boundaries of community organizations have been determined (a situation not true in all cities), and (3) it has a consolidated city-county government.

    B. Social area analysis describes the distribution of populations over census tracts and the variation between tracts in terms of economic status, urbanization, and segregation.

    C. Block modeling partitions the members of a population into mutually exclusive and exhaustive subsets, or blocks.

    D. For both analyses the unit of analysis is the census tract.

III. The results should show whether the combination of social area analysis and block modeling yields a more complete description and analysis than either does by itself.

A. Factor analysis of eight census variables should yield distinct factors, or constructs, for the 183 tracts.
B. Two different block models, one based on only three relationships and one based on those three plus four more, should distribute the census tracts into similar blocks.

[Outl. 7.3]

A. Flaws in social area analysis
1. It does not treat census tracts as independent units.
2. It does not deal with other census tracts as parts of the environment.
3. It does not deal with interaction between the residents of census tracts.

7.16 Usually the most efficient way to outline is to use specific sentences at the first and second levels of importance, and sometimes the third. At lower levels, use topics. The value of specific sentences is that they force clarification of thoughts, and clarification is especially important at higher levels of importance. For example, in Outline 7.1 topic *VI, transportation resources,* tells a reader nothing about the resources. In contrast, the following sentence summarizes what you have concluded about the resources:

IV. Transportation resources in Smallcity are so inadequate that without a city bus system, 45 percent of the population would have no transportation available.

The value of topics is to help keep track of lists like the ones in Section III of Outline 7.1. Often, writing complete sentences only wastes time because in the draft, the items in a list end up as several items in a series in a single sentence. Or they might end up in displayed lists of incomplete sentences, preceded by open squares, like those in Section 7.23.

Organizational Patterns

7.17 *Kinds.* The general organizational patterns are order of time, order of place, groups of various sorts (men, women, mice, Democrats), order of increasing or decreasing importance, and order of emphasis by position. Time order displays information by date; geographic order, by location; categories, by group. Order of increasing importance, typical of mystery stories and scientific reports (discussed in Sections 8.10 through 8.13), presents the least important information first and then builds to a conclusion by presenting the most important information last. Outline 7.2 uses order of ascending importance. Order of decreasing importance, which does just the opposite, is typical of reports that start with a long abstract or summary of conclusions and recommendations. Order of emphasis by position mixes the last two options by presenting some important information first and then building to a conclusion. A typical example is a scientific report preceded by a short abstract. Outlines 7.4 and 7.7 mix kinds of organization in the proper way; Outlines 7.5 and 7.6 mix the kinds of information improperly. If you want more detailed information on patterns of organization, see Tichy (1966, pp. 67–83), Lesikar (1974, Chapter 3), and Sachs (1976, Chapter 9). Outlines help you to write documents in patterns that will make sense to readers and meet their needs. Nevertheless:

□ Remember that the basic reason for outlining is to help *you* organize and clarify your thinking.

7.18 *Principles.* Within the outline for a complete manuscript, you can use one basic pattern at the first level of importance, another at the second, another at the third, and so forth. For example, if you were writing about trends in the use of mass transportation between 1900 and 2000 and wanted to compare different regions, you might begin with Outline 7.4.

[*Outl. 7.4*]   I. Introduction

        II. 1900–1919: Use of mass transportation from 1900 through the end of World War I
        A. In the industrial Northeast
           1. Trolleys
           2. Trains
           3. Buses
           4. Subways
        B. In the rural South
           1. Trolleys
           2. Trains
           3. Buses
           4. Subways
        C. In the agricultural Midwest
           1. Trolleys
           2. Trains

    3. Buses
    4. Subways
  D. In the West
    1. Trolleys
    2. Trains
    3. Buses
    4. Subways

III. 1920–1945: The period between the wars
  [Repeat second- and third-level topics from Section II.]

IV. 1945–1955: The good years

V. [Repeat second- and third-level topics from Section II.]
  1956–1965: Suburban sprawl and the decline of mass transportation
  [Repeat second- and third-level topics from Section II.]

VI. 1966–1980: UMTA and the increasing involvement of federal, state and local governments
  [Repeat second- and third-level topics from Section II.]

VII. 1980–2000: Conclusions and prospects for the future
  A. Conclusions
    1. By region use the four regions as fourth level of importance and the types of transportation as the fifth level
    2. For the nation as a whole
  B. Prospects
    1. By region [use the four regions as fourth level of importance]
    2. For the nation [use the four types of transportation as categories at the fourth level of importance]

At the first level of importance, time order organizes the information, and on this topic you reap a bonus. Without altering the time order, you can save the most important information—conclusions and prospects—for the climax, so the outline also has some features of order of increasing importance. A short summary at the beginning would add the benefits of order of emphasis by importance. At the second level of importance in most sections, the organizing pattern is geographic; at the third level, categories of mass transportation.

7.19 What often leads people astray when they outline is the way they think. A few lucky people get ideas precisely in the order of an outline. The rest of us think in patterns like the spokes of a wheel. For example, thinking about the industrial Northeast might bring to mind contrasts in development of the four geographic areas; the contrast between commuter trains and passenger trains for long trips; and the Metroliner that serves Boston, New York, Philadelphia and Washington, and features both kinds of service. If thoughts like these were competing for your attention, the beginning of Section II in Outline 7.4 might start to look like Outline 7.5.

[*Outl. 7.5*] II. 1900–1919: Use of . . .
　　　　　　　A. In the industrial Northeast
　　　　　　　　1. Trolleys
　　　　　　　　2. Trains–what we can learn from the development of trains in different areas
　　　　　　　　3. Differences in passenger and commuter trains
　　　　　　　　4. The Metroliner and the BosWash Megalopolis
　　　　　　　　5. Buses

Or perhaps:

[*Outl. 7.6*] II. 1900–1919: Use of . . .
　　　　　　　A. In the industrial Northeast
　　　　　　　　1. Trolleys
　　　　　　　　2. Trains
　　　　　　　　　a. Contrasts in development of the four areas and how differences in railroad systems show differences in the areas
　　　　　　　　　b. Differences in commuter and passenger trains
　　　　　　　　　c. The Metroliner and the BosWash Megalopolis

7.20 The possibilities are endless, but what is important is the sneak attack your thoughts have launched on your outline. At the third level of importance, you intended to organize by categories of transportation, but in Outline 7.5 you found yourself with smatterings of geographic order (the comparison of trains in different areas), with subcategories of train (passenger, commuter, Metroliner), and with time order (the development of railroad systems up to the Metroliner). Had you recognized that you were introducing new organizational principles, you might have used Outline 7.6; however, although that would have preserved the integrity of order at the third level of importance, you still would have had a variety of organizational principles at the fourth level. Regardless of the level at which different patterns compete, they will have the same effect—when you begin writing, you will find yourself getting off the topic, repeating some information over and over, having difficulty with transition from section to section, and so on.

7.21 You need to stick with your patterns of organization, yet you don't want to lose valuable ideas. To cope with this problem:

- □ Never use two patterns simultaneously to organize the topics that supposedly divide a topic at a higher level.
- □ Record the stray ideas on 3 × 5 or 4 × 6 file cards, one idea per card.
- □ Using organizers if you have lots of stray ideas, arrange the cards in the order you intend to use them so that the ideas resurface at the proper time.

Often people who think they can't outline are having trouble only because they have unwittingly mixed two or more organizational principles at the same level. Using just one and recording stray ideas on cards solve the problem.

7.22 *Alternatives.* Suppose, now, that instead of general trends over time, you wanted to compare trends in different *forms* of mass transportation, by area, over time. In this case you would want categories of transportation at the first level of importance, geographic order at the second level, and time order at the third level. In brief, the result might look like Outline 7.7:

[*Outl. 7.7*] I. Introduction
 II. Trains
  A. The Northeast [and three more regions as B, C, and D, respectively]
   1. 1900–1919 [and remaining time periods as 2, 3, 4, etc.]
 III. Trolleys
 IV. Buses
 V. Subways
 VI. Conclusions and prospects

7.23 Outlines 7.4 and 7.7 are just two of the many possible ways to organize the same information. On most topics your situation will be exactly the same. You will be choosing an outline from among several possibilities—some that are more appropriate, some that are less appropriate, and some that seem about the same. Sometimes choices will be arbitrary, but usually you can choose on the basis of:

□ Who your readers are.
□ Which aspects you want to emphasize.
□ What kinds and amount of information you have.

Time order is particularly useful when you have reasonably complete information and you want to examine trends. Geographic and categoric order are especially useful for comparison, contrast, and analysis of differences. Order of ascending importance is traditional for scientific reports. Order of descending importance and order of emphasis by importance are valuable when, as with most business reports, you must grab your reader's attention at once and give essential information rapidly. For further discussion, see Sections 3.30 through 3.32.

7.24 *Organizational patterns and tables.* Once you have chosen an organizational pattern, let it govern tables and illustrations as well as text. Tables 5.1 and 5.2 in Chapter 5 show tables that follow the same principles as Outlines 7.4 and 7.7, respectively. Sections 5.23 through 5.25 explain how to create parallel order in tables and text.

Number and Placement of Topics at Each Level

7.25 The number and placement of topics at each level of importance strongly influence a document's nonverbal messages (discussed in detail in Sections 11.19 through 11.33). In general:

□ For documents you expect to be longer than seven typed pages, plan no more than three to five topics at the first level.
□ Expect the greatest number of subtopics in the most important section of the document.
□ When all other factors are equal, in each group of subtopics place first the subtopic you want to emphasize most.

For example, the outline for a 30-page technical report might have three major sections: discussion of problem, explanation of method, and results and conclusions. Or the writer might create separate sections for the results and the conclusions. Among the subtopics of *conclusions,* he or she would place the most important conclusion first. For a related discussion of nonverbal messages, see Sections 12.7 through 12.13.

8 Standard Outlines: Uses, Kinds, and Preparation

8.1 Standard outlines, common in much scientific and technical writing, are all-purpose, general outlines that impose order on all information of a specific type. For example, the standard outline for research reports is used by researchers in all disciplines—social and behavioral sciences, natural and physical sciences, engineering, medicine, and so on. Modifications abound, but the basic pattern (shown in Outline 8.1) remains pretty much the same. Some standard outlines, such as the outline for research reports, outlines for technical reports (such as Outline 8.8), and outlines for user documentation of computer systems (Outlines 8.9 and 8.10), are known and used by many organizations. Others, like Outline 7.1, which was developed for reports on transportation systems In small cities, are used only by organizations that do a specific kind of work. Many organizations develop standard outlines that only they use. In general, the longer the document, the more useful standard outlines are.

Why Use Standard Outlines?

8.2 Standard outlines are popular for one basic reason—they allow writers and organizations to apply assembly-line techniques to writing reports, proposals, and instructions without losing quality of writing, logical flow of argument, consistency in style and format, and attention to unique features. The reasons are:

1. Because they provide both organization and detail, they spare writers the need to spend time defining reader, purpose, scope, and plan for a document.
2. Because writers can use them as a checklist of information they need and questions they must answer, they know when they have finished research.
3. When time is pressing, managers can divide the work among several employees without fear that the results will overlap or fail to integrate easily.
4. Because researchers, writers, editors, typists, and managers know the outlines, supervision is easier and faster, and errors and omissions are more likely to be caught and corrected before the finished document has left the office.
5. Drafting is easier and faster because information is complete and in proper order.
6. Because the outlines impose limits on the kind and amount of research, they make costs reasonably easy to estimate and control.
7. The uniformity of documents makes supervision and quality control relatively easy.
8. Uniformity also helps readers because they can always find the same kinds of information at about the same place in every document.

Reader, Purpose, Scope, and Plan

8.3 Whenever you use a standard outline, the kind of reader, the purpose, and the scope (described in Sections 7.4 through 7.10) remain the same as in every other document based on the same outline. The plan also starts out the same; writers change it only when they find items that don't apply or items they need to add to the outline. Sections 8.29 and 8.30 explain how to make these changes.

Checklists for Research

8.4 By acting as checklists, standard outlines make research more efficient. The more detailed an outline, the more useful it is as a checklist. To use an outline as a checklist:

1. As you find information on a topic, write a note on a copy of the outline.
2. When you find that a topic doesn't apply, scratch out the topic and write an explanatory note to yourself. (When you write the report, omission of seemingly obvious topics usually requires an explanation.)
3. When you find information on an important topic that is *not* on the outline, find an appropriate place for it (for help in finding a place, see Section 8.29). Write a note for your own benefit and keep a separate list of these topics so the general outline can be improved for later use. Outlines kept on a word processing system are easy to update.

Division of Labor

8.5 Sometimes the anticipated, final size of a document and the nearness of a deadline force managers to assign parts of the work to several people. When division is necessary, use the following guidelines:

1. Try to match the assignments with staff members' interests. People usually work more efficiently and write more effectively about topics they like and are familiar with, than about unfamiliar or uninteresting topics.
2. Assign the largest, continuous blocks of work possible, such as whole chapters or at least everything on one topic at the first level of importance. (Section 7.12 describes levels of importance.) The larger the assignments, the easier it will be to produce a smooth, final document from the parts.
3. Assign a single editor, technical writer, or other employee to integrate the parts and edit. For help, see Sections 11.19 through 11.33 and Chapter 14.
4. See Sections 2.7 through 2.14 for other shortcuts.

Supervision and Control

8.6 *Of writing.* Give a copy of the outline to all employees who will be working on the document. This includes proofreaders, typists, and editors. Let them know someone else is responsible for double-checking and quality control generally, but ask that all others report to the responsible person if something obvious seems missing. On rush jobs especially, tables, illustrations, and even pages of text easily get lost (often they turn up mixed with the pages of earlier drafts).

8.7 Keep a copy of the working outline, with notes, attached to the draft of sections and chapters. The outline helps supervisors and critics to do their work faster and better by eliminating guesswork.

8.8 *Of time.* To help you estimate time and cost of future documents of the same type, everyone who works on a project should keep a record of time spent on it. Often, especially with the first few documents of a type, brief notes on the type of work (for example, typing rough first draft, correcting final copy) help managers to analyze time and costs and find ways to reduce both. For instance, after discovering that correction of typographical errors takes longer than the initial typing, or that retyping pages by hand requires repeated use of proofreaders' time, many managers have decided to purchase word processing equipment.

Organizer and Reminder for Writing

8.9 When you are ready to write a first draft, simply spread the outline on your desk and begin dictating. The outline and detailed notes from research keep you in order and prevent you from forgetting details. Even when you type your own drafts, the work will be faster because you have everything in front of you.

Outlines Based on the Scientific Method

Outline for Reporting Research Results

8.10 For articles, research reports, proposals, and some monographs, most scientists use some version of Outline 8.1 because it helps to convey information without bias, makes information easy to find, and makes refereeing for publication easier and faster. (Outline 7.2 in Chapter 7 is an adaptation of Outline 8.1.)

[*Outl. 8.1*]   I. Problem statement
            A. The problem

      B. Theory, including hypotheses
  II. Method
      A. Description of data and method
      B. Variables
      C. Analytic techniques
  III. Results (including tables)
  IV. Discussion (including tables)
  V. Summary

8.11 *Problem statement.* In the problem statement:

1. Present specific questions; show why they are important.
2. Tell what researchers know about these questions.
3. Cite only the most pertinent documents.
4. Overall, move from general issues to the specific problem.

One sentence for each issue, supported by one or more references to pertinent literature, is often adequate.

8.12 *Description of method.* The method section describes research in enough detail that someone else could repeat the research. When a description of the method has been published before, writers either (1) cite the document that describes the method or (2) cite and then summarize the method briefly. There are several possible outlines for the method section. Sections 2.31 through 2.35 in Mullins (1977) list four possible outlines and describe how to choose among and use them.

8.13 *Results and discussion.* The results and discussion follow the method section as either one section or two separate sections. Mullins (1977, Sections 2.36 through 2.39) shows three possible outlines and tells when and how to use them. The general principles for writing results are:

1. Never present raw data.
2. Give all the data needed to test the hypotheses stated in the introduction, but no more.
3. State clearly whether, on the basis of the evidence, you are accepting, rejecting, or modifying the hypotheses you started with.
4. State clearly the reasons for accepting, modifying, or rejecting.

Outlines to Present
New Theories and Method

8.14 Scientists and technicians also use a standard outline when they want to describe and discuss a new theory or method. The basic outline is:

[*Outl. 8.2*]   I. Problem statement
　　　　　　　II. Exposition
　　　　　　　III.Discussion
　　　　　　　　　A. Improvement over earlier theories methods
　　　　　　　　　B. Implications for future work
　　　　　　　IV.Summary

8.15 Writers who want to demonstrate how a new method works with data can make the following change in Section II:

[*Outl. 8.3*]   II. Exposition
　　　　　　　　　A. Description of method
　　　　　　　　　B. Description of data
　　　　　　　　　C. Demonstration

Writers who want more detail on either version can find it in Mullins (1977, Sections 2.41 and 2.42).

Standard Outlines for Proposals

8.16 Proposals usually follow the requirements of the organization that has requested the proposal or bid or otherwise offered funds. Different organizations have different requirements, but most expect proposals to follow the guidelines specified because similar formats make evaluation and comparison easier. Writers who chafe under the guidelines and offer, instead, a proposal in a different format only reduce their chances because:

□ They risk not including required information, or when included, the possibility that readers might not find it.
□ They work harder than is necessary, and they may miss a deadline.
□ They may even risk an organization's refusal to evaluate.

8.17 Therefore, whenever you apply for a grant or submit a proposal for a bid or contract:

- □ Always get as much information as possible on the program from which you want funds.
- □ Look for outlines. When none are explicitly given, devise one that fits the description as closely as possible.
- □ Follow the outline in as much detail as possible. When some part of a required outline does not apply to your project, state that fact and say why. The inapplicability may not be obvious to reviewers.

Research Funds

8.18 Proposals for research funds often follow an outline that emphasizes elements in the problem statement and method sections of Outline 8.1. For example, the National Science Foundation requires that applicants for basic research funds describe their proposed work along these lines:

[*Outl. 8.4*] I. Objectives and expected significance
II. Relation to the present state of knowledge in the field, to previous work done on this project, and to related work in progress elsewhere
III. General plan to work
 A. Broad research design
 B. Experimental methods and procedures
IV. Bibliography

Funds for Instructional Uses

8.19 Similarly, schools' requests for funds to support instructional programs usually have to follow a standard outline. For example, the NSF's CAUSE program (Comprehensive Assistance to Undergraduate Science Education), which offers grants for instructional purposes, explicitly asks that proposals follow Outline 8.5 closely.

[*Outl. 8.5*] I. Needs and project objectives
 A. Needs addressed by proposal and how they were determined

      B. Project objectives as a consequence of assessment of needs

      C. Relationship between project objectives and CAUSE objectives

II. Project plan and logistics

      A. Detailed description of each activity

      B. Chronological sequence of activities, including time allotted to each (give a timetable)

      C. Justification of costs associated with each activity except project management and evaluation

      D. Justification of request in light of recent advances in science education materials and techniques

III. Management and evaluation

      A. Management procedures

      B. Critical decision points

      C. Distribution of responsibilities and percentage of time committed to project by staff

      D. Qualifications of personnel, including staff and consultants (include vitae in appendixes)

      E. Justification of costs for management and evaluation personnel

      F. Evaluation plan

         1. Provisions for internal monitoring, including feedback and modification procedures

         2. Provisions for a summative look at the project, including productivity, cost effectiveness, improvements in undergraduate science education, and increases in institutional capability for self-assessment

IV. Merit and justification of activities

      A. Relevance of scientific content

      B. Educational value

      C. Merit over alternative lines of action

      D. Long-term effects of plans on students and departments

      E. Potential for transferability of project outcomes to similar institutions

Technical Proposals

8.20 A technical proposal often includes all of the sections listed in Outline 8.6. Part or all of sections repeated in other proposals, like *VIII, IX,* and *X,* often become boiler plates (discussed in detail in Chapter 9).

[*Outl. 8.6*]   I. Summary
        II. Introduction
       III. Problem statement, or statement of task
       IV. Technical description, proposed approach, technical approach, or technical analysis
        V. Plan for management, or organization of program
       VI. Plan for program, or schedule
      VII. Conclusions
     VIII. Capabilities and experience, or qualifications
      IX. Resumes, or curriculum vitae, of personnel
       X. Facilities and equipment
      XI. Appendixes

Shnitzler (1973, p. 10) lists additional sections that technical proposals sometimes contain.

Business Systems Proposals

8.21 When you are trying to sell a potential client a new business system, an outline like Outline 8.7 will help you state clearly the problem, course of action, benefits and risks, and present elements in logical order. When you present the same basic system over and over to different companies, add details to the outline (as in Outline 7.1) and write boiler plates for parts that either stay the same or change very little.

[*Outl. 8.7*]   I. Executive summary
        II. Identification of the business problem
       III. Identification of business scope and objectives
       IV. Information requirements
        V. System concept
       VI. Recommendations for a new system
      VII. Justification and evaluation of costs
     VIII. Alternatives
      IX. Assessment of risk
       X. Project management

Andres (1978, pp.39-41) describes this outline in modest detail.

Outlines for Technical Reports

8.22 Technical reports often follow standard outlines. For example, Outline 7.1 is a standard outline for the first chapter of a four-chapter technical report that evaluates transit systems in small cities. The other three chapters describe the local transit system (Chapter 2), present alternatives for future service (Chapter 3), and make recommendations (Chapter 4). The outlines for these chapters are as detailed as Outline 7.1. In addition, these chapters also have varying amounts of boiler plate ready for use at a moment's notice. To save still more of writers' time and effort, this basic outline has been modified for use with reports on transit systems in larger cities, with reports on transportation for elderly and disabled people, and with management audits of transit systems.

8.23 Another, but more general outline for technical reports is:

[*Outl. 8.8*] I. Foreword
II. Conclusions
III. Recommendations
IV. Discussion
V. Appendixes

The foreword gives general background and describes the subject, scope, and purpose of research. The conclusions summarize results, and section III can include recommendations for both future research and applications. The first three parts are prepared with busy managers in mind. The rest of the report is for people who are continuing the work or who want to know the details. Richards and Richardson (1941) discuss the various purposes of this outline in an excellent article that is short, readable, and available from the Society for Technical Communication.

Outlines for Instructions and Instructional Manuals

8.24 Even simple instructions, such as how to use a can opener or how to change a typewriter ribbon, can usefully follow an outline that begins with the first step a user must take and ends with the last step.

8.25 Outlines for instructional manuals, such as guides for users of computer systems, also can follow standard outlines. Outline 8.9 is recommended by John Vaughn (1979), a consultant who specializes in documentation for corporate data processing systems.

[*Outl. 8.9*]   I. Input
          II. Output
          III. Glossary

Vaughn's reasoning is that users only want to know how to make the system work—how do you wind it up (input) and what do you get out (output). The glossary explains essential terms. *Why* the system works (flow charts, program statements, and the like) is of no more interest to users than an explanation of internal combustion engines would be to most buyers of a new car. *Why* belongs in a manual for programmers who will have to maintain and alter the system.

8.26 Sometimes user manuals need a slightly more elaborate outline, such as Outline 8.10.

[*Outl. 8.10*] I.   Foreword
       II.   Explanation of necessary mechanics (such as how to get on or off a remote system via terminal, how to set up a card job). For example:
          A.   Terminals are located in [give locations].
          B.   Figure 1.1 shows a terminal with all keys and switches labeled.
          C.   To LOG ON the system, follow steps 1 through 9 in order; when something unexpected happens, read Section 1.00 before going further.
             1.   Make sure the cord is plugged into the wall.
             2.   Turn on the machine (push to your left the switch that sticks out from the bottom, right-hand corner of the terminal; Figure 1.1 shows the switch).
             3.   Wait two minutes for the terminal to warm up.
             4.   Turn the BRIGHTNESS and CONTRAST knobs clockwise until the small, square rectangle of light (the CURSOR) has appeared and is comfortable for your eyes.
             5.   Type X and then the RETURN key. Wait for a hyphen (-) to appear in the farthest left column of the screen.

6. Then type W and RETURN and wait for the computer to respond with general information and then a request for your account number.
7. Type in your account number, initials, and password, separated by commas but no spaces. For example: *1234,abc,pswrd*.
8. Then type RETURN and wait for the system to respond with a PORT number.
9. Now perform your first task.

D. Things that can go wrong and what to do about them. [Give a list of general system error messages and what the user should do about them.]

III. Questions users want the system to answer; for each question, how to ask (input) and what comes back (output). For example:

A. To ask questions about a student's transcript, such as: What is John Student's grade point average?
1. On the terminal keyboard type [fill in] and wait until the central computer responds by displaying a copy of student's academic record on the screen.
2. Look at the number on line 6, column 14; that is the grade point average.
3. Actions you might want to take next:
   a. Write the number on a piece of paper.
   b. Clear the screen by typing the SHIFT key and the CLEAR key simultaneously.
   c. Correct the GPA by [list steps]
   d. Request a printed copy of the record by [lst stpes]
4. Error message you might get [list all error messages this action might elicit and what the user should do about them.]

B. Questions about financial aid, such as: Has Ann Student ever received financial aid? [Follow the same procedure as for the previous question.]

IV. Glossary, in tabular form, of all error messages and what the user needs to do to correct the error.

V. Glossary of technical terms. This does *not* replace an explanation in text where terms are first introduced. The glossary is needed by users of later sections who have forgotten, say, what CURSOR means.

8.27 Other information might be related, but if users don't need it to get and change information, it doesn't belong in a users' manual. Programmers who write documentation for users sometimes need to be reminded that what they take for granted is precisely what users need—and, often, little more.

How to Develop and Change Standard Outlines

Development from Scratch

8.28 Development of a standard outline can begin with the first document of a type. Much of the development and maintenance can be done by technical writers. The steps are:

1. Make a careful, detailed outline of the first document.
2. Correct inconsistencies, type (on a word processing system, if possible), and circulate copies to others who are working on similar topics or who know the topic well. Attach a note that asks readers to suggest additions, corrections, and changes, and expect several changes to come from the next four or five similar reports.
3. Correct the outline and place a copy in the procedure manual.
4. Circulate copies to all researchers who are assigned similar topics and require that they follow the outline. Ask that they consult with you or with the manager in charge of maintaining outlines before making any changes. Explain that consistency enhances the speed and quality of research, typing, and production of reports.
5. Scan completed reports for paragraphs and sections that change little or none and that can, therefore, become boiler plates.
6. Explain use and maintenance of standard outlines to each new employee.
7. To help employees adapt outlines to specific situations, give them a list of guidelines like the ones in Section 8.29.

Modification to Fit Situations

8.29 Most reports require some changes from a standard outline. For example, researchers who used Outline 7.1 often had to add to Section *II.B.* a fifth category—secondary school students—because many of them used the public bus system and all paid a reduced fare. Other researchers found that Section *III.E.* could not be subdivided because the cities had no major employers, no commercial centers, and no plans for the future; all development was residential. A few cities had unique features—one community had a large, nationally known recreation area; another had nationally known architectural features. To make changes in an outline:

1. When you need to add a feature, look first for a list of similar items; for example, "young people" fits into the list of categories in Section *II.B.*
2. When no similar list exists, look for a similar kind of category. For example, "recreation areas" would fit well in Section *III.E.* because they are large, specific locations that draw daily commuter traffic. "Architectural attractions" would fit the same category if they drew tourists. When not, the writer might mention them in Section *I,* with "description of the area."
3. When items don't apply, scratch them out and write a note to remind yourself why.
4. When you delete all but one of several items that subdivide a category at the next higher level of importance, reword the higher level category to include the single subdivision. For example, a writer left with only "housing" in Section *III.E.* changed "locations of industry, commerce, and housing" to "residential areas." When the area under study had only a single, consolidated school that served all grades, the writer changed Section *III.C.* from "educational facilities" (followed by a list of schools) to, simply, "Jones Consolidated School."
5. Mark all modifications with a large, red "M" on the outline. This will help the supervisor who checks the writing.
6. When you turn in part or all of a draft, attach to it the outline you worked from (or a copy of that outline, if you still need the original).

Tailoring an Outline

8.30 The last steps, which involve tailoring the outline to fit a specific location, are:

1. Throughout the outline change general terms to specific names.

For example, insert names of rivers, bridges, geographic features, housing subdivisions, and so forth.

2. At the first and second levels of importance, change topics to specific, complete sentences. For example, a topic sentence for Section *II* might be: "The population of Smallcity, which has been shrinking since 1950, is mostly composed of people 65 years old or older whose average incomes are less than the federally established poverty level."

These changes enable writers to make a smooth transition to writing a draft. They also permit writers to retain the advantages of mass production (via the standard outline) without losing the unique features that make, say, Smallcity different from another small city in the state.

9 | Boiler Plates: Purpose, Kinds, and Preparation

9.1 Boiler plates are paragraphs, sections, chapters, and appendixes that writers can use in reports, proposals, and other technical documents with few or no changes from one manuscript to the next. For example, a technical appendix on routine procedures for cleaning and maintenance of buses probably needs no changes. A chapter on how to use a specific kind of CRT (cathode ray tube) computer terminal probably needs no changes from one set of instructions to the next. A chapter on recommended management procedures probably would require the writer to change only the name of the company or organization receiving the recommendations. The longer the document and the more frequently your organization writes similar documents, the more useful boiler plates are likely to be.

9.2 In general, the number of changes writers can make conveniently depends on whether the document has been typed on word processing equipment (discussed in Chapter 4), and, if so, on whether:

- The system is line- or scroll-oriented (definitions in Section 4.15).
- The system can perform global, or string, searches (defined in Section 4.17).
- The equipment is supported by a powerful enough computer that writers can use programs like the ones described in Sections 4.8 through 4.10.

Examples of Boiler Plates

9.3 Some kinds of boiler plate are useful in reports, proposals, and instructions. Others can be developed for one or two of these categories, but not all three. Among the generally useful boiler plates are:

- □ Cover.
- □ Front matter; title page, table of contents, list of tables, list of illustrations, and preface can easily become boiler plates and act as checklists.
- □ Title pages for parts and chapters.
- □ Descriptions, as of relevant state laws, types of equipment and procedures (for example, to gather data, to install a sink or car washer, to get support from registered voters).
- □ Technical appendixes.
- □ Glossaries of technical terms.
- □ Bibliographies.
- □ Formats for tables and illustrations.

9.4 Closely related to boiler plates are boiler plate forms, whose purpose is to gather information in the same form and thus make using it easier. Examples are forms for:

- □ Checklists and instructions.
- □ Organizational structure for managing a project.
- □ Gathering information on resumes (described in detail by Breslin 1973).
- □ Estimates of time and cost.
- □ Preprinted pages with, say, TABLE OF CONTENTS or ILLUSTRATIONS on it.

For Reports

9.5 When a firm repeats the same kind of report over and over for different contractors, additional boiler plates, such as the following, can speed up the writing and improve the quality of the report:

- □ Release page.
- □ Introductory chapters that describe general purpose and organization and may need changes only in the name of the contractor or organization that is the subject of the report.

▢ Recommendations; such as specific management techniques and short- and long-range future plans.

Proposals

9.6 Proposals usually were due yesterday, if not sooner. Anything the proposer can do in advance will save wear and tear on nerves and give everyone a bit more time on work that cannot be standardized. Teigen (1973), Stoddard (1973), and other articles in *Proposals and Their Preparation* give excellent suggestions for preparation and use of boiler plates. The following list includes some of the more likely candidates for boiler plates for proposals:

▢ Introductory section that describes organization of the proposal.
▢ Descriptions of your organization, why it is best for the job, what unique resources it has, what especially qualified people, and so forth.
▢ Resumes; short and long forms.

For more suggestions, read Caird (1973), Stoddard (1973), and Ullman (1973).

Instructions

9.7 Complex instructions, such as user manuals for a computer system, also may benefit from boiler plates. Examples, based on computer documentation, are:

▢ Description of user manuals and how to keep them up-to-date.
▢ Description of equipment, such as a kind of computer terminal, and how to use it.
▢ Description of how to punch cards.
▢ Description and list of control cards for specific jobs.
▢ Description of how and where to get printout.
▢ Description of a general system that users must enter before gaining access to a subsystem or program.
▢ Description of error messages and how to correct them.
▢ Glossary of technical terms.
▢ Summary sheets for experienced users.

In addition, color coding the boiler plates helps users find information quickly. For example, front matter might always be cream-colored; the description of equipment, buff-colored; error messages, light yellow; and so on.

Why Use Boiler Plates?

9.8 When you meet resistance to boiler plates from frustrated writers who consider prewritten material an affront to their creative talents, remind them of the purposes of technical writing (given in Section 1.9) and then show them the reasons in Sections 9.9 and 9.10.

The Obvious Reasons

9.9 Among the more obvious reasons for using boiler plates are:

- They save the writer's time.
- They save typing and proofreading time.
- They save reproduction costs; boiler plates that require *no* changes can be reproduced in greater quantity at lower cost per copy and stored for later use.
- Because they don't need to be retyped, they prevent new typographical errors from creeping into the text.
- They can be written well because writers can justify spending more time, and technical writers and editors can justify more effort, with material that will be used over and over.
- They can be modified slightly, even without word processing, with judicious use of cutting, taping, and masking (the original looks terrible, but when the masking has been done properly, the copies are perfectly clean).
- Word processing enables more extensive modifications without loss of quality.

The obvious advantages add up to shortcuts that save time and money without loss of quality.

The Less Obvious Advantages

9.10 The less obvious advantages take effect more slowly. The most important of these are:

- Because readers get the same information in the same form over and over, they can read through documents more rapidly. For example, people who are already familiar with some programs on a computer system, but are learning another, will be able to read quickly through the user manual, stopping only to learn the features and steps that are *different* from what they already know.

□ Writers improve their writing because reading through well-written boiler plates over and over gradually impresses on their minds good sentence patterns and paragraph structure, and correct format and design.

How to Develop Boiler Plates

9.11 Ideas for boiler plates can come from anyone in an organization. For example, typists and proofreaders might recommend pre-printed forms for front matter, tables, and illustrations because they are the people who prepare and check final copy. To develop boiler plates most efficiently:

□ Be sure everyone you supervise knows what boiler plates are and how they can help make work easier and faster.

□ Watch for repeats; the second time you use the same information, mark it in a copy of the document and write a brief desription on a list.

□ Anticipate; when you know your organization will be doing several documents of the same kind, make some guesses in advance about likely boiler plates.

□ Similarly, when your organization has boiler plates for one type of document and is beginning work on new documents that include some of the same kinds of information, cull from the earlier documents sections you could adapt for the new documents.

9.12 You can justify spending extra time and effort to prepare boiler plates well. When possible, have technical writers and editors work on them (see Sections 11.19 through 11.33 and Chapter 14 for help). The steps are:

□ Circulate drafts and ask for criticism and suggestions.

□ Ask typists and proofreaders to watch carefully for typos and to ask if something seems wrong.

- When boiler plates include instructions, test them thoroughly on users and make the necessary changes after each test. Don't consider them final until users who have had no previous experience with the instructions can follow them perfectly.
- For each document, keep a list (in a procedure manual) of boiler plates that tells where they fit in the document and what, if any, changes have to be made when they are used.
- When boiler plates have been typed on word processing equipment, also record information that tells you where they are stored (usually diskette, cartridge tape, or magnetic tape), and what file or index names you need to retrieve them.

9.13 When boiler plates have not been prepared on word processing equipment, have the final typed copy prepared to cope with change as easily as possible. For example, when you will have to change the name of one company or city for another, keep relatively short the lines of typing where the names occur. Then, when typists prepare the new lines, long names won't cause the line to protrude Into the right margin.

9.14 Even after you consider a boiler plate finished:

- Make it office policy to keep a list of suggested improvements.

A carefully prepared boiler plate will elicit relatively few suggestions, but especially when it has been prepared on word processing equipment, improvements will be relatively easy to make. Why settle for less when you can have the very best?

How to Use Boiler Plates

With No Changes

9.15 When a boiler plate requires no changes, even of chapter or appendix numbers, and also constitutes a whole unit (like a chapter or appendix):

- Take advantage of the savings in time and reproduction costs to reproduce large quantities; collate, staple, and gang-punch for notebooks (when necessary); and store for use as needed.

The work can be done at times when the workload is not heavy, and your office benefits from a more even workload all the time. Caird (1973), Eames and Chesnut (1973), Stoddard (1973), and Ullman (1973) give many useful suggestions for proposal writers who need to make the best use of boiler plates to speed writing and to even out workloads when a deadline isn't imminent.

9.16 With "modular" boiler plates—such as a paragraph or a few pages—that must be incorporated into a larger unit, such as a chapter, advance reproduction makes no sense. Instead:

- □ Have a few copies on file, ready to cut and tape into the unit at the proper place, or to read in from storage on a word processing system. (Magnetic card word processing systems are especially useful for work that involves frequent use of short sections.)
- □ Reproduce with the rest of the unit.

With Changes

9.17 Boiler plates that require changes postpone some work until the last minute. After you have made changes:

- □ Proofread the changes and correct errors.
- □ When you have cut or pasted sections onto pages, be sure you have masked the sections so the reproduction won't show where you made the additions.

9.18 Before you reproduce the copy:

- □ Have a proofreader read the copy for obvious errors and omissions.

It is embarrassing to send to one company a document in which one or more pages still contain the name of a previous company. When work is rushed, it is all too easy for one or two errors to slip through uncorrected. When the document has been prepared on word processing equipment, a typist may be able to make a string search (explained in Section 4.17) to check.

III. WRITING
AND REVISING

10 Drafting Text, Titles, Front Matter, and Summaries

10.1 Writers prepare better drafts, which are easier for typists to follow, when they know and use proper style and format. Therefore, read Sections 11.19 through 11.33 and Chapters 14 and 15 before you begin drafting. While you are drafting, don't try to be creative. When you are using a standard outline, use phrases and even sentences from it. When boiler plates for sections exist, don't rewrite them. Don't even retype them. Using them as is, with as few changes as possible, is one way to work smarter.

10.2 Sections 10.3 through 10.15 discuss ways to draft chapters and appendixes that are not boiler plated. Sections 10.16 through 10.23 describe procedures and equipment. Sections 10.24 and 10.25 describe drafting of titles and front matter. Sections 10.26 through 10.29 describe preparation of abstracts and summaries. Not all of documents have all of these parts. In general, the longer the document, the more parts it has. For example, memo reports often present everything in a page or less. In contrast, a document with several chapters needs a title page, table of contents, abstract or summary, and main text as well as appendixes.

No Outline Necessary (but It Helps)

10.3 Write drafts of all other text matter—chapters and appendixes—in whatever way and place, at whatever time, and with whatever equipment helps you work most efficiently. When dealing with very

139

long manuscripts, most writers prefer to draft just one major part, such as a chapter, at a time. Many writers find that they prefer one method with a first draft and others with later drafts, or different methods with different topics. Most methods of drafting fit into one of a few categories.

From Beginning to End

10.4 *With a complete outline.* Starting with a complete, detailed outline, some writers begin with the first major topic and progress in orderly fashion through the outline, following it in every detail, to the end of the manuscript. For example, a writer using Outline 7.1 (in Chapter 7) would begin by writing about geographic area and would finish by describing other, relevant kinds of transportation.

10.5 This is the most efficient way to write, especially when you dictate drafts. You can talk faster than you can handwrite or type, and the outline keeps your information in order. Therefore:

□ Whenever you are using a reasonably complete outline, force yourself to dictate and follow the outline closely even if you have never tried dictation previously.

CAUTIONS: (1) As you dictate, recheck the outline frequently. Otherwise, like the writer who produced Outline 7.5 (in Chapter 7), you may find your thoughts wandering off the central topic. (2) If you are not using a standard outline and you have not previously had good luck writing from outlines, don't force yourself to use this method because that may prevent you from ever getting started. However, keep in mind as you use other methods that your ultimate goal should be to write from a detailed outline.

10.6 *With major sections defined.* Some writers write from beginning to end, but they don't want to be bothered, initially, with all the detail in Outline 7.1. The most they want is general ideas and the order of the ideas. So they use an outline somewhat like the one in Outline 8.1 (in Chapter 8), which has topics at the first level of importance, but very few topics at lower levels.

By Blocks

10.7 *The basic method.* A very popular method is to write major sections in blocks. The procedure usually works in this way:

1. Write the easiest part first.
2. Write the second easiest part next, and so forth.
3. Write the hardest part last.
4. When all parts have been completed, prepare a detailed outline from the parts.
5. Prepare a complete first draft following the detailed outline.

10.8 For example, if you were using Outline 8.1, you might draft the method section while you were doing the research. You might prepare tables next and use them as a basis for writing results. Discussion might come next, the problem statement next, and the conclusions last. Finally, you would put everything together in a single draft. The advantages of this procedure are that:

1. Beginning with what you know best may help you over the biggest hurdle of all—getting words on paper. And that advantage compensates for any loss of efficiency.
2. Each succeeding part is often made less difficult by the previously written parts.
3. Many writers who follow this procedure eventually find themselves outlining and writing from beginning to end.

10.9 The major disadvantages are a physically messy draft, overlapping sections, discontinuous writing style, and the need for substantial rewriting.

10.10 To prevent loss and chaos:

- When you write on paper, keep pages in a notebook, separated by dividers, or in a large folder with several pockets.
- When you write on 5 × 8 file cards, use a large file box and dividers.
- Write the title for each part on a divider.

10.11 *A variant.* A few writers use a variant of this procedure that avoids some of the disadvantages. They write a section and then set it aside. Later they rewrite it and write the next section. They repeat this procedure several times, sometimes reediting previously edited sections. As a result, when they have written the last sentence of the last section of the first draft, the manuscript is finished.

By Bits and Pieces

10.12 *The basic method.* Some people dislike any kind of formally organized procedure. If you are one of these:

1. Begin with what you know best and write in bits and pieces.
2. Use paper and a notebook, or 5 × 8 cards and a file, and tape, paste, or a stapler.
3. From time to time, sort and organize the pages or cards.
4. As you gather enough information to establish topics at the first level of importance (Section 7.12 describes levels), label a divider for each major section. For example, research scientists might begin with *problem statement* or *method;* as details emerge, identify and label dividers with topics at the second level of importance. For example, *subjects* and *procedure* might be subtopics of *method.*
5. Place completed pages or cards in the proper section of the notebook, folder, or file box.
6. Gradually, a detailed outline of each section will emerge, and you will be able to prepare a complete first draft.

10.13 *Advantages and disadvantages.* Authors who use this method treat manuscripts like jigsaw puzzles. Putting together the recognizable parts eventually helps make all the other pieces fit because there are fewer pieces, specified limits, and diminishing space into which the pieces can fit. This procedure is inefficient and repetitious. Nevertheless, even when you have to write this way, you are working more efficiently than people who share your inability to write by outline, but who are still trying to begin at the beginning.

10.14 When you have drafted in blocks or in bits and pieces, preparing a first draft will seem more like "prerevision" than like writing.

Different Methods for Different Drafts

10.15 When you are trying to write a draft, remember that not all topics and drafts are alike. For example:

□ Standard outlines and familiarity with a topic make it easier to write from beginning to end.

□ Second and third drafts usually are easier to write. There is nothing sacred about any method. What matters is that you find a satisfactory way to work. For each manuscript and draft, choose a method for drafting that suits your tastes, your skills, and your topic.

Trying Different Procedures and Equipment

Setting

10.16 As you work:

□ Experiment with physical surroundings and time of day until you find out what setting works best for you.

□ Try to write without interruptions such as telephone calls and administrative responsibilities.

□ When you draft, don't edit.

When you make a mistake, keep writing, just as if you were lecturing or giving a paper or presentation. You might restate a sentence and then go on, but you would not stop. You are your own worst enemy when you give in to the time-consuming urge to correct the tense of a verb, complete a reference, polish a sentence, or devise a transition. Moreover, you may well delete material in a subsequent revision and thus lose the time put into editing it.

Coding

10.17 When you are through with this and subsequent drafts, type a draft number and date on the upper left-hand corner, for example, 11/6/80. As you progress from draft to draft, the code will help you to keep drafts separate. When the document has been typed on word processing equipment:

□ Use the automatic running head for the date, and change it every time you work on the file.

CAUTION: When you do word processing on a large, central

computer, always check the date before you begin work on a file. Large systems sometimes break down, destroying the files you have created or changed during the last day or two. Knowing that fact allows you to retrieve the most recent version from a back-up tape or disk.

Mechanical Ways to Write

10.18 *Handwriting.* Handwriting is slow, but it can be useful for producing a complete draft from prewritten bits and blocks. When you handwrite, double-space.

10.19 *Typing.* Normal typing speed more closely matches thinking speed than handwriting does. Typed drafts are more legible than handwritten ones, and you are less tempted to edit as you write. When you type drafts, use double- or triple-spacing. When you triple-space, use legal-size paper (8 1/2″ × 14″). It shows paragraph length better and does not need to be changed as often. One scientist found a novel solution to paper changing: he used a "scroll" of white shelf paper, which he later cut into 11-inch lengths!

10.20 *Word processing.* Word processing, described in detail in Chapter 4, automates the typing process. Available on many computer systems (large, mini, and micro) as well as in systems intentionally developed as word processers, the increase in typing speed and improvement in quality are so dramatic that writers owe it to themselves to learn about systems that may be available to them. The author types in text along with commands for paragraphing, tabulation, centering, and so forth. Corrections, even moving sections of text from one part of the manuscript to another, can be made automatically via an editing system. The advantage is that retyping of an entire manuscript is never necessary. The result is that revisions are easy and proofreading and errors are kept to a minimum. The greater the number of revisions, the greater the advantages of word processing equipment over ordinary typing.

10.21 *Dictating.* Some writers dictate their first drafts, using either standard dictation equipment or a tape recorder with transcribing equipment. The reasons are:

- Most writers can think and talk faster than they can handwrite or type.
- Dication equipment prevents the need for dictators to tie up their time *and* a secretary's when they draft.
- Dictation is exceptionally efficient when writers draft from a detailed outline or from prewritten pieces.
- When writers use tank-type dictation equipment (described in Section 4.27), the typist can be transcribing just a short distance behind.
- The typed transcript is ready for editing.

Machine dictation is so much faster than other methods, especially for writing drafts, abstracts, and summaries (described in Sections 10.26 through 10.29), that all writers should try this method. Be aware, however, that the sheer joy of having a complete first draft, together with the beauty of a professional typing job, may lull you into thinking that revision is unnecessary. Yet, in truth, dictated drafts usually need more editing than do typewritten drafts.

10.22 *Lecturing.* Some writers draft by lecturing if they happen to be discussing a topic with a class or other audience. To use this method:

1. Obtain a recorder with transcribing equipment and running time of at least 30 minutes without a change.
2. Test the recorder in the room and adjust the volume and other controls.
3. To prevent interruptions, ask an assistant to turn and change the cassettes or tapes.
4. Have a typist transcribe the lecture.

This technique is particularly useful when you are writing something like a textbook or trade book, or an article that is for a nonspecialized audience.

Getting Perspective

10.23 When you are through writing the first draft, let it "cool" for a few days. That is the only way to get enough distance to revise the manuscript.

Titles and Front Matter

Titles

10.24 When the exact title has not been prescribed by your organization or by a funding agency, draft a title that:

- □ Summarizes the topic briefly and simply.
- □ Uses no abbreviations.
- □ Mentions important variables, procedures, findings, perspectives, or whatever else distinguishes the document.

In general, avoid "cute" titles with multiple levels of meaning. The reason is the need to communicate clearly, without the possibility of misunderstanding. When an organization repeats the same kind of study over and over, writers can use a boiler-plated title in which only specific names change. For reports that will be made public in any way, or that have to be cataloged for electronic retrieval, a second reason is the requirements of abstracting services and information-retrieval systems, which catalog and retrieve documents by mechanically searching titles for keywords.

Front Matter

10.25 Short documents usually don't need elaborate front matter. The longer ones usually need, in addition to a title page, a table of contents, sometimes lists of tables and illustrations, and sometimes a preface. If your organization produces long documents frequently, save time and effort by preparing boiler plate forms and even boiler plates, if employees frequently produce documents of the same kind. For help in developing boiler plates, read Chapter 9. For help with stylistic detail, read Sections 11.19 through 11.33 and Chapter 14.

Abstracts, Summaries, and Executive Summaries

10.26 The longer a report or proposal, the greater the need for a brief, concise abstract or summary that:

- □ Lets potential readers decide whether they want to read further.

□ Lets interested but busy readers glean the essence of the document without reading it thoroughly.

Often writers have no choice about summaries and abstracts because their organization or a sponsoring organization requires one or the other.

10.27 Most writers write abstracts and summaries after they have finished drafting the rest of the document, and many don't write them until the rest of the document is being typed in final form. The disadvantage of writing the summaries after final typing has begun is that the writer no longer has the possibility of changing the main text without considerable cost in time and effort. Yet the exercise of drafting abstracts and summaries, which must be clear, brief, and specific, often reveals flaws in the main text. When you want to benefit from the chance to recheck the document and still use many sentences from the document:

□ Draft abstracts and summaries after you have finished a final draft of the document, but before final typing. Even for a long document, copying usable sentences directly from the document shouldn't delay typing for more than a day.
□ When the document has been typed on word processing equipment, mechanically copy the sentences directly from the document files to a summary file.
□ When you are pressed for time, have a technical writer draft the abstract or summary for you.
□ Dictate (for help, see Section 10.21).
□ Develop boiler plate formats that other writers can use like a sentence completion test. For example:

> This report describes [fill in].
>
> The major conclusions are [give a list].
>
> The major recommendations are [give a list].

Technical writers and editors can save organizations considerable time by drafting abstracts and summaries. They can save even more time by streamlining procedures with modular boiler plates and boiler plate forms (discussed in Chapter 9).

Abstracts and Summaries

10.28 Abstracts and summaries can range in length from four or five sentences to a page or two. Their basic purpose usually is to give potential readers a way to decide whether to read the rest of the document. Sentences must be specific, for example:

> This report on transportation in Smallcity shows that the bus system provides convenient, frequent service at reasonable rates.

NOT

This report describes bus transportation in Smallcity.

Most of the time, pulling together specific topic sentences for major sections yields an adequate abstract. When detail is necessary, usually it is for the conclusions or recommendations or both. For more help on summaries, see Brown (1973, pp. 313-314, 334) and Lesikar (1974, pp. 15, 30).

Executive Summaries

10.29 Executive summaries are longer than abstracts and summaries and often are the only part read. They can range from 10 to 50 pages in length and often are bound separately from the main report. A good rule of thumb for writing them is to include information that an executive would need to make decisions. For example:

- A list of reasons or problems that caused the study.
- Some detail about findings, but much more about recommendations.
- Little, if anything, about how the study was done.

Others will use the details about method and implementation, but to get them they will have to read the report. In many ways, then, the executive summary is much less balanced than the abstract and short summary, which give approximately equal space to different parts of the report or proposal. Some parts are summarized briefly while others are summarized in detail.

11 Tools for Revision: Readability Measures, Criticism, and Nonverbal Messages

11.1 Most writers know that careful revision is the only way to get the results they want. What they don't know is *how* to revise and *how* to know whether they are revising successfully. This chapter resolves both difficulties by giving specific steps for revision and specific tools for evaluating success. The tools and steps are useful on all documents, regardless of length.

11.2 The basic purpose of every step and tool is to help you conserve readers' mental energy. Writing teachers have long known that readers come to a document with a fixed amount of mental energy. When it's gone, it's gone. The practical implication for writers is:

□ The more mental energy it takes to dig meaning from sentences and paragraphs, the less energy readers have left to do something with what they learn and the more likely they will quit in exhaustion.

The amount is different for every reader, and the devilish part is that writers have no way to estimate the amount. The goal of revision, then, is to make sure that nothing about writing style stands between the reader and the information in the document.

11.3 The steps in revision, in order, are:

1. Measure the readability of the first draft.
2. Decide overall use of style, format, and artwork to enhance communication of your message.
3. Evaluate organization (change if necessary).
4. Add headings and subheadings to reflect the outline.
5. Cut out repetitive sections.
6. Evaluate and revise tables, illustrations, and associated text.
7. Improve the clarity of sentences.
8. Have a clean draft typed and measure readability.
9. Correct grammatical errors.
10. Take out unnecessary words.
11. Measure readability.
12. Check editorial style and consistency.
13. Type and proofread.
14. Correct and copy.

Doing the steps out of order wastes time. For example, suppose you correct grammatical errors or take out unnecessary words (steps 9 and 10) before doing one or more of steps 3 through 6. Then, when you do the earlier steps, you throw away several paragraphs or pages. When you do that, you also throw away the time you spent correcting the grammatical errors and wordiness in those paragraphs and pages.

11.4 As you revise, use readability measures and critics to help you evaluate progress. In addition, pay careful attention to the mechanics of editorial style and to format (how text looks on pages) because both can communicate strong nonverbal messages that either enhance or detract from what the document says in words. Style and format affect the readability of a document almost as much as the length and complexity of words and sentences do.

Readability Measures

Readability and Good Writing

11.5 Readability formulas can help you judge whether you are successfully helping readers to conserve mental energy. Technically, readability tests only measure the amount of education a reader must have to understand a piece of writing; and, as Hirsch (1977) has pointed out, even technically the measures have limits. However, they also can help you decide whether readers will be able to understand a document without doing battle with each sentence. The reason is that the basic variables in the formulas—length and complexity of words and sentences—reflect the basic goal of revision: conservation of readers' energy by making the structure of text as simple as possible.

Calculations

11.6 When you are calculating by hand, try the SMOG index (McLaughlin, 1969). Although it measures only sentence and word length, it gives you a rough idea how close you are to a readable draft. The instructions are:

1. Take 10 sentences from the beginning, 10 from the middle, and 10 from the end of your draft.
2. In all 30 sentences, count the total number of words with three or more syllables (the only exception is proper names).
3. Take the square root and add three.

The resulting number should be no higher than 11 or 12, and often lower. For example, textbooks for college freshmen are written at levels no higher than 9 or 10. Darwin's *Descent of Man* has a readability level of 10. As a general rule, the number should be at least two less than the number of the lowest grade you expect your least educated readers to have completed. For example, if you are writing instructions for stock boys with only an eighth-grade education, you should try to obtain a readability level no higher than 6. If the readability level is any higher, you run the risk of having the stock mishandled.

11.7 In an article in *Management Accounting*, Richard John (1976) suggests a more elaborate way to assess readability. The first steps, which analyze difficulty of words, are:

1. Count the total number of words in a sample of text. (Unlike the SMOG index, John's measures don't require a fixed, minimum amount of text.)
2. Count the number of words that have more than two syllables.

Don't include verbs made into three syllables by adding "ed," "ing," or "es," and omit proper nouns (capitalized) and compound words made up of easy elements (for example, bookkeeper, dishwasher).

3. Divide the number of words with more than two syllables by the total number of words. When the result is .3 or higher, more than 55 percent of American managers won't understand the writing.

11.8 The next steps, which involve analyzing sentences, are:

1. Count the number of sentences in the sample.
2. Divide the total number of words by the number of sentences.

When the result—the average length of sentences—is more than 13, many managers will have trouble understanding the writing. This fact doesn't mean that only short sentences are good; it *does* mean you need to use short ones whenever possible and save the longer ones for ideas that you can't express any other way.

11.9 Similarly, type of sentence affects clarity. Simple sentences, like the first one in this paragraph, contain only one main clause; they have no subordinate clauses. Compound sentences, like the second one in this paragraph, have at least two main clauses, often joined by "and," "or," "but," or a semicolon or comma. Complex sentences, like the last sentence in Section 11.7, contain a main clause and one or more dependent, or subordinate, clauses. Some sentences, like the last one in Section 11.8, are both compound (note the semicolon) and complex (note "that" in both clauses, and the implied "that" between "mean" and "you"). Complex ideas always require a fair number of complex sentences. Your goal, then, is to use simple sentences wherever possible to conserve readers' energy and hold their interest. Then they will have energy left to cope with the longer words and the longer and more complex sentences that are essential to your ideas. John advises:

▫ Don't let compound sentences make up more than 20 percent of the total sentences.
▫ Don't let complex sentences make up more than 40 percent of the total.

11.10 Writers averse to calculations can try Gunning's (1968, pp. 42-43) simple rules for achieving readability. They are:

- Consider who your reader will be.
- Avoid long sentences.
- Use long words as little as possible.

11.11 When you have access to a computer, obtain from General Motors a copy of the program STAR, which is a computerized version of the Flesch Index. The program is written in BASIC.

The Hidden Agenda

11.12 Good writing is hard work, especially for people who are just starting to try to improve their writing. Readability measures help by introducing a reward system and allowing writers to monitor their progress. Perhaps most important, writers who use readability measures regularly soon become conditioned to using the long words and sentences only when they are absolutely necessary. Many writers find it helpful to calculate a readability measure:

- Before starting to revise the first draft
- After taking the steps discussed in Chapter 12.
- After taking the steps discussed in Chapter 13.

The first measure gives a starting point; the second tells whether the writer is making progress; the third, whether he or she has reached the goal.

Critics and Critisism

Why?

11.13 The basic reason to seek and use criticism is that "two heads are better than one". You may find criticism hard to accept, especially the first few times, and you may even be tempted to question the critic's intelligence or parentage. Don't be surprised at this response. Many others have felt exactly the same way, but the truth still remains: criticism is invaluable for helping you write better and faster. A good critic:

- Contributes a different viewpoint from yours and so sees things you might not have made clear or might have left out unintentionally.

□ Stimulates your thinking by asking questions and making suggestions.
□ Helps you finish manuscripts faster by reading and criticizing during the times you are cooling the draft. When you begin revising, then, you have some distance from the manuscript *and* some questions to ask about it.
□ In an organization, helps to assure accuracy and prevent violation of organizational rules.
□ Helps you improve your writing by asking questions that make you think more logically and by rewriting sentences to clarify meaning. When the critic is a technical writer or editor, this benefit is even greater.

Furthermore, when you return the favor, you will find out that you aren't the only one who writes lousy first drafts or skips important steps unintentionally!

When and What to Request

11.14 *When.* There are three points at which you can usefully ask for criticism. They are:

□ Right after the first draft, before you have done anything to it. CAUTION: You can ask for this kind of help only when you have worked with someone for a while. Most critics can read a writer's first draft easily only when the two have had experience working with each other.
□ After you have done the steps in Chapter 12 (3 through 6 in Section 11.3) and had a clean draft typed so the critic can read it easily.
□ After you have done the steps in Chapter 13 (7 through 10 in Section 11.3) and had a clean draft typed. At this point, when you are writing instructions, *don't* test them on a co-worker. Instead, ask for help from someone who will have to use them.

11.15 *What to ask for.* When you ask for help on either a first draft or a draft on which you have done the steps in Chapter 12:

□ Ask for general criticism of organization and substance.
□ Ask especially that the critic mark sections that seem to repeat other sections, and sections that introduce information the reader was unprepared for.

Experienced critics, especially technical writers and editors, also will be able to mark locations in the document where they were expecting you to introduce topics that never appeared.

11.16 When you ask for criticism on a later draft, try to find someone who has not previously read the document. Then:

- Ask the critic to check the logic of the organization and to mark any sections that seem redundant.
- Also ask that he or she mark sections that lack enough headings and subheadings; sentences that aren't clear; technical language you have used unnecessarily; grammatical errors, and so on.
- When you use technical writers or editors as critics, give them permission to rewrite and reorganize. You will benefit from an individually tailored lesson in good writing.
- When comments and corrections of the same kind occur over and over, list them on a card and post it above your desk. Use the suggestions as a guide to better writing.
- As you correct the faults, cross them off the list and replace them with new ones.

How to Ask for Help

11.17 The best way to ask for help is in person. Take with you a written list of sections and sentences you think may be unclear, questions about organization, sections you think may violate security or company policy, and so forth. Next:

- Give the critic the written list of concerns.
- When you have a deadline, state it and ask whether the person can meet it. Asking in advance (step 11, Section 2.3) can help assure the availability of a given critic, such as your supervisor, when you need it.
- Express thanks when the critic returns comments and offer to return the favor.
- When you act as a critic, be as tactful as possible. Try to offer constructive suggestions, not just criticism.

What to Do with Criticism

11.18 You will probably find criticism hard to accept, especially if you have not had previous experience with it. Therefore:

- Remind yourself that it saves you the time needed to find all mistakes and ambiguities on your own. Also remember that criticism of a manuscript isn't personal criticism.

□ Take all criticisms seriously. Even when critics don't describe a problem correctly, almost always they have pointed out a legitimate problem that you need to fix.

□ Treat criticisms as indications of nonverbal messages that all readers will get even though you didn't write them and didn't intend them.

□ When a comment doesn't make sense even after considerable thought, ask the critic to elaborate.
  CAUTION: Restrict yourself to clarification; don't debate.

Style, Format, and Artwork

11.19 Style, format, and artwork are not separate entities, as this heading may imply. Indeed, the three are powerful tools that writers can use jointly to enhance their written messages. The separation is made here only to emphasize the distinctive features of each. With all three, a writer's dominant concerns should be:

□ Use of style, format, and artwork to make nonverbal messages enhance written messages.

□ Simplicity. For example, when a choice is between underlining and not underlining a set of words in text, don't underline.

□ Consistency. For example, when you capitalize one chapter title completely, capitalize all chapter titles completely. Don't use initial caps only on some of the titles.

□ Distinctiveness. For example, when you capitalize chapter titles completely, don't treat first-level headings the same way. If you do, you run the risk that readers will mix them up visually.

Editorial Style

11.20 "Editorial style" refers to rules for mechanical details of format such as spacing lines, typing references and headings, and presenting tables and equations. These rules affect every aspect of every page of all documents—short or long, from the title page through the index. The following list shows the most common styles and the abbreviations used in this book. Complete information on

American Chemical Society [1]	AChemS
American Institute of Physics [2]	AIP
American Mathematical Society [3]	AMathS
American Medical Association [4]	AMA
American Psychological Association [5]	APA
American Society for Testing and Materials [6]	ASTM
American Sociological Association [7]	ASA
Council of Biology Editors [8]	CBE
Journal of The American Statistical Association [9]	*JASA*
Manual of Style, humanities [15]	MSH
Manual of Style, natural science [15]	MSN
Modern Language Association [10]	MLA
Sage journal style [11]	Sage
Suggestions to Authors [12]	SA
Turabian [13]	Turabian
U. S. Government [14]	GPO

each style is contained in documents listed in the bibliography. The documents are coded with the bracketed number listed with each style.

Sometimes your own organization prescribes the style—often called the "house style"—and sometimes an outside funding organization requires the style.

11.21 *The importance of consistency.* Some styles are similar and there are many versions of each style, but the only guides for typing are little more than brief asides in style sheets, pamphlets, and books addressed to writers. Nevertheless:

- □ Neatness, consistency, and faithful use of a prescribed style make a favorable, although often subconscious, impression on readers.
- □ Failure to meet these criteria may cause readers to reject even the most carefully researched and written report or proposal simply because it looks sloppy (therefore, the contents probably are sloppy).
- □ Most important, inconsistent attention to detail means inconsistent nonverbal messages.

For example, when you use side headings to display subtopics of a center heading and you or a typist mistakenly treat one of those subtopics as a paragraph leader instead, readers will assume, incorrectly, that the paragraph leader subdivides the preceding side heading. For information on subordinate and coordinate topics, see Sections 7.12 through 7.14. For information on headings and subheadings, see Sections 12.15 through 12.17.

11.22 *How to insure correct style.* Writers of technical documents, especially those for publication, must follow exceptionally detailed rules. Yet many writers have to use a different style for every document, and only a few rules hold for all styles. For all other aspects of typing each document, every writer must eventually specify a host of specific rules.

11.23 What supervisors and writers need is a checklist of the details, by category, about which they must give their typists specific instructions. Before you give your next document to a typist:

1. Read this chapter, Chapters 14 and 15, and the first 12 pages of the document.
2. From topics in Chapter 14, make a checklist of items to which typists will need answers. Table 11.1, a checklist for the manuscript of this book, is an example. The sample pages are in the Appendix.
3. Get (1) a copy of instructions for the style you are to use and (2) copies of example pages that show front matter pages (when the document is long enough to require front matter), headings, subheadings, tables, illustrations, notes, and documentation.
4. For consistency, make decisions about items on the checklist on which the style and example sheets either are ambiguous or give no guidelines. Make the simplest choices possible and mark examples in the sample pages.
5. Give the typist the style sheet, the example pages, and your list of answers to questions on the checklist. Insist on faithful execution of your instructions. Sometimes it helps to explain the importance of consistency.
6. Ask the typist to save the list of answers.
7. When the typist returns the document and checklist, look for places where the typist didn't carry out instructions exactly. Talk with the typist to find out what the misunderstanding was, and then rewrite the instructions more clearly.
8. From the revised list, make, or have an assistant make, a checklist of specific answers that you and other writers in your organiza-

tion can use for that style. Reproduce and distribute the master list.
9. Use one copy for each new document in that style. The result will be greater consistency and fewer questions with less effort.

When a checklist like Table 11.1 comes with sample pages that have vertical and horizontal spacing marked, it reduces the possibility of misunderstanding between writers and typists.

11.24 On subsequent documents:

1. Read the first 12 pages of the document. Use either this chapter or a general checklist as a guide, following the instructions in Section 11.23.
2. With each document in a style for which you do not have a general checklist, follow steps 6 through 8 in Section 11.23 so that you will have general lists in the future.

Format and Design

11.25 Some aspects of format, such as the space between paragraphs and headings or whether tables may be typed on pages with text, are prescribed by rules of style. Usually, however, writers can make choices about format because it has to do with the layout of pages, use of space and displayed lists, use of columns, balance of text with pictures, width of columns and pages, and so forth. Like style, format is important because a pleasing layout appeals to readers and makes comprehension easier. Thoughtfully used, it also communicates strong nonverbal messages. Therefore:

☐ If you are not familiar with principles of format, consult technical writers and designers. Ask them to explain *why* they make each change or recommendation.

11.26 *Principles for using format.* Sections 5.28 through 5.45 explain principles for designing effective tables. Sections 6.34 through 6.56 explain the principles that govern design of effective illustrations. The rest of this section illustrates some of the ways writers can treat single-column text pages that don't include illustrations. When you need multicolumn pages and pictures, consult a designer.

TABLE 11.1 *Example of Style Sheet*

1. Margins: 1 1/2 inch left (for holes and binding); 1 inch right margin; 1 inch top to running head and page number, which should be on same line; and 1 1/4 inch bottom margin. Below running head skip a space before beginning text unless the page begins a section of front or back matter or a chapter, in which case skip an inch.

2. Running head: Top left corner of every page, with date first, type of document second, author's name third, and publisher and date last. Flush with left margin. Example:

    09-10-79, Book, Mullins, Prentice-Hall 1980

3. Page numbers: On Front Matter, sequential lowercase roman numbeals beginning with "i" for the title page. No number typed on title page or first page of table of contents, list of tables, list of illustrations, preface.

    Main test through back matter: Sequential arabic numerals beginning with "1" for first page of first chapter. No page number typed on part pages or first page of chapters, appendixes, indexes, bibliographies, or illustrations even though these pages count in the numbering.

    Placement: top, right-hand corner of pages, one inch from top of page and right edge.

4. Front Matter: Follow models in attached Sample Pages 1 through 5. Follow details exactly—placement on page, centering, capitalization, vertical and horizontal spacing as marked, lining up decimals in section numbers and table and illustration numbers, and so forth.

5. Part pages: Follow model in Sample 6.

6   Title pages of chapters, appendixes, etc.: Follow pattern in Sample 7.

7. Headings: Follow patterns in Sample pages 7, 8, and 9.

8. Second and subsequent pages of chapters, appendixes, etc.: Follow pattern in Sample pages 8 and 9.

9. Pages with instructions in playscript format: Follow model in Figure 11.2.

10. Tables: For treatment of number, title, turnover lines in title, horizontal lines, column heads and boxheads, row stubs, and notes: follow patterns in Sample page 10, including capitalization and spacing, vertically and horizontally. In regression tables follow title pattern in Sample page 10 and body pattern in Sample page 11.

11. Citations in text and tables: Follow patterns in Sample pages 9 and 10.

12. Lists of references: Follow patterns in Sample pages 9 and 10.

13. Notes: None

11.27 The basic rule is:

☐ Determine format by what you want to emphasize most, second most, and so forth.

Section 11.20 above shows a fairly simple example. In it the capital letters and ample space emphasize the abbreviations. The reason is to make cross-reference easy. For example, when you want to find out the meaning of an abbreviation used in Chapter 15, you can easily refer to Section 11.20, scan the right-hand column for the abbreviation, and then find the matching full title (and source information) on the left.

11.28 Figure 11.1, which shows a page from a report, demonstrates a way to emphasize features at several levels of importance. The

---

last sentence of previous paragraph.

Capital Expenditures

This is a sentence of introduction.

Other Equipment

Supervisor's car. A supervisor's car would allow the manager to check buses on routes, to pick up parts from local dealers, and to attend official meetings. It could also be used to bring drivers to and from the bus transfer point at the beginning and end of shifts.

Shelters and signs. Bus shelters at major traffic generators would protect travelers from bad weather. Bus stop and bus route signs would make it easier for people to find bus routes and would advertise the service to people who do not use transit. Similarly, posting the times at the bus stops for major traffic generators would both help to reduce waiting time for riders and advertise the service to nonusers.

Automatic bus washer. An automatic bus washer would reduce the time needed to perform routine daily maintenance. The washer could also be used by other city departments; however, UMTA would provide 80% funding only for the proportion of total cost allocated to the transit system. For very few vehicles, then, a bus washer might not be an economical investment.

Service van. A service van would be used for emergency road calls when transit vehicles broke down. It could also be used to pick up parts too large for the supervisor's car. A simple tow could be added

---

FIGURE 11.1 Example: Page of text with paragraphs and headings

surrounding space, centering, and underlining combine to make the first-level heading, *Capital Expenditures,* the most important feature on the page. Similarly treated except for being flush with the left margin and therefore visually subordinate to *Capital Expenditures, Other Equipment* is a second-level heading and the second most important feature on the page. Third most important are the paragraph leaders that show subdivisions of the second-level heading. The fourth most important feature is the text. The writer used headings and subheadings because she wanted the outline of recommendations to show clearly. She used the paragraph leaders, even though they weren't necessary, because she knew that the officials reading the report would want to know about those specific recommendations immediately. The paragraph leaders help readers find recommendations without a hunt through the section on *Other Equipment.*

11.29 Figure 11.2 shows a page of text whose format, a "playscript" (Matthies 1963), is designed to enhance communication of instructions. On that page, the most important feature is the first-level heading, which is centered, underlined, and numbered (to make cross-reference easy). The second most important feature is the column titles, *Actor* and *Action,* which tell readers who does what. The next most important feature is the actors, who are emphasized by the amount of space that surrounds each actor. The space and the use of a separate column also show clearly when steps in a process stop being the responsibility of one actor and become the responsibility of another.

11.30 The text in the right-hand column is the next most important feature, and within this column specific features distinguish various aspects. The numbers tell the order of actions. Many readers will not pay attention to the specific numbers, but the fact of numbering communicates that the steps have a built-in order. The indented numbers that have letters attached are substeps and sometimes groups of substeps. Again, many readers will not notice the actual numbers, but the fact of numbering communicates order, and the indentation communicates "subcategory." Where choices might exist, the use of capped OR, centered within the column, will catch readers' eyes and signal the possibility of an alternative. The capitalized words signal technical terms. The writer used this device to tell readers that these words are used in special ways. Readers who

Begin with either Step 1 (when small square contains a question mark) or Step 2 (when small square contains a cross).

Actor		Action
Operator	1.	When small square contains question mark,
	1a.	Pushes down ALT key.
	1b.	While holding down ALT, pushes SYS REQ key.
Computer	1c.	Changes question mark to cross. (If small square continues to contain question mark, calls 000-0000 for help.)
Operator	1d.	Goes to step 12.
	2.	When small square contains a cross,
	2a.	Presses and holds ALT, then pushes SYS REQ key.
Computer	2b.	Changes square with cross to solid
Operator	2c.	Goes to Step 3.
		OR
Computer	2d.	When cross changes to question mark, had no link to CICS.
Operator	2e.	Repeats Step 2a until computer responds with a cross.
	2f.	Goes to Step 12.
Operator	3.	To find out whether link is to PROD or TEST, types: CLME
	4.	Presses ENTER key.
Computer	5.	Responds with message in Figure 1, Part A, which says terminal is fully linked to PRODUCTION CICS.

FIGURE 11.2   Example: Text page that lists instructions

don't know the special meanings have been told earlier about the glossary that lists all technical terms. Note that the writer did *not* use headings at second and third levels to subdivide the text. If she had, they would have conflicted visually with the list of actors in the right-hand column; the result would have been confused readers.

11.31 The writer was able to make initial choices about many of these features. The choices were based on simplicity—how to communicate all the information without excessive use of transitions, repeated definitions, and so forth. Once she has made those choices, however, she must follow them consistently throughout the rest of the document. Eventually her employer might require all instructions to follow these patterns.

11.32 *How to insure consistency.* To insure consistency, from both herself and typists, the writer needs to include these specifications in a style sheet like the one recommended in Section 11.23. Specifications can even include tab settings and might include a brief reference to the reasons for choices to keep typists from deciding independently that, for example, the format wastes a lot of space on pages and something else would be better. In addition to insuring consistency:

□ A style sheet for an entire document also helps writers find potential conflicts and do something about them before final typing begins.

For example, some writers completely capitalize first-level headings, but that practice usually conflicts with treatment of chapter titles, for which most writers use all caps. Similarly, some writers use capitalized words for emphasis, but a writer who made that choice would then have to find another way to emphasize technical terms.

11.33 Technical writers, editors, and designers usually can help writers make these decisions and then standardize them across a range of documents. Because they work with a range of documents across an entire organization, they can make more informed choices about style and format than writers familiar with only a narrow range. Editors and designers who have had experience with publishing houses often are exceptionally good resources because their knowledge includes printed as well as typed documents.

Artwork

11.34 The uses and principles for using artwork are the same as for style and design, and writers can use a style sheet to keep track of choices. However, unlike choices about layout of typed pages, execution of artwork usually isn't something that writers can automate in the way choices about layout often can be incorporated as macro commands in a word processing system (for explanation, see Section 4.15, Chapter 4). In general, avoid artwork because it involves unusual time and expense. When it is necessary, perhaps for a logo or for labels on complicated illustrations, consult a professional. Their technical knowledge of type sizes and styles and of shadings is not something most writers have.

Summary

11.35 The basic principles of revision can be summarized as follows:

- □ Two heads are better than one.
- □ Like people, manuscripts communicate nonverbal messages.
- □ Poor writing reflects poor thinking.
- □ Small is beautiful, and less is more.
- □ Your primary purpose is to inform, not to entertain.
- ⊔ You must budget long words and sentences like money.
- □ Variety is *not* the spice of technical and scientific writing.

Chapters 12 through 14 give specific techniques to help you carry out these principles. Chapter 12 describes steps 3 through 6, which help writers cut out peripheral text, shape the focus of the document, and display organization. Chapter 13 discusses steps 6 through 12, which help writers get rid of ambiguous sentences, grammatical errors, and wordiness. Chapter 14 describes the kind of editing and double checking that writers should do, especially on longer or more important documents, before having the final copy typed.

12 Revision: Clearing Away the Underbrush

12.1 This chapter describes steps in revision that apply to all documents regardless of length: evaluating and revising organization; evauating and revising tables, illustrations, and associated text; using headings and subheadings; cutting out summaries and repetitive statements; making drastic cuts in length; using appendixes effectively; finding a good starter; and checking unity of paragraphs. The longer the document, the more important the steps. There is an excellent reason for doing these steps before revision that involves sentence structure and choice of words:

- □ There is no sense spending time on sentences and words that, later, you might eliminate from a document because you've decided to eliminate the section they're in.

Evaluation of Organization

Evaluation of Reader, Purpose, Scope, Plan

12.2 Skim the document quickly. Even a one-page monthly report might be incorrectly focused. Try to identify clearly the intended reader, the purpose in writing, and the scope. For help, see Sections 7.4 through 7.10. Write a topic sentence in fewer than 50 words.

12.3 When you find reader, purpose, scope, and plan hard to identify, take the steps listed below. They work on any document, whether yours, a student's, or a fellow worker's. They work especially well when the document is not yours because writers find each other's errors faster than their own.

1. Skim the document.
2. In the margin (when there is space) or on a piece of paper, briefly summarize the topic of each paragraph and its connection to the paragraph just before it. When there is no logical or apparent connection, say so. Figure 12.1 shows an example of what the notes could look like.
3. On a separate piece of paper, outline the document to the third level of importance. (For a discussion of levels, see Sections 7.12 through 7.14.) Use a topic outline and try to write legibly. Don't look at previous outlines and don't try to evaluate or reorganize. Just try to find out what the document actually says.
4. Try to write the central theme in 50 words or fewer. You should find only one such theme; other themes, or topics, should be subordinate to it. If you have not yet identified the reader, try again.
5. Now evaluate the plan of organization by marking on your outline places where topics repeat, where topics seem out of place, or where topics placed at the same level of importance don't seem to be equally important.

12.4 When you are working with a partner:

□ Try to be tactful.
□ Try to suggest ways to correct specific problems.
□ Don't discuss a partner's document with other people. What you say to each other is confidential.

12.5 Using as a basis the outline and comments from the exercise in Section 12.3, decide whether the document says what you wanted it to say. When it doesn't, revise the outline so that you put together all the information on the same topic in the most effective order. (For help, read 7.11 through 7.25.) Scientists might find helpful the outlines in Mullins (1977, Sections 2.28 through 2.40). Others might find helpful the outlines in Chapters 7 and 8 of this book. When you are ready to reorganize:

□ Tape or staple the pages together in the new order.

6. Little effort, if any, was made to interpret results to improve teaching-learning situations nor to modify the objectives. *Detailed repetition of earlier work; not necessary*

The experiment being reported in this article was motivated by the results of the survey just described. Specifically, because the survey revealed a big gap between what should be and what actually existed, it might be that what ought to be could not be achieved. The research was, therefore, a study undertaken to follow the requirements of the specific model, thereby testing its workability or fitness for use. *Reason for new study*

THE REPORT

The study being reported took up the entire 1979-80 academic session, October 1979 to June 1980. The participants were the 265 second-year Education students of University, and the course involved was Development of Curricula. *Time of new work setting*

Step I: Determination of Present Status

In order to determine the degree of students' knowledge, ability and skills in relation to the course, background information was requested regarding the bases of their entry into the University. This was with a view to determining those who had had some familiarity with studying in general. Table 1 shows analysis from this first step. *Testing students' background. Later analysis never uses Table I*

From the above, the number of students who had been previously exposed to Education in general was 88 as outlined below: *Students' previous education. Analysis never uses this breakdown*

Grade 13 level: 7
Grade 14 level: 18
Grade 15 level: 9
ABC level: 54

Total: 88

It was assumed that those who had some previous classwork on education would somehow know something about development of curricula. *Assumptions about relation between previous education and knowledge about curriculum development*

FIGURE 12.1   Example: Marginal notes for evaluating organization

□ When you have thought about more than one new order, try all of them. (Use a different copy of the old draft for each.)

□ Compare the drafts and choose the one you like best.

12.6 Repeat steps 2 through 5 in Section 12.3, and:

□ Make sure the reason for the order is clear.

□ Make sure topics at the second and third levels of importance are relevant, understandable in context, and of equal importance relative to each other.

□ Ask whether the outline is appropriate for the intended audience and is the most efficient one possible.

□ Make sure the central theme is clearly stated in the abstract (when there is one), in the introduction, and in a brief summary at the end.

Evaluation of Nonverbal Messages

12.7 Three aspects of a document give strong, nonverbal messages that writers can use to communicate more efficiently and effectively: number of topics at first level of importance, relative amounts of space given to topics and subtopics, and placement, or order, of topics at the same level. Often, when a critic isn't understanding your message and you can't figure out why, the problem is that nonverbal messages are contradicting the written message. Although often overlooked, nonverbal messages are especially important because they have strong effects on whether a document communicates exactly, and only, the message the writer intended.

12.8 *Number of topics at first level.* In all technical writing (except instructions with long lists of steps):

□ Count the number of topics at the first level of importance and the total number of pages.

The more topics at this level, the less the effect of any single one and the less likely that the document presents a strong, cohesive single theme. This effect is not nearly as important in written instructions, which usually divide necessary steps into relatively short units identified by a single, topical heading and usually do not try to make a cohesive argument.

12.9 Use the following criteria for deciding whether you have too many topics at the first level of importance:

□ Average one topic at the first level for every seven or eight pages. For example, a 35-page report or chapter usually shouldn't have more than five topics at the first level. Very short reports (2 to 8 pages) usually should have 2 at most.

□ Don't expect the pages to distribute equally to topics. For example, in 35-page scientific reports (see Outline 8.1, Section 8.10), the problem statement may take up as few as 3 or 4 pages; the discussion, as many as 18 to 20.

□ When you find yourself with too many topics relative to the total length of the document, reevaluate.

□ When in doubt about effect, ask a critic to read the document and give you an opinion.

□ Violate the general rule when the resulting effect would be what you want.

12.10 *Allocation of space.* The number of sentences, paragraphs, or pages on a topic communicates how important the writer thinks the topic is. In general:

□ In any report or proposal or chapter, give more space to all topics at the first level of importance than to any topic at the second or third level.

□ Give the greatest amount of space to the most important topic. For example, in research reports the most important parts are the findings and discussion.

□ When a major topic at the first level of importance has fewer pages allocated than a topic at a lower level of importance in another section, consider the reason and the effects before making changes.

For example, in research reports, discussions of just one set of several findings may take more space than the entire problem statement. In the report on a company's financial condition, the discussion of any single recommendation in a chapter on recommendations may take up more space than the earlier chapter that described the company. Both situations would be perfectly appropriate because the most important parts of the reports should be the findings and discussion (in the first report) and the recommendations (in the second).

12.11 In contrast, in a report on transportation in Largestate, you might have written a long section that describes transportation in Smallcity and a shorter section that describes transportation in Largecity, but Largecity's transportation has always had a stronger effect on transportation in Largestate. A critic, responding to the draft, might have asked why Smallcity is so important, because the report gives no special reasons. You didn't think Smallcity was important either, and you might have wondered about the reason for the question. The reason is, simply, that you gave Smallcity more space than more important cities like Largecity—probably by describing in the report many of Smallcity's charming features. The critic simply picked up the nonverbal message communicated by the excessive length at which the document described Smallcity. The solution is either to add comparable details about the more important cities or to delete the details about Smallcity. Unless you make use of the features later in the report, usually the best solution (and the least work) is to delete the details about Smallcity.

12.12 Use the following mechanical measures to evaluate allocation of space:

- ▫ Count the number of pages or paragraphs, or measure inches with a ruler.
- ▫ Compare the relative length of sections at the first level of importance. Make sure the one you want to emphasize is the one you give the greatest amount of space.
- ▫ Compare the relative lengths of subsections within sections at the first level of importance. Sometimes all will be equally important; when one is more important, probably it should be longer than the others.

This is not an excuse to pad, with summaries and repetition, the writing on more important topics. In fact, padding to increase length will have the opposite effect—boring readers and even causing them to skip the important topics (see discussion in Sections 12.18 and 12.19). If the topic is important, you should have enough to say that you will need all the space you can justify. Writers of research reports may want to consult Table 5.1 in Mullins (1977), which gives approximate lengths of major sections in scientific reports.

12.13 *Placement.* Especially when a document appears to offer more than one possible organizational pattern, consider the nonverbal message that arrangement of topics can convey. For example, Susan Smith is writing the six-month evaluation of a new employee, John Brown. He has performed outstandingly in a few areas and well in others, and is weak in three. She wants to keep him and get him a raise. An effective arrangement of topics would be: (1) recommendation, in one or two sentences, first paragraph; (2) reasons for recommendation, with outstanding features first and the good ones next, together with their benefits for the organization; (3) weak features last, briefly mentioned, but with her plan for action to strengthen Brown's abilities. Putting the recommendation and strong features up front emphasizes them. The same principle applies to longer documents. For example, if a document describes several cities and no inherent feature, such as geographic order, dictates the order in which you discuss them, the nature of your recommendations might make you want to emphasize deliberately one or two of the cities. If so:

- □ Place them either first or last, where they are more likely to be remembered by readers. Items in the middle of lists stand out less.

Evaluation of Tables and Illustrations

12.14 The next step is to check all tables, illustrations and associated text. Tables and illustrations are most likely to occur in longer documents. The basic principles are:

- □ Take out all tables and illustrations you haven't discussed and all tables with fewer than 9 entries in cells (defined in Section 5.7).
- □ Consider taking out tables with between 9 and 15 entries and describing the data in text. With so few entries, text usually is equally clear and also takes up less space.
- □ Insert any tables and illustrations you have discussed but not included.
- □ Make sure the associated text discusses and elaborates, and doesn't simply repeat entries in the cells.
- □ Present illustrations in the most effective form (for help, see Chapter 6).
- □ Present tables in the most efficient formats (for help, see Sections 5.13 through 5.22).
- □ Make sure the organization of tables supports your outline (for help, see Sections 5.23 through 5.27).

▫ Make sure tables and illustrations are properly designed and in proper style (see Sections 5.28 through 5.45 for help with tables and 6.34 through 6.56 for help with illustrations).
▫ Make sure words and terms are consistent with words and terms in text.

Headings and Subheadings

12.15 In most technical writing, use headings and subheadings to display the organization of the document. Because they are set off from text and emphasized with features of design such as underlining (in print, italics), capitalization, boldface, and so forth, they grab the reader's attention and thus help readers find topics of interest easily and quickly. In documents of two or three pages, headings at the first level only usually will be enough. In short reports, use headings only to the second level of importance. In longer reports, in general:

▫ Insert headings at the first, second, and (sometimes) third levels of importance.
▫ Make topics at the first level reflect changes in topic as determined by your outline.
▫ Make topics at lower levels reflect coordinate and subordinate relationships between topics.
▫ Make headings topical, grammatically parallel, no longer than half a typed line, and stylistically correct.

Figure 12.2 shows examples of headings at all three levels in three different styles. Section 14.12 shows a sample summary of specifications for style of headings and subheadings. When you use unfamiliar style requirements, you will find a similar summary helpful.

12.16 Headings and subheadings are especially important in proposals for grant and contract funds. Writers who follow an agency's required outline (discussed in Sections 8.16 through 8.19) and reflect it in headings and subheadings show that they have followed the guidelines faithfully. The headings also help reviewers find topics quickly and thus may elicit a more favorable review than otherwise would occur. An additional benefit for writers is:

PART A: APA STYLE

Method

Design of Study

Subjects

Number of subjects.

Sampling procedure.

Procedures

Data sources.

Instruments used.

Administration.

Instructions to respondents.

Controls.

Variables

Analytic Techniques

Results

PART B: ASA STYLE

METHOD

Design of Study

Subjects

Number of subjects.

Sampling procedure.

Procedures

Data sources.

Instruments used.

Administration.

Instructions to respondents.

Controls.

Variables

Analytic Techniques

RESULTS

METHOD

DESIGN OF STUDY

SUBJECTS

Number of Subjects

Sampling Procedure

PROCEDURES

Data Sources

Instruments Used

Administration

Instructions to Respondents

Controls

VARIABLES

Analytic Techniques

RESULTS

FIGURE 12.2 Examples: Headings and subheadings in three styles. Taken from the method section of a report on research done by the scientific method.

□ Headings and subheadings reduce the need for summaries and transitional sentences and clauses, so they help keep proposals shorter and crisper.

For example, in the following pairs of sentences, the first example is what one writer was using before he changed to subheadings. The second is after insertion of subheadings.

A third set of attitudes that may affect judges' willingness to convict or acquit men accused of rape relates to the degree to which they subscribe to the view that women are the sexual property of their husbands or fathers. Judges who endorse such views should be more willing to convict when an alledged rapist has violated some man's property rights.

Women as sexual property. Judges who believe that women are the sexual property of their fathers or husbands should be more willing to convict when an alleged rapist has violated some man's property rights.

The data presented in Figure 4 show the average total activity counts for the members of each group in each area for the period from 1962 to 1975. The figure shows two patterns.

Group development and activity. Figure 4 shows two patterns.

12.17 In instructions, a single topical heading, centered, often is best because readers can visually confuse subheadings in other locations with lists of steps.

Repetition: The "Bulletin-Board Syndrome"

12.18 The Lord's Prayer contains 56 words; the Gettysburg Address, 266; the Ten Commandments, 297; the Declaration of Independence, 300; and a more recent U. S. government order that set the price of cabbage, 29,111! In most drafts, summaries and restatements cause the greatest number of unnecessary words. Therefore, *don't* take the old preacher's advice to "tell 'em what you're gonna tell 'em, tell 'em, then tell 'em what you done told 'em." Most repetition and summarizing is only a lazy writer's attempt to compensate for sloppy writing. Summaries, repetitions, and restatements, which are rather like tacking on the same bulletin board several announcements of the same event, only compound the effect of bad writing by putting readers to sleep or, at best, putting their minds on "hold," waiting for the next piece of new information. The fewer lines you need to make a point clearly, the more effect it will have. In general:

- □ Restrict summaries and restatements to the abstract (when there is one), the introduction, and the concluding one or two paragraphs (in a short document) or the concluding chapter.
- □ Check quotations. Often they duplicate points made in text. Many quotations are so badly written that writers can paraphrase more clearly and briefly than they can quote.

12.19 To keep readers' attention, depend on:

- □ Clear organization.
- □ Headings and subheadings.
- □ Numbered lists.
- □ Other displayed lists of items preceded by bullets or other device, such as the open squares that precede items in this list.

◻ Occasional examples and anecdotes.

When you finish this step, you may find that the draft is only half as long as your first draft was. After these revisions, you will almost always need to have a fresh copy typed.

Drastic Reductions in Length

12.20 When, at this point, the document is still 20 percent or more longer than it should be, you will have to make drastic cuts in either the scope or the amount of detail. There is no other way to excise, systematically, this much of a document.

Cutting Scope

12.21 Cutting scope is the easier of these techniques, although, unfortunately, the less likely. It requires cutting the number of topics at the first, second, and third levels of organization (Sections 7.12 through 7.14 explain levels). For example, if the document based on Outline 7.4 (in Chapter 7) is too long, you might either cut the pages based on Sections II and III (the time periods from 1900 through 1945) or rewrite to compress the discussion into many fewer pages. If the document based on Outline 7.7 (also in Chapter 7) is too long, you might cut discussion based on trolleys (*III* in the outline). Sometimes pages cut in this fashion make up another, independent document. On occasion they make up an appendix, such as an appendix on historical background, but writers still must compress the information into fewer pages

Cutting Detail

12.22 Cutting detail is harder than cutting scope because it requires cutting topics at the fourth through sixth levels of importance— reducing the amount of detail in which you discuss a topic. Often that means cutting out every third or fourth paragraph, many tables and illustrations, most quotations, and many footnotes. Usually the pages never make up a separate document, but an extensive unit of information, such as historical background or a complex research method, might make up an appendix.

12.23 To make this kind of work easier:

1. Make a detailed outline to the sixth level of importance.
2. Mark sections at the fourth level or below.
3. Find and mark the sections of text that match the sections on the outline.
4. Cut the sections; at most, summarize briefly and eliminate detail.

Using Appendixes Effectively

12.24 In technical documents, balancing nonverbal messages with some readers' need for detail often requires skillful use of appendixes that separate the detail from the main text. Consider using appendixes for the following kinds of text:

- ☐ Complicated research methods, descriptions of data, variables and coding, construction of indexes, questionnaires used to gather data, descriptions of unusual analytic procedures, and qualifications and conditions when they apply.
- ☐ Printed matter, such as schedules.
- ☐ Complex derivations of formulas used in the main text, detailed breakdowns of cost estimates, tabular material, and so forth.
- ☐ In research proposals: vitae, breakdowns of expenses in various categories, guarantees that human subjects will not be exploited.
- ☐ In instructional manuals: instructions that will interest only a few people, or variants of a procedure that are useful under certain conditions. For example, a COBOL manual might have an appendix for readers who are using Control Data equipment, another for readers with Burroughs equipment, and a third for readers with IBM equipment.
- ☐ Also in instructional manuals: glossaries of technical terms and error messages, and summaries for quick reference.

Bait: A Good Starter

12.25 Before tossing out lines, fishermen often throw chopped bait, called "chum," onto the surface of the water to attract fish. Writers can do the same thing with an anecdote, illustration, quote, or example (stories in news magazines often use this technique). Often, a good starter is an anecdote tied to the problem solved, procedure introduced, innovation reported, or need for research proposed. For example:

> For years Joe Smith spent his first 30 minutes at work doing. . . . Now, with NewWidget, he is assembling . . . just five minutes after he arrives. This report tells how researchers developed NewWidget, . . .

12.26 For help in learning how to write interesting lead sentences and paragraphs:

- □ For a few weeks read the lead paragraph or two of articles in news magazines.
- □ Pay attention to which articles keep you reading and how the writer started the article.
- □ Adapt the techniques you learn for your own work.

12.27 Another good technique is the rhetorical question, such as: Do you know *why* Jimmy can't read? Readers won't expect to give an answer, but they *will* be prepared to have you give them one (or more). Still another is a surprising statement, such as: Nearly 80 percent of all auto accidents occur within 20 miles of the driver's home.

12.28 On the occasions when you get no ideas for a starter, simply plunge into the topic. Don't spend a lot of time winding up.

Paragraphs

12.29 Check each paragraph, making sure it has:

- □ A single, unified topic that is either implied clearly or explicitly stated at either the beginning or the end of the paragraph.
- □ The most important element at either the end or the beginning; don't bury it in the middle.
- □ Each sentence logically linked to the others in the paragraph.
- □ A clear link to the paragraphs that precede and follow.

When you have trouble with transitions between sentences, cut apart the sentences in a paragraph. Ask a critic to try to reassemble them. If he or she gets the order right, your transitions are adequate. If the order is wrong, ask why. The answers will suggest the transitions you need.

$\boxed{13}$ Revision:

Weeding and Pruning

13.1 The steps in this chapter move from work with a whole manuscript to work with paragraphs, sentences, and words. The goal is to help you achieve a clear, simple, and brief style in which no feature of the writing stands between the reader's understanding and the information you want to communicate. Never lose sight of the most important feature of effective writing—the idea you want to express in each sentence, paragraph, or section. Often the best way to deal with an error is to throw away the sentence that contains it, rewrite it, or rewrite the paragraph that contains it. For this reason:

□ Treat all problems with sentences not as isolated problems with clarity, grammar, or brevity but rather as indicators that the central idea still hasn't been expressed clearly.

Enhancing Clarity

13.2 Grammatically perfect sentences still can be totally incomprehensible. Writers can correct this problem by following the steps in Sections 13.3 through 13.33, summarized in Table 13.1. If you are pressed for time:

□ Consider getting help from an experienced technical writer or rewriter or manuscript editor. Look for someone with at least

TABLE 13.1 *Checklist for Improving the Clarity of Writing*

1.	Use of headings and subheadings in place of transitional sentences and paragraphs.
2.	Use of transitional words and phrases between sentences and paragraphs.
3.	Proper expression of sequences in time.
4.	Use of informative introductions to tables and illustrations.
5.	Use of active voice.
6.	Avoidance of unnecessary long sentences.
7.	Avoidance of unnecessary long words.
8.	Subjects and verbs close together.
9.	Consistent use of general and technical words.
10.	Sparing, proper use of technical language.
11.	Elimination of Latin phrases and abbreviations.
12.	Elimination of indecisiveness.
13.	Elimination of double negatives.
14.	Elimination of pompous self-reference by author.

two years' experience and who can work with ideas. Editors who work sentence by sentence usually don't do this kind of work well.

Because the writer or editor is always making changes that may affect substance, read the manuscript carefully when the work has been done and respond to any written notes or questions. For more help, see Chapter 14.

Transitions

13.3 Transitions help readers to move smoothly from one idea to the next and to understand the relationship between ideas. In proposals, reports, chapters, and articles, they also must help readers to locate quickly topics they want to explore more deeply. In instructions, writers often use displayed, numbered lists to show clearly the steps in a sequence. In reports and proposals, which require more unbroken paragraphs, writers can make transitions clear with:

☐ Headings and subheadings, used like the ones in this book.
☐ Transition words and phrases instead of clauses and sentences. Table 13.2 lists some useful words and phrases.
☐ Careful use of properly sequenced verb tenses.
☐ Introductory sentences that give information, especially when

TABLE 13.2 *Categories of Transitional Words and Phrases*

Type of Connection	Examples
Comparison, contrast	but, however, in comparison, in contrast, on the contrary, likewise, similarly, still, whereas
Conclusion to argument	accordingly, consequently, hence, therefore, thus
Coordination	and, ; [semicolon], : [colon]
Different physical location	adjacent to, beyond, here, near, opposite to, there
Different times	afterward, after an hour (day, week, month, fiscal year, quarter, etc.), before, immediately, meantime, meanwhile, then
Equal importance	first (second, third), also, and, equally important, furthermore, moreover, or, in addition
Example	for example, for instance
Same time	also; at the same time; simultaneously; while . . .
Subordination	although, as, as if, as though, because, if, since, so that, that, though, unless, until, when, whenever, where, wherever, whether, while
Summary; intensification	briefly, in any event, in brief, indeed, in fact, in particular, in short, in summary, of course, to sum up

the discussion is about tables and illustrations that accompany the text.

13.4 Better use of verb tenses usually involves nothing more than identifying the time sequence of events. Combinations of a perfect tense (a form of "to have" together with a past participle) and a past tense express action at two times in the past; a combination of the present perfect and the future express sequences to occur in the future. Use of progressive tenses enables writers to express simultaneous actions without complicated explanations. For example:

[1]   After she *had checked* the oil, she *washed* the windows.

[2]   After she *has checked* the oil, she *will wash* the windows.

[3]   While the gas *was being* pumped into the car, she *checked* the oil and *washed* the windows.

13.5 Informative sentences give readers some of the actual information in a table or illustration. In the examples below, sentences

[1] and [2] are fillers; the other five sentences provide information as well as transition to a new idea.

[1]	Table 1 shows data on railroads.
[2]	Figure 2 shows trends in the birth rate.
[3]	As Table 1 shows, the Northeast has the greatest amount of railroad track.
[4]	Table 1 shows that the Northest has the greatest amount of railroad track.
[5]	The Northeast has the greatest amount of railroad track (see Table 1).
[6]	Figure 2 shows that the birth rate has been dropping by ? percent a year.
[7]	The birth rate has been dropping by ? percent a year (see Figure 2).

In first drafts, sentences like those in the first group help writers move into discussion of a table or illustration, and in lectures they help listeners move to a new topic, but in writing they slow readers down. Writers can tighten their writing by checking the text around tables and illustrations and changing from useless sentences to informative ones.

Use of the Active Voice

13.6 Complete sentences have actors (someone or something that acts) and action words, or verbs, that tell what happened. Some sentences also have objects—persons or things affected by the action. When writers use the active voice, the actor is the subject of the sentence. In the passive voice, the object is the subject, and the actor normally appears in a prepositional phrase that begins with *by*, although writers sometimes omit the phrase and thereby create a sentence that is ambiguous, misleading, or inaccurate. The following three examples of the same sentence are in the active voice, correct passive voice, and incorrect passive voice respectively:

[1]	John Smith wrote the accounting program in three weeks.
[2]	The accounting program was written in three weeks by John Smith.
[3]	The accounting program was written in three weeks.

Of the three sentences, [1] is the shortest and most interesting. The second sentence is longer and less interesting; the third is less interesting and also misleading and inaccurate, especially if someone cares *who* wrote the program.

13.7 Writers have a distressing tendency to litter sentences with the passive voice, even though it usually muddies the meaning, because:

- The active voice makes crystal clear who did what to whom (but if John Smith's program didn't work, he may not want to advertise his responsibility, so he hides behind the passive voice).
- Writers are unsure of either themselves or their results or both (so they use the passive voice to conceal that fact from readers).
- For decades the passive voice has defaced reports and proposals in all fields, supposedly to promote "unbiased" reporting (so neophytes who once wrote easily in the active voice find themselves conditioned into the passive).
- Sometimes the reason for findings or situations isn't clear (so writers take refuge in the passive rather than tackle the difficult job of explaining *why* the ambiguity exists).
- Using the active voice often means digging out additional information to clarify ambiguities (and writers don't want to take the time).

The irony of the situation rests in the reverence for unbiased reporting. Truth is best served by clear, unambiguous statements in the active voice, even if a few of them begin with *I* or *we* (depending on whether one or two authors are involved).

13.8 Using the active voice and eliminating the passive is a mechanical technique that, almost automatically, helps writers cure other writing problems such as wordiness, repetition, separation of subjects and verbs, and ambiguity. Getting rid of the passive voice does not always require rewriting the sentence with the actor (object of the preposition *by*) as the subject. Rarely do writers need to use *I* as the subject. Sometimes writers can eliminate a sentence completely or eliminate it by including some of it in another sentence. For example, a writer concerned with John Smith's accounting program might eventually write:

[4]   Smith's accounting program, written in three days,
        doesn't compile properly.

                          OR

[5]   Smith's accounting program doesn't compile properly
        because he had only three days to write it.

The choice depends on what information the writer wants to emphasize.

13.9 To find out how much you use the passive voice:

- Skim something you wrote; circle every form of the verb *to be;* these include *am, be, been, being, is, are, was,* and *were.* The forms that come attached to past tense forms of verbs (*found, dug, discovered, wound,* and so on) are passive verb forms.
- When a document has been typed on word processing equipment, especially equipment backed by substantial computer power, do a string search (defined in Section 4.17) for the forms of *to be.*
- Try to eliminate enough passive verbs so that fewer than 10 percent of the total sentences use the passive voice. Section 13.11 lists the few situations in which the passive voice is useful.
- In the long run, consider having either the manufacturer of the equipment or one of your programmers write a program to do the search automatically, print the affected lines, and identify blocks of lines by page number. You can then rework the sentences at your desk and have a typist enter corrections.

Having computer programs to locate problems means that the writer spends time only on corrections. Mullins (1980) gives detailed information on the process and programs written for a CDC 6600 computer. For writers who always work under pressure of deadlines, the difference in amount of time spent may determine whether the job gets done at all.

13.10 The following simple exercise can make an astonishing difference in writing:

1. Rewrite three pages of any manuscript.
2. Try not to use any form of the verb *to be.* This eliminates not

only the passive voice, but also sentences with *am, are (was, is, were,* and such) as the main verb.

Writers who have relied heavily on the passive voice may find that rewriting even three pages takes several hours. Often they feel uncomfortable with the naked clarity of the resulting prose. (One of my students even had a severe "identity crisis:" "I've *always* been a passive person," she protested, one page into the exercise.) However, the results are worth it. You will find yourself promoting nouns and adjectives to verbs. The active voice will give your prose new life and vitality. You will probably also find that the end product is at least 10 percent shorter than the previous draft. (My student with the identity crisis cut nearly one-third of the text from her thesis—and thus saved more than $100 on the cost of the final typing!) You may even find, to your pleasure, that people compliment you on your "interesting reports," because use of the active voice often is the major factor that keeps people reading and learning.

13.11 Under only a few situations will you find the passive voice desirable; these include:

□ When the actor is obvious, unknown or unimportant (for example, "when size of population was controlled" . . .)
□ You want to stress the object, use a weak form of the imperative, present a thought deliberately, or give variety in a passage otherwise composed completely of active-voice verbs.

Spend these uses carefully. Under most circumstances, use the active voice.

Long Words and Sentences

13.12 Writing sentences that are both long and effective requires exceptional skill and years of practice, which most business and research writers lack. Therefore, try to keep most sentences short—come to a full stop (period, semicolon, question mark, or exclamation point) every two typed lines or less. This doesn't mean that all sentences need to be short; writing sometimes becomes choppy when they are. It *does* mean spending longer sentences carefully and taking the time to build them with care. Example [2] below is much clearer than example [1].

[1]   With allowances made for certain limitations and lapses,
           the exercises showed that the evaluation model on which
           the course was based is workable and that a university
           course can be consciously planned, pursued, and evaluated
           beyond the ordinary or well-known processes.

[2]   Although limited, the model works. With it teachers can
           plan, teach, and evaluate university courses more effectively
           than with other models.

Sentence [1] has many more problems than length alone, but concentrating on breaking up the sentence resolves the other problems, such as separation of subjects and verbs. Interestingly, short sentences sometimes sound choppy only to the writer. Whether they sound choppy to readers depends on whether the flow of ideas is logical and clear. Checking for choppiness is one way a critic can help. For help in reducing sentence length, see Sections 11.5 through 11.12.

13.13 Similarly:

□ Always choose the shortest, simplest words possible.
□ Whenever possible, don't use words longer than two syllables.

Why *utilize* when you can *use,* or *contemplate* when you can *think about* something? There will always be some long words you can't avoid; eliminating the rest simply helps readers grasp your message as easily as possible. Short words also may prevent embarrassment. One supervisor described as "deciduous" an employee who made decisions easily. The boss fired back this query: What in hell is the employee falling off of?

Separation of Subject and Verb

13.14 Separating subjects and verbs by more than half a line places an unnecessary burden on readers. For example, readers of sentence [1] below have to wait nearly two and one-half lines before they find out that the exploration "began." The absence of internal punctuation adds to the difficulty of understanding.

[1]   Exploration of the possibility of developing a replacement for

GOSYSTEM which was designed and implemented in 1969 began in the early fall of 1977.

[2]   In October 1977 we began exploring the possibility of developing a replacement for GOSYSTEM, which had been designed and implemented in 1969.

An even clearer, briefer version of the same sentence is:

[3]   In late 1977 we began to think about replacing the eight-year-old GOSYSTEM.

13.15 When you rewrite, avoid the passive voice. Place the subject and verb next to each other; in no case separate them by more than half a line. Often it helps to rewrite the sentence completely to get rid of excess verbiage, as in sentence [3] above. Often the words that separate the subject and verb aren't necessary anyway.

Appropriate Language

13.16 For both general English and technical terms, a good rule to follow is—the harder your topic, the simpler and more consistent your language should be. Therefore:

□ As much as possible, restrict yourself to one- and two-syllable words. Then, when you have to use longer words, especially technical words, they will be more effective.
□ Do not vary your prose or in other ways be creative in your writing. You may be bored by the same words, but your reader won't be. Remember that your purpose is to inform, not entertain.

Technical writing must be lean, simple, and clear. If, for example, you call part of a train a "coach" in one paragraph and a "car" in the next, readers will inevitably wonder if you mean the same thing or something different.

13.17 Choose words and phrases carefully; check meanings in the most recent *Webster's New Collegiate Dictionary* unless you are certain. Table 13.3 lists words and phrases that writers frequently misuse or confuse with each other. When the document has been typed on word processing equipment:

TABLE 13.3 *Words and Phrases Frequently Confused with Each Other*

Words and Phrases	Meaning (Brief) or Proper Use
abjure, adjure	*abjure:* put aside, repudiate; *adjure:* to command, solemnly direct
accelerate, exhilarate	*accelerate:* to quicken; *exhilarate:* to gladden
adapt, adopt	*adapt:* to conform to one's own purposes; *adopt:* to take and make one's own as is
adverse, averse	*adverse:* bad; *averse:* opposed
affect, effect	As verbs, *affect:* to influence or have an effect or impact on; *effect:* to bring about, accomplish, execute, or cause. As nouns, *affect* has a specialized meaning in the field of psychology; *effect:* result or consequence
allude, elude	*allude:* mention; *elude:* escape
alternate, alternative	Have different meanings. Most commonly, *alternate* is an adjective; *alternative,* a noun. Check *Webster's* before using.
allusion, reference	*allusion:* indirect mention; *reference:* direct mention
attorney, lawyer	*attorney:* person designated by another to transact business for him or her; *lawyer:* a person who practices law. An attorney does not need to be a lawyer
avenge, revenge	*avenge:* to mete out punishment for a wrong, with the intent of restoring the balance of justice; *revenge:* to retaliate resentfully, with the intent of obtaining satisfaction
avert, avoid	*avert:* to prevent; *avoid:* to stay clear of
basis, bases	*basis* is singular; *bases,* plural
beside, besides	*beside:* at the side of; *besides:* in addition to
blatant, flagrant	*blatant:* obnoxiously loud; *flagrant:* openly evil or scandalous
bloc, block	*bloc:* a coalition of people with the same goal; *block:* a mass of matter with an extended surface, plus many other meanings. See *Webster's*
callus, callous	*callus:* a noun (bump on foot); *callous:* an adjective (without feeling)
can, may	*can:* ability to do; *may:* permission to do it
compare to, compare with	*compare to* connotes basic similarity; *compare with,* basic dissimilarity
compose, comprise	*compose:* make up; *comprise:* encompass. Example: Once parts have been *composed,* the whole *comprises* the parts.
consist in, consist of	*consist in:* define or set forth an identity; *consist of:* introduces the parts that make up a whole
continual, continuous	*continual:* over and over again; *continuous:* unbroken
councilor, counselor	*councilor:* member of a council; *counselor:* a person who gives counsel
criterion, criteria	*criterion* is singular; *criteria,* plural
datum, data	*datum* is singular; *data,* plural. *Datum* is not common usage: in its place use *observation, fact,* or *figure*

Words and Phrases (cont.)	Meaning (Brief) or Proper Use (cont.)
definite, definitive	*definite:* precise; *definitive:* beyond argument
denote, connote	*denote:* means; *connote:* implies
different from, different than (for things and people)	*different from* is correct (see Bernstein 1972, pp. 139–141)
disinterested, uninterested	*disinterested:* impartial; *uninterested:* not interested
ecology, environment	*Ecology* is the study of relationships between organisms and their environment
either, each	*Either:* one or the other; *each:* both
formula, formulas	*formula* is singular; *formulas,* plural
hypothesis, hypotheses	*hypothesis* is singular; *hypotheses,* plural
impact	*impact* when used as a verb
imply, infer	speakers *imply;* hearers (readers) *infer*
incredible, incredulous	*incredible:* not to be believed; *incredulous:* skeptical
index, indexes	*index* is singular; *indexes,* plural (*indices* is rarely used)
its, it's	*its;* possessive of it; *it's* contraction of *it is*
less, fewer	Use *less* for quantities, like sand, whose parts cannot normally be separated; use *fewer* for items that can be counted (e.g., nuts and bolts, reports)
Like, as, as if	*Like* does not mean *as* or *as if.* In general, use *like* to compare phrases and clauses that contain a verb (e.g. this boltcutter works well *as* a boltcutter should)
medium, media	*medium* is singular; *media,* plural
method, methodology	*method:* what people use to do a job; *methodology:* the study of methods
oral, verbal	*oral* refers to human utterance; *verbal:* applies to spoken or written words (connotes reducing ideas to writing)
optimal, optimum, optima	*optimal* is an adjective; *optimum,* a singular noun; *optima,* a plural noun
over, more than	*over* refers to spatial relationships; *more than* is used with figures. For example; He earns *more than* not *over)* $20,000 per year
Per cent, percent, percentage	*per cent,* in U. S. usage, is an incorrect spelling of *percent,* which should always be preceded by a number. *Percentage:* a given proportion in every hundred; stated as — *percent.*
phenomenon, phenomena	*phenomenon* is singular; *phenomena,* plural
principal, principle	*principal:* first, dominant, leading; *principle:* a guiding rule or basic truth
refute, response	*refute:* argue successfully; *response:* answer (no implication of success in argument)
that, which	*that:* begins a restrictive clause, which is essential to meaning of sentence; *which:* begins descriptive clause, which is not essential, and usually is preceded by a comma

Words and Phrases (cont.)	Meaning (Brief) or Proper Use (cont.)
under, less than	*under:* refers to spatial location; *less than:* used with figures. Example: he earns less than (not *under*) $10,000 per year
whose, who's	*whose:* possessive of who; *who's:* contraction of who is

□ Do string searches (defined in Section 4.17) for the words in the left-hand column so you can check usage and change those that are incorrect.

If your organization is blessed with powerful equipment, chances are either the manufacturer or a programmer in your firm can develop a program that will search entire texts automatically and give writers a list of the words and phrases that occur, the lines they are in, and the pages they are on. Writers can make any changes necessary on text pages, and typists can make the corrections for them.

Technical Language

13.18 When writers use technical language properly, it functions much like idioms and cliches in general English: it packs a lot of generally shared meaning into a few words, and thus enhances clarity. Improperly used, it becomes jargon and does more to blur than to enhance meaning. For example, words like *infrastructure, dimension, viable, functional,* and *systematized* can make even the simplest topic seem hopelessly complex. Technical and scientific reports, proposals and instructions share with government documents an almost total inability to use technical language properly. Aaronson (1977) compared jargon with terms in jive talk, such as *turn on, outtasight* and *freak out,* which are vague substitutes for ordinary words, but they "allow members of a particular subculture to exclude outsiders" from communication (Aaronson 1977, p. 8).

13.19 *Reasons for overuse.* The reasons for this situation, which are much like those for overuse of the passive voice, are:

- □ Plain English makes perfectly clear who did what, how, and when (and who is, therefore, responsible).
- □ Individuals have been steeped in "bureaucratese" for so long they've been conditioned into using it themselves.
- □ Writers aren't sure of either themselves or their findings or both; generous layers of technical language make it harder for readers to discover that fact (or anything else, for that matter).
- □ Writers think that technical language makes them sound important, or at least knowledgeable. In fact, it just makes readers put down a document in frustration. Writers who use plain English are the ones judged knowledgeable.

One writer described as "the higher illiteracy" the proliferation of jargon and other forms of gobbledygook in government and other documents. One critic of this chapter was more blunt. He has concluded that the amount of jargon is inversely proportional to the writer's intelligence (or at least, common sense).

13.20 *Principles of good use.* No matter what audience you are writing for, avoid any form of technical language if you possibly can. There are at least two reasons why. First, many readers will not know what you mean and so will be baffled rather than impressed by your knowledge. Second, many terms are ambiguous. For example, in reports on mass transportation, *ridership* can refer to statistics about either number of riders or number of trips taken, to either round trips or one-way trips, or to any combination of these variables. Because writers *know* what *they* mean, often they don't think about the kind of question readers might have. (Finding these ambiguities can be one benefit of having a critical partner.) The only exception to this rule is documents, such as research articles in specialized journals, that are intended solely for a narrow audience, and even those become much more understandable when writers keep technical language to the minimum.

13.21 General English equivalents for many technical terms aren't hard to find. For example, why *conceptualize* when you are *thinking*? (*Conceptualize* is a technical term associated with theory building and should be reserved for that purpose.) Why use *domain* when *area* is what you mean? Why *configuration* instead of *pattern*? If, like many writers, you are so accustomed to these pomposities that you don't even notice them:

□ Try reading Edwin Newman's *Strictly Speaking.*

He pokes holes in so many, so effectively, that you may come away with a built-in wince that activates at any excuse—including your daily attempt to relax with a newspaper.

13.22 A more specific rule is: don't use technical terms from disciplines or work areas other than your own. For example, *parameter* is a technical term in mathematics and not a synonym for *boundary* or *limit.* The worst examples probably are terms borrowed from computer science. Regardless of topic, writers in all areas freely describe *input, output,* and *thruput.* A dean at the University of Cincinnati became so fed up with *input* and *feedback* that he imposed a 25-cent fine on writers who used these words in manuscripts that were being reproduced by the university's duplicating center. Next on the list of forbidden words: *proactive, interface, bottom line, facilitate, utilize,* and *impact* when used as a verb.

13.23 Don't create terms. You may know what you mean, but If a term isn't in the dictionary, others won't know. Some may guess or borrow and use the term in ways you didn't intend. The word *operationalize* is a perfect example of this phenomenon. As of 1979 it still hadn't been included in *Webster's New Collegiate Dictionary,* but hardly a government document exists that doesn't try to "operationalize" a program (start it up), or a social science document that doesn't talk about "operationalizing" concepts (matching concepts with variables to test a theory). Applied social scientists use the term freely in both senses and in others not so clear. Often, even a close reading doesn't yield information on what the writer meant. One of my enterprising undergraduates gleefully took to placing bets with the social science faculty where she worked; if they could find *operationalize* or *operationalization* in *Webster's,* she'd buy them a bottle of wine; if they couldn't, they'd buy her one. She hasn't paid for a bottle of wine in quite some time!

13.24 Although some technical ideas have more than one technical term attached to them:

□ Don't use them synonymously; you will only confuse readers if you do.
□ When you feel compelled to show the alternatives, do so the

first time you use a term. Use parentheses or a footnote and write a sentence like:

(also called "oldwidget")
1. Also called "oldwidget."

□ After the first mention, use the preferred term only. Don't repeat references to other terms.
□ When you have to deal with many synonymous terms, each invented by a different, prior writer in your field, expand the "also called" statement to include all terms together with citation of the original source of each.

13.25 Don't use a word in both its common and its technical senses. For example, *valid* is a technical term in research that means a variable measures what you want it to measure, so anyone connected with research should not also use the term in its general sense as a synonym for *correct* or *true*. In social science, *factor* is a technical term associated with *factor analysis*. Social scientists, then, should not use the word as a general synonym for *variable* or *thing* as in:

> Several *factors* influenced the decision.

13.26 In general, when writing for specialists on your topic, don't define terms that are common knowledge among these readers. With less common terms, define and cite a source that defines and explains. When you write for anyone else, eliminate technical terms where possible. For any that you must use, define and explain, and cite a source. Don't be concerned that readers, especially technical peers, will judge you ignorant. Readers don't look for technical language; they read for ideas. When you make ideas clear and easy to grasp, that's what readers will notice.

Latin Terms

13.27 Avoid Latin words and abbreviations in citations and in general sentences. Writers frequently misuse even the most common ones—i.e. (that is) and e.g. (for example). Most writers also misuse *cf.*, which doesn't mean "see" but "compare," and connotes difference, not similarity. Even if you use terms correctly, many readers

will misunderstand. Why give them the chance when plain English
is just as easy?

Indecisiveness

13.28 *Seems, apparently, appears to,* and the like abound in the
manuscripts of writers who are (1) unsure of themselves or of their
work or (2) trying (unsuccessfully) to demonstrate modesty. Therefore:

□ If x *is more important than* y, say so. Don't weasel by saying that
x *seems to be more important than* y.

Readers assume that facts and opinions belong to the writer unless
he or she explicitly attributes them to someone else. Some writers
feel intensely uncomfortable with flat statments because they've
been conditioned to use indecisive words. Nevertheless, if you are
one of these writers, make the effort to use decisive words. Indeci-
siveness casts doubt on what you've written because:

□ If your writing implies that *you* lack confidence in your work,
can you expect it to persuade anyone else?

13.29 When genuine doubt exists:

□ Use an indecisive word, but also give an explanation.

For example, you could report a given result as "apparently" true,
but caution that it also could be due to a specific, uncontrolled
variable or to temporary electrical failure in the lab. Or, Jones made
one statement in Chapter 3 and a contradictory one in Chapter 7,
but gives no reason for the difference. A few creative writers use
indecisive words effectively in other ways—to show sarcasm, for
example—but these uses don't serve the purposes of technical
writing. Equally important, most technical writers lack the skill to
use these words effectively in other than straightforward ways.

Double Negatives

13.30 Like indecisive words, double negatives are weaselers used
by uncertain writers. Therefore:

▢ If it is *not incorrect to say that Brand X isn't safe,* say so:

Brand X isn't safe.

Leave to experienced nontechnical writers the more complicated and legitimate uses of double negatives.

Author Self-Reference

13.31 When you need to refer to yourself:

▢ Be direct. Say *I* (if you are a single author) or *we* (if you have one or more coauthors).

Indirect statements like "the writer [author, present writer] found that" are relics of a mercifully bygone era. So also is use of *we* by single authors. Occasional use of the first person singular is not only appropriate; it may keep the writer from executing a painfully tortured sentence in the passive voice. Furthermore, it doesn't either add or remove bias in reporting. Writers who remain uneasy with the first person singular might enjoy reading van Leunen's (1978) thoughtful "Scholarship: A Singular Notion," in the May 1978 *Atlantic.*

General Help with Clarity

13.32 Daily exposure to bad writing takes its toll (no one knows this better than the technical editors and writers who spend their days rewriting it). Before long, the best of the worst begins to look downright good. To combat this phenomenon:

▢ Take a small daily dose of any kind of good, plain nontechnical writing.

As little as 15 minutes a day will suffice. Almost any type of writing will do. If you have trouble recognizing excellent writing, try one or more of the following works as starters. If you like reading aloud to children, try E. B. White's stories, especially *Charlotte's Webb.* Or Laura Ingalls Wilder's *Little House* books. Among news columnists, Stewart Alsop wrote well, and Shana Alexander's editorials in *Newsweek* always were well written. Articles in *Atlantic* and *Sports Illustrated* usually are well written. Works on writing by H. J. Tichy and Theodore Bernstein are not only well written; they also teach principles of good writing. If you prefer lighter reading, try E. B. White's *Letters,* or anything else by White. Hall (1979) is a complete, bibliographic catalog of White's works through 1978. If you like sports, Bill Bradley's *Life on the Run* is good. For bedtime and in-the-bathroom readers, White's letters and essays, Bradley's vignettes, and Bernstein's works have a major advantage: they come in short snatches that won't keep you reading to find out how a plot resolves itself.

13.33 When you read articles and books in your field, study treatment as well as information. An introduction that you like or a table, illustration, or argument that you find especially clear may be based on a principle or pattern that you can apply to own writing and teach to students and subordinates.

TABLE 13.4 *Checklist of Troublesome Grammatical Problems*

1.	Dangling introductory modifiers.
2.	Misplaced modifiers.
3.	Incomplete comparisons.
4.	Comparisons completed unnecessarily.
5.	Incorrect treatment of direct quotations.
6.	Overuse and misuse of quotation marks.
7.	Use of sexist language.
8	Misuses of nouns as modifiers.
9.	Misspelling.
10.	Overuse of underlining.
11.	Incorrect capitalization. Uses a grammar book. In general, if you cannot find a rule that specifies a capital letter for a word, leave it lowercased.
12.	Misuse of numbers for words and words for numbers.
13	Disagreement (singular or plural) of subjects and verbs and of subjects, verbs, and objects. Use a grammar book.

Grammar

13.34 Careful revision to enhance clarity eliminates most problems with grammar. This section will not substitute for a good, detailed grammar book such as Perrin's (1972) *Writer's Guide and Index to English.* The purpose is only to list some of the most common problems writers should eliminate from their manuscripts. Table 13.4 is a checklist for quick reference. When you are pressed for time:

□ Consider getting help from a technical editor.

Try to find someone with at least a year's experience as a copy editor, preferably with experience on documents like yours, although that isn't essential. Look for a persnickity nitpicker who works sentence by sentence and has a solid foundation in grammar. For more help, see Chapter 14.

Dangling Introductory Modifiers

13.35 Dangling modifiers and their close cousin, the misplaced modifier, may well have caused more unintentional humor than any other kind of grammatical error. These danglers earned their name by hanging precariously off the beginning of sentences, and they cause laughter by not referring unmistakably to the word or words they logically modify—the subject of the sentence. An advertisement delivered this choice morsel to my desk:

[1]   Lying on top of the small intestine, you will perhaps
        make out a nearly invisible thread.

And I had thought yoga put people in strange poses! The writer probably meant to convey the idea that when the surgeon took a close look, he or she would find a nearly invisible thread lying on the small intestine. Unfortunately, the structure of sentence [1] makes "you" [the surgeon], the subject of the main clause, the actor that "lies." Remember, then:

□ When the first part of a sentence is a modifying phrase that begins with a verb form, the implied actor is the subject of the sentence.

13.36 Correcting the problem means changing the subject of the sentence. Sometimes writers have to rewrite sentences completely. Sentence [1] is better written as:

[2]   You will see a nearly invisible thread lying on top of
        the small intestine.

13.37 Writers often cause dangling modifiers, such as the one underlined in sentence [3] below, by trying to express a condition or a time sequence in the modifier and then using a passive-voice verb in the main clause—another good reason for writers to use the active voice whenever possible. As a result, the actor associated with the modifier is not the subject of the sentence. Instead, if the actor appears at all (in sentence 3, it doesn't), it is usually as the object of the preposition *by,* toward the end of the sentence (for more information on the passive voice, see Section 13.6). For example:

[3]   *Assembling the steps in the program correctly,* whether it
          works can be determined.

[4]   The programmer must assemble the steps properly
          before he can find out whether the program works.

Sentence [4] corrects sentence [3] by using the active voice and putting the programmer (the implied actor in sentence [3]) into the picture. Sentence [5] shows an error that is particularly common among writers who use equations, list hypotheses, state assumptions, and so forth. The sentence is incorrect because *assuming* doesn't mean *if.* Furthermore, Y doesn't "assume." Writers can write a clearer, briefer sentence if they use the "if . . . then" structure of sentence [6].

[5]   Assuming X is . . . , Y is . . . .

[6]   If X is . . . , then Y is . . .

13.38 Most of the time, dangling modifiers begin with a verb form that ends in "ed" or "ing," but sometimes they begin with other descriptive words. The sentence may even be in the active voice. Examples [7] and [8] show a typical problem sentence and a way to correct the problem.

[7]   Melted by the intense heat, firemen couldn't open the door.

[8]   Firemen couldn't open the door because the intense heat
          had welded the door to the door frame.

When you revise, check the relationship between the action in introductory modifiers and the subjects of sentences. Don't melt the firemen!

Misplaced Modifiers

13.39 Like dangling modifiers, misplaced modifiers are words, clauses, and phrases whose place in the structure of a sentence causes them to modify the wrong word or group of words. The writer's job is to rewrite so that the modifier is in the proper location. In the following examples, sentence [2] is a corrected version of [1].

[1]   Put the broom in the building in the closet.

[2]   Put the broom in the closet in the building.

The first sentence could be correct only if the closet were very large and the building very small.

Incomplete Comparisons

13.40 Incomplete comparisons can cause ambiguous sentences. For example, sentence [1] below leaves readers wondering whether teenagers are as likely (1) to commit suicide as to murder adults (sentence [2]) or (2) to commit suicide as adults are (sentence [3]).

[1]   Teenagers are as likely to kill themselves as adults.

[2]   Teenagers are as likely to kill themselves as to kill
          adults.

[3]   Teenagers are as likely as adults to kill themselves.

13.41 Once the writer has specified the elements being compared, however, the tendency is to repeat completions unnecessarily. Unnecessarily completed comparisons only add words and make manuscripts harder to read. The result is tiring to readers and causes them to begin skipping words, phrases, and even sentences with the result that they might miss something important. Very careful workers are especially likely to complete comparisons unnecessarily. Example [4] includes comparisons completed unnecessarily. In example [5], the unnecessary comparisons have been removed.

[4]   The research compared boys and girls. On the average,
          boys were taller than girls and weighed more than girls, but
          girls ran faster than boys and completed intricate tasks more
          quickly than boys.

[5]   The research compared boys and girls. On the
         average, boys were taller and weighed more, but girls ran faster
         and completed intricate tasks more quickly.

CAUTION: Don't remove unnecessary comparisons until you are
past the stage of moving sections around!

Use of Quotations

13.42 Technical documents should contain few, if any, quotations.
Those included can be either integrated with text or blocked and set
off from it. The general rules are:

- When the quotation is longer than seven typed lines, block it.
- When the quotation is shorter than five typed lines, integrate it
  and use quotation marks around it.
- When the quotation is between five and seven typed lines, block
  only the ones you want to emphasize strongly.
- When you omit words, make changes, or add emphasis, follow
  the conventions described in Sections 15.16 and 15.17.

Use of Quotation Marks

13.43 Documents peppered with quotation marks imply that the
writers didn't take time to express themselves clearly and precisely.
In technical writing, use quotation marks only for:

- Quotations included in the body of a paragraph.
- Technical terms not familiar to your readers, in which case give
  a source (see Section 13.26).
- Words used ironically, to mean the opposite. For example: The
  engine "worked," but only during the trial runs.
- Definitions. For example: "analog" means . . . .

Avoid colloquial terms, even with quotation marks. They only signal
laziness. For example, sentence [1] below, published in a reputable
journal, could have been better expressed as sentence [2].

[1]   Smith proposed his "sets of relations" model to explain . . .
[2]   Smith proposed sets of relations to explain . . .

Use of Sexist Language

13.44 Sexist language has been imbedded in American culture for so long that many writers find it hard to avoid. This book demonstrates various ways to avoid sexist language—use of plural pronouns, use of alternating male and female subjects in examples, use of *he* or *she* (*him* or *her*), and so forth. The easiest cure for sexist language is to send for the best available guide, which also happens to be free. To get a copy of *Guidelines for Equal Treatment of the Sexes in McGraw-Hill Book Company Publications* (McGraw-Hill, n.d.), write to:

> Public Information and Publicity Department
> McGraw-Hill Book Company
> 1221 Avenue of the Americas
> New York, N. Y. 10020

This readable publication is packed with examples to cover all conceivable publications. You might want to have a technical writer prepare a modified version that applies specifically to common situations in your organization.

Noun Modifiers

13.45 Try to avoid using nouns to modify other nouns. Newspaper headlines, which string together nouns like so many boxcars on a train, have dulled our sensitivity to the resulting ambiguities. If you need help in resensitizing yourself, try reading *Strictly Speaking* (Newman 1974). And try to figure out what the noun modifiers (*italicized*) in the following examples were trying to communicate.

[1]   *Indian expert* (expert on American Indians? or India?
or Indian who is an expert on [something]?)

[2]   *Third party billing process summary* (summary of process
for billing third parties? instructions for billing third parties?)

[3]   *Change form process summary* (is this a summary
of process for using change form? or summary of process
for changing forms?)

[4]   *Conversion plan diagram* (diagram of plan for conversion)

[5]   A *population ecology* perspective on *organization-environment* relations is proposed as an alternative to the dominant *adaptation* perspective.

My best guess about [5], rewritten as sentence [6], shows that no single principle applies to clarification of noun modifiers. Sometimes the answer is an adjectival form of the noun, such as *ecological*. Sometimes the answer is a prepositional phrase, such as *of relations*. And sometimes complete rewriting is necessary, in which case the writer's basic concern, as always, should be the central idea.

[6]   On relations between an organization and its envivonment, an ecological view is more useful that the more commonly used type of analysis that is based on adaptation.

Spelling and Underlining

13.46 Every writer needs a good dictionary. A valuable additional resource is Table 6.1 in the University of Chicago Press's *Manual of Style* (1969), which is a spelling guide for compound words. For each category of words, it tells when to hyphenate, when to spell as two words, and when to spell as one word. In general:

□ Underline only the most obscure foreign words and phrases, headings and subheadings, and book, journal, and report titles.
□ Keep underlining for emphasis to a bare minimum. It rapidly loses its effect.

13.47 Writers are especially prone to misspell or misuse the words and phrases listed in Table 13.5. Therefore:

□ Scan manuscripts for the words in the left-hand column. Replace wrong words with the words on the right.
□ When a document has been prepared on word processing equipment, try the procedures listed in Section 13.17.

Rules for Capitalization

13.48 For headings, subheadings, and titles of books, chapters, articles, and other manuscripts, the general rule is:

□ Capitalize the first word, the last word, and the first word after a colon; all nouns, pronouns, verbs, adjectives, and adverbs; and all prepositions that contain more than four letters.

The most common exception to this rule is reference lists and

Table 13.5 *Words Frequently Misspelled or Misused*

Incorrect	Correct
acknowledgement	acknowledgment
afterwards	afterward
ageing	aging
alright	all right
analyse	analyze
an hypothesis	a hypothesis
behavior	In the abstract, is singular
bi-polar	bipolar
Black, White	Not proper nouns; when referring to race or skin color, always *black* or *white*. The correct proper nouns are *Negro* and *Caucasian*.
can not	cannot
clearcut, clear cut	clear-cut
co-author	coauthor
co-education	coeducation
co- compounds	Spell solid as in preceding two examples; only exceptions are words like *co-worker*, in which lack of hyphen might cause mispronunciation
comparitive	comparative
controled, controling	controlled, controlling
co-ordination	coordination
demolish (or destroy) completely (or totally)	demolish, destroy (adding *completely* or *totally* is redundant)
descernable	discernible
dichotomy	Does not mean *gap*
grey	gray
head up	head
hopefully	Does not mean "If all goes well. . . ." "Hopefully I will finish the report by Friday" means "On Friday, when I finish the paper, I will be in a hopeful state of mind."
interaction	In the abstract, is singular
labelled, labelling	labeled, labeling
mid-point	midpoint
non-directive	nondirective
non-schizophrenic	nonschizophrenic
non- compounds	Spell solid, as in the previous two examples.
ommission	omission
only	In general, place *only* just before the word you want it to modify
originil	original
over-aggressive	overaggressive
plurals of words ending in *x*	End with *xes*, not *ces*. For example, *appendixes*, not *appendices*
post-test	posttest
pre-test	pretest
programing	programming
re-examine	reexamine

Incorrect (cont.)	Correct (cont.)
recieve	receive
represent	Does not mean "is"
results of	Follow with a noun such as *calculation, research, observation,* but not with a name. "Results of Smith" is wrong: "results of Smith's research" is correct
re-unite	reunite
self-	Always hyphenate when using *self* as a prefix
sizeable	sizable
suggest	does not mean *show*
towards	toward
unique	Means *one of a kind;* use no modifiers (e.g., more, most)
Use *'s* to form possessive singular of all nouns	Examples: Bent's, Jones's (not Jones'), Billings's (not Billings')
wave length	wavelength
while	Does not mean *when*
yeild	yield

bibliographies in certain styles (discussed in Sections 14.24 and 14.25). When you use capital letters consistently, you will get speedier and more consistent work from typists.

Figures or Words

13.49 Rules for using numbers and words confuse both typists and writers because two different conventions exist and many people don't realize that they apply to different kinds of writing. Check the rules below to learn what applies. When you follow the rules consistently, you will help typists prepare your manuscripts faster and more consistently. In general:

□ Rules for nontechnical writing most often apply to nonscholarly documents and to documents in the humanities, languages, history, and nonquantitative social sciences because such documents contain few numbers. Also, book publishers prefer these rules.
□ Rules for technical writing most often apply to documents in business, mathematics, natural and physical sciences, engineering, behavioral sciences, and quantitative social sciences.

13.50 *Nontechnical writing.* In nonscientific documents:

- □ Spell out exact numbers less than 100.
- □ Use figures for numbers 100 or above.
- □ Use figures for numbers grouped within a sentence or several sentences in a sequence when *any* of the numbers is 100 or more.

13.51 The exceptions are:

- □ Parts of a book or article: p. 3, Part 2, Table 4.
- □ Decimals, fractions, percentages, years, eras (such as 44 B.C., A.D. 66), time expressed with A.M. or P.M., monarchs and popes (such as George VI, Pius XII), family names (such as John D. Rockefeller IV).

13.52 Use words for:

- □ Round numbers in the hundreds, thousands, or millions.
- □ Any number at the beginning of a sentence.
- □ Centuries and decades (twentieth century, forties).
  EXCEPTION: Use 1960s, *not* nineteen sixties or 1960's.
- □ Governments, political divisions, military units: Third Reich, Ninety-Fifth Congress, Sixth Ward, First Precinct, Third Army.

13.53 Use both figures and numbers to express very large round numbers: 4.3 billion, $4 million, $6.5 billion.

13.54 *Technical Writing.* In technical writing, for cardinal numbers (1, 2, 3; one, two, three) and ordinal numbers (1st, 2nd, 3rd; first, second, third), use words for:

- □ The numbers zero through nine, except as noted below.
- □ Any number that begins a sentence.

13.55 Express in figures:

- □ Numbers 10 or greater.
- □ Any numbers that are units of measurement or time, ages, times, dates, percentages, fractional or decimal quantities, ratios, arithmetical manipulations, exact sums of money, scores and points on scales, numbers referred to as numerals, page numbers, series of four or more.

□ Numbers that refer to the same unit and are grouped within a sentence or several sentences in a sequence *when any* of the numbers is 10 or more.

□ All percentiles and quartiles: 4th (not fourth) percentile.

13.56 In general, use arabic numerals unless the roman numeral is part of an established term, such as Type I and Type II errors (APA 1974, pp. 41–43).

Eliminating Wordiness

13.57 Although pressure of time sometimes forces writers to skip the steps needed to achieve brevity, the briefer a document is, the more likely it will be read and have the effect the writer wants. A good copy editor can perform these steps for a writer. Most of the steps, listed in Table 13.6, are discussed earlier in the book. Only the others are discussed here. The basic purpose is to tell how to take out the wordiness that creeps into manuscripts because during drafting, the writer needed a way to move his or her thinking from one section or sentence to the next. In the final draft, these elements only stand between the reader and the writer's message.

Unnecessary Repetition and Restatement

13.58 Often, clues to repetition are statements like "as was stated earlier," "as has already been shown," "that is," "i.e.," and sometimes a semicolon between two clauses. For example:

[1]   Thus, urban families are less likely than rural families to think that a working mother has little commitment to her family; commitment to family and commitment to work are less likely to be seen as opposite ends of a scale.

Although the words are different, the idea in the clause before the semicolon is the same as the idea in the clause after. Because the first clause states the idea in a clearer, plainer way, the writer should simply change the semicolon to a period and delete the rest of the sentence.

TABLE 13.6 *Checklist for Achieving Brevity*

1.	Delete unnecessary summaries. See Sections 12.18 and 12.19.
2.	Delete unneeded quotations; paraphrase instead. See Section 12.18.
3.	Remove repetitive clauses, sentences, and paragraphs.
4.	Change passive-voice sentences to the active voice. See Sections 13.6 through 13.11.
5.	Look for tables that could be presented more efficiently in text; textual material that could be presented more efficiently in a table; unneeded tables; and tables that could be combined.
6.	Remove unnecessary footnotes. See Section 12.22.
7.	Remove unneeded comparisons (see Section 13.41), descriptions and modifiers.
8.	Remove verbal repetition of mathematical symbols.
9.	Using the list in Table 13.7, remove wordy phrases.
10.	Read the manuscript out loud to yourself to catch awkward phrases and glaring errors.
11.	Calculate a new SMOG index.

Unnecessary Descriptions and Modifiers

13.59 A writer's topic often comes with a variety of qualifiers and modifiers that, when repeated over and over every time the topic is mentioned, burden the manuscript and discourage readers. For example, a writer whose topic is "transportation of postdoctoral students in high energy physics from universities in North America and Europe" need not repeat all of these descriptors with every use of word *transportation*. Researchers with carefully chosen samples sometimes have even more descriptors. To prevent wordiness:

▫ State all qualifications the first time you define or describe. Thereafter, use only the noun (*transportation, sample,* and so on).

The only exceptions occur when writers have several of the same noun with different descriptions. In that case, find a short way to refer to the noun (*students' transportation,* for example) and use it when necessary to tell readers which topic you are talking about.

13.60 Look also for unnecessary one- and two-word modifiers. For example, in the following pair of sentences, the modifiers in brackets aren't necessary. By the time readers have reached the second sentence, they know that *parents' norms* is the independent variable and *occupational goals* is the dependent variable.

> The parents' norms influenced the boys' occupational goals (see Table 2). Other studies also have reported no effect [of parents' norms] on boys' [occupational] goals but have reported an effect on girls' [occupational] goals.

13.61 As a general rule, use any modifier sparingly. Words like *very* and *quite* weaken rather than strengthen sentences. For example, of the two sentences below, the second is stronger.

[1]   The data were quite wrong.

[2]   The data were wrong.

The first sentence has the ring of "protesting too much." In contrast, the meaning of the second is intensified by the simplicity of the flat statement.

13.62 Terms in mathematical equations pose a special case. The purpose of symbols and letters is to simplify reference. Therefore, once you have introduced a term and explained the meaning:

□ Don't repeat in text the verbal representations of the terms. For example, if Rb stands for rate of births, use only Rb after you have introduced the term and its meaning.
□ The only exception: After a gap in use of several pages or chapters, repeat the term and its meaning once as a reminder to readers.

Wordy Phrases

13.63 More generally, the author who has written *from the point of view of* may not think automatically of *for* as a briefer, crisper way to say the same thing. Or, if X is *in close proximity to . . . ,* he or she may not think about substituting X *is near . . . .* Table 13.7 lists some common wordy phrases and briefer substitutes. The steps are:

□ Scan the manuscript for the phrases on the left; replace them with the phrases on the right.

□ If you have word processing equipment, investigate automation of the search and replace procedures.

Section 13.17 describes a similar application; the difference for Table 13.7 is that many of the replacements can be done by the computer.

TABLE 13.7 *Common Wordy Phrases and Briefer Equivalents*

Wordy Phrase	Suggested Change
accordingly	so
accounted for by	due to, caused by
add the point that	add that
aggregate	total
a great deal of	much
along the line of	like
a majority of	most
analyzation	analysis
an example of this is the fact that	for example
another aspect of the situation to be considered	as for
a number of	about
approximately	about
are of the opinion that	think that
as per	Delete
as regards	about
as related to	for, about
assist, assistance	help
as to	about (Or, omit)
attempt	try
at the present writing	now
based on the fact that	because
chemotherapeutic agent	drug
collect together	collect
commence	begin
communicate	write, telephone (i.e., a specific verb)
concerning, concerning the nature of	about
consequently	so
construct	build
demonstrate	show, prove
depressed socioeconomic area	slum
donate	give
due to the fact that	because
during the time that	while
employ	use
endeavor	try

Wordy Phrase	Suggested Change
except in a small number of cases	usually
exhibit a tendency to	tend to
facilitate	ease
few [many] in number	few [many]
final conclusion	conclusion, end
firstly [secondly, etc.]	first [second, etc.]
for the purpose of	for, to
for the reason that	because
from the point of view of	for
future prospect	prospect
help and assistance	help
hopes and aspirations	hopes
if at all possible	if possible
implement	do, start
inasmuch as	because
in case, in case of	if
In close proximity	near
in favor of	for, to
initial	first
initiate	begin, start
in light of the fact that	because
in order to	to
(have an) input into	contribute to
inquire	ask
in rare cases	rarely
in [with] reference to, in regard to	about
in relation with	with
in terms of	in, for (Or, omit)
In the case of	Can usually be dropped
in the case that	if, when
in the course of	during
in the event that	if
in the first place	first
in the majority of instances	usually
in the matter of	about
in the nature of	like
in the neighborhood of	about
in the normal course of our procedure	normally
in the not-too-distant	soon
in the opinion of this writer	in my opinion, I believe
in the vicinity of	near
in view of the [above], [foregoing circumstances], [fact that]	therefore

Wordy Phrase (cont.)	Suggested Change (cont.)
involve the necessity of	require
is defined as	is (will frequently suffice)
is dependent upon	depends on
it is clear [obvious]	therefore, clearly, [obviously]
it is observed that	Delete
it is often the case that	often
it is our conclusion in light of investigation	we conclude that, our findings show that
it should be noted that the X	the X
it stands to reason	Omit
it was noted that if	if
it would not be unreasonable to assume	I [we] assume
leaving out of consideration	disregarding
locate	find
linkage	link
make an examination of	examine
marketing representative	salesperson
mental attitude	attitude
modification	change
mutual compromise	compromise
necessitate	require, need
not of a high order of accuracy	inaccurate
notwithstanding the fact that	although
numerous	many
objective	aim, goal
obtain	get
of considerable magnitude	big, large, great
of very minor importance [import]	unimportant
on account of the conditions described	because of the conditions
on account of the fact	because
on a few occasions	occasionally
on the grounds that	because
outside [inside] of	outside [inside]
partially	partly
perform	do
perform an analysis of	analyze
personal friend	friend
positive growth	growth
presently	now
prior to, in advance of	before
proceed	go
proceed to investigate, study, analyze	Omit *proceed to*

Wordy Phrase (cont.)	Suggested Change (cont.)
(the data-gathering) process	*Process* can usually be dropped
prompt and speedy	prompt, quick, speedy
purchase	buy
refer to as	call
relative to this	about this
remainder	rest
renovate like new	renovate
resultant effect	effect
short minute	minute, moment
solid facts	facts
subsequent to	after
successful triumph	triumph
sufficient	enough
synthesize	unite
taking this factor into consideration, it is apparent that	therefore, therefore it seems
terminate, termination	end
that is, i.e.	Usually can be deleted If writer has written clearly the clause or phrase to which it refers
the data show that X	X . . .
the existence of	Usually can be deleted
the foregoing	the, this, that, these, those
the fullest possible	Omit, or use *most, completely,* or *fully*
the only difference being that	except
the question as whether	whether
there are not very many	few
tire and fitigue	tire
to be sure	of course
to summarize the above	in sum, in summary
transmit	send
under way	begun, started
usage [other than language]	use
utilize	use
veritable	true
visualize	foresee
within the realm of possibility	possible, possibly
with reference [regard, respect] to	Omit (or use *about*)
with the exception of	except
with the result that	so that
with this in mind, with this in mind it is clear that	therefore

13.64 In certain contexts, some words can simply be dropped. For example, the *nature of work* and the *space factor* don't say anything more than *work* and *space* by themselves. You can describe *a person of an unpleasant character* much more effectively if you simply say that he or she is *an unpleasant person.* Why talk about *weather conditions* when you can talk about *weather,* about the *research process* when you can talk about *research,* or about the *soft quality of the fabric* when you can talk about the *soft fabric?* In your own writing, watch for similarly useless appearances of *nature, factor, character, conditions, process,* and *quality.* You will probably be surprised at the number you find and at the way your writing improves when you take them out. When you've mastered these, look for other useless words in similar constructions.

The Next Steps

13.65 When you finish this step:

- □ Read the manuscript out loud to yourself to catch any awkward phrases and glaring errors.
- □ Do an editorial check (for help, see Chapter 14).
- □ Calculate a SMOG or other readability index. If it isn't at least 12 or lower, have a co-worker read the manuscript for clarity.
- □ To measure your progress, compare the index with the first index you calculated.
- □ Have a clean draft typed.

IV. PRODUCTION

14 Editorial Checking

14.1 This chapter discusses steps that are especially important on longer documents, documents for wide distribution in- or out-of-house, and important documents for distribution outside the originating organization. (These steps are relatively unimportant on small and informal documents.) The editing functions described in this chapter help to prevent incompleteness, inconsistency, error, and embarrassment. Authors can do these checks for themselves, but the best policy is either to have technical editors or writers do them, or to encourage authors to do them for each other. Other people are always better than authors at finding problems in manuscripts. The functions are checking completeness; minimal copyediting to ensure integrity, correct unacceptable errors, and clarify illegible material; checking format and mechanical style; checking language; and substantive editing. When you begin checking:

□ Never make the mistake of trying to do all these steps at once. You will only do a bad job on all of them.

JPL (1976), available free from the Jet Propulsion Laboratory, shows how one organization tailored these steps to the needs of its documents.

14.2 This chapter is written for checkers, in part to help writers understand the checker's viewpoint. In addition:

□ Follow these instructions when you check a co-worker's manuscript.
□ When circumstances dictate that you do your own checking, use
these guidelines, but take a break of at least a day from writing
to help alter your perspective.

And encourage your supervisor to hire editorial help!

Minimal Copyediting

Completeness

14.3 Checking completeness might include making certain that a
document has a letter of submission, an abstract, cover and title
page, preface, acknowledgments, release statement, table of contents, running heads, sequential page numbers, figure captions, table
titles, appendixes, and bibliography. Other checks involve detail.
For example, does the table of contents contain at least the first-
order headings in the document? Do lists of tables and illustrations
contain all table titles and figure captions? Are all references complete enough that readers could locate the sources cited? To help
with this job:

□ Make a master list of items your organization requires, reproduce
it, and attach a copy to each document when it is ready for
checking.

Checking Integrity

14.4 Check integrity to make sure the parts of a document match.
Especially in long documents, prepared by more than one writer,
parts can get mixed up, misnumbered, and mistitled. Sometimes
writers leave out parts, expecting that someone else is to supply
them. Double checking always catches enough errors that organizations are well advised to make a complete checklist, reproduce it
in quantity, and attach one to the front of a document as soon as it
is ready for checking. When you have a word processor that
automatically creates tables of contents and lists of tables and
illustrations (as described in Section 4.9), you will be able to skip

many of these steps. For example, when the computer has created the table of contents and lists from the text, there is no possibility of error in the first two items below, and probably not in the third. Similarly, string location checks (much like the string change actions described in Sections 4.7 and 4.17) can allow easy checking of items like the fourth and sixth.

14.5 Use the following list as the basis for developing your organization's own list for checking integrity:

□ Table of contents; make sure numbers and wording agree with numbers and wording in chapter titles and headings.

□ Lists of tables and illustrations; make sure numbers and wording agree with numbers and wording in table titles and captions. (Check main titles only; there's no need for detailed, explanatory material in the lists.)

□ Page numbers; make sure numbers in the table of contents and lists of tables and illustrations agree with the page numbers in the body of the document.

□ Citations; make sure every table, figure, reference, note, and appendix is mentioned in text. Conversely, make sure every mention in text correctly identifies an existing table, figure, reference, note, or appendix. Also make sure unpublished documents have been treated properly (guidelines are in Sections 3.19 through 3.24).

□ Sequential numbering; make sure chapters, pages, tables, figures, references, equations, notes, sections, paragraphs, and appendixes have sequential numbering or lettering with no duplications and no gaps. For example, when tables are numbered sequentially by chapter (2.1, 2.2), a chapter shouldn't contain tables 2.1 and 2.3 but no 2.2.

□ Consistent numbering; make sure numbering doesn't change styles. For example, when page numbers are to be arabic, one chapter shouldn't have roman numerals.

□ Identical titles; make sure each title is unique; no two tables or illustrations may share the same title.

□ Cross-references; make sure elements cross-referenced (tables, figures, paragraphs, and so on) exist and are correct.

□ Running heads, feet, titles; make sure running heads, feet, and titles exist and are consistent with document title, chapter titles, and headings.

☐ References to future volumes; when the document is part of a series, warn the writer about specific references to the content of future volumes. (Plans may change several times before the volume is written.) Check the preface, foreword, and text.

☐ Prior references; in later volumes, check actual content with the earlier reference; when the two don't agree, the author needs to add a clarifying note.

Screening for Unacceptable Errors

14.6 The next step is to eliminate errors such as disagreement between subjects and verbs, incomplete sentences, incomprehensible statements (sometimes caused by missing material, but sometimes caused only by poor writing), and format errors such as handwriting on illustrations that are intended as camera-ready copy.

Clarification

14.7 Clarification is especially important for text that is to be set in type. Clarification might include identifying and marking mathematical symbols, showing where super- and subscripts go, and marking where to break an equation. Other possible steps include marking the tops of figures and specifying details that must remain clear when an illustration is reduced.

Format and Style

14.8 When you check format and style, you need a copy of the writer's format and style sheet (described in Section 11.23, example in Table 11.1). When the document is to be printed, you also need a copy of A *Manual of Style*,[1] by the University of Chicago Press (1969), which specifies printing details.

14.9 The importance of a carefully prepared format and style sheet cannot be overemphasized. Good copy editors are possessed by a basic urge for consistency and neatness. When in doubt, they choose the simplest options—often the choices most familiar to them but

[1] A new edition is due for publication in July 1981.

not necessarily what you want. When you don't specify your needs and give reasons for them, your document may return to you neatly checked and internally consistent—to standards you didn't intend to meet. For example, skim the table titles in Chapter 5 and the figure captions in Chapter 6 of this book. Note the variety in format and style. This is normally very poor practice; it was done only to illustrate possible variations without adding to the length of the book. When I turned the illustrations over to a draftsman, however, he very carefully conformed all captions to a style he liked. He was accustomed to writers who didn't know style from stile, and he simply assumed that I was just one more in that long line!

Organization of Manuscript Parts and Page Numbers

14.10 *Separate pages.* Certain parts of long documents, listed below, always or nearly always begin on separate pages.

PROPOSALS

Front matter
    Cover page
    Table of contents
    Abstract
Body
    First page of text
    Each table
    Each illustration
    Notes
Back matter
    List of references
    Bibliography
    Budget
    Each appendix

BOOKS, REPORTS,
AND INSTRUCTIONS

Front Matter
    Title page
    Release page
    Acknowledgments
    Table of contents
    List of tables
    List of illustrations
    Preface
Body
    Abstract or summary
    First page of each
      chapter
    Each table
    Each illustration
    Notes to each chapter
Back Matter
    Each appendix
    Bibliography or list of
      references
    Glossary
    Index

Mark all parts that begin on separate pages, arrange pages in proper order, and assign page numbers.

14.11 *Treatment of page number.* Specify the pages that have numbers typed on them, the type of number, and the placement. In general:

- ◻ Use roman numerals for front matter (defined in Section 2.3, Step 5).
- ◻ Use sequential arabic numerals for the body through the appendixes and bibliography.
- ◻ Type the page number on pages with tables; omit typed numbers from camera-ready illustration pages.
- ◻ When numbers are to go in the corner, specify three-quarters of an inch from the top of the page, flush right.
- ◻ When reproduction is to be on both sides of the page, write instructions that tell the typist to alternate the page number from right corner (on right-hand, or *recto*, pages) to left corner, flush left (on left-hand, or *verso*, pages). Odd-numbered pages usually are recto; even-numbered, verso.
- ◻ Specify whether you want a typed number on the first page of the table of contents, lists of tables and illustrations, chapters, appendixes, and bibliography.

Titles, Headings, and Figure Captions

14.12 For chapter and appendix titles, headings and subheadings (described in Sections 12.15 through 12.17), table titles (Sections 5.40 and 5.41), figure captions (Sections 6.36), and all other titles, specify the style for:

- ◻ Capitalization (first letter of first word only, first letter of all important words, completely capped).
- ◻ Underlining (in print, italics).
- ◻ Treatment of "turnover" (second and subsequent) lines in titles and captions.
- ◻ End punctuation, if any.
- ◻ Space above and below.
- ◻ For headings and subheadings, the relative positions of first, second, and third levels. Figure 12.2, Section 12.15 shows just three possible variations.

□ Also check style specifications for distinctiveness (described in Section 11.19). For example, if both chapter titles *and* first-level headings were capitalized completely, it would be easy for readers to mix them up visually.

Often you will find that the writer hasn't treated all headings at the same level in the same way, and you will have to ask for clarification. When the writer has given you the outline for the document, you might find helpful a brief summary that describes the relationship between outline levels and headings. The following example is for headings in APA style, shown in Part A of Figure 12.2.

When a heading goes with	Type it	It is a topic at the
An outline topic at the roman numeral level of importance	Centered, left to right on page	First level of importance
An outline topic at the capital letter level of importance	Flush with left margin	Second level of importance; divides a topic at the first level
An outline topic at the arabic numeral level of importance	As a paragraph leader, period at end; caps on first word only	Third level of importance: divides topic at the second level

Documentation

14.13 *Author (date) documentation.* Author (date) documentation is one of three common forms of documentation. Check the entire document for consistency on the following items (Section 11.20 gives the full names for the styles abbreviated here):

□ Punctuation between name and date when both elements are inside parentheses. For example:

(Jones, 1977)   APA, ASA, SA, Sage
(Jones 1978)   CBE, *JASA*, MSN

□ Punctuation between date and page number. Variations are:

Jones (1975:3)	ASA, CBE, SA, Sage
Smith (1975, p.30)	APA, *JASA*, MSN

□ Use of and or ampersand between names:

Lee and Lin (1978)	APA, ASA, CBE, *JASA*, Sage
Lee & Lin (1978)	SA
Lee and Lin (1978:6)	ASA, Sage
(Lee and Lin 1978, p.6)	*JASA*, MSN
(Lee and Lin 1978:6)	CBE
(Lee & Lin, 1978:6)	APA, SA

□ Use of brackets when part or all of a citation is enclosed within parentheses along with a short comment. Variations:

Lee (1975; one . . .)	APA, SA, Sage
Lee ([1978]; one . . .)	ASA
(Lee, 1975; one . . .)	APA, SA, Sage
(Lee 1975; one . . .)	CBE, MSN
(Lee [1978]; one . . .)	Not common

□ Within parentheses, use of a comma to separate dates for two or more documents by the same author, and a semicolon to separate the data on documents by different authors. For example:

(Lee, 1975, 1976)	APA, ASA, SA, Sage
(Lee 1975, 1978)	CBE, *JASA*, MSN
(Lee, 1975; Lin, 1978)	APA, ASA, SA, Sage
(Lee 1975; Lin 1978)	CBE, *JASA*, MSN

□ Use of et al. or *et al.* to replace the names of second and subsequent authors in references to documents written by more than two authors. Some styles, such as ASA and CBE, require use of first author's last name and "et al." in place of all other names for *all* references to a document. Others, such as APA, require all names for the first citation of a document with more than two authors. In all subsequent citations, authors must cite only the last name of the first author and "et al." MSN permits use of "et al." only for citation of documents with more than *three* authors and only for second and subsequent citations. For example:

Lee et al. (1977)
Lee, Lin, and Lyn (1977); and Lee et al. (1977)
Lee, Lin, Lyn, and Low (1977); and Lee et al. (1977)
(Lee et al., 1977)
(Lee et al. 1977)

Writers should not use "et al." when doing so would produce an abbreviation identical to that for another document. For example, in the second and third examples just above, Lee et al. (1977) is used to abbreviate the citation of two different documents. When you find two identical abbreviations:

☐ Call the writer, point out that fact, and suggest use of all names each time to prevent ambiguity.

14.14 Also make certain the writer punctuated references within the sentences to which they are attached. For example:

That finding is clear (Jones 1974).
That finding is clear (Jones, 1974).

NOT

That finding is clear. (Jones 1974)
That finding is clear. (Jones, 1974)

14.15 *Citation of document by number.* Some styles—for example, ASTM and AMathS—require writers to show documentation by inserting a bracketed or parenthesized number in the text. A very few styles use neither. Instead, writers treat the number cited in text just like a footnote number. Different styles establish the number different ways. For example, ASTM uses the number established by the order in which the writer first cites the document. Thus, if Smith's paper were the object of the third and the ninth citations, you would use the superscript 3 both times. In contrast, AMathS cites the number established by the document's position in a bibliography whose entries are (1) alphabetized by last name of author and (2) subsequently numbered in that order. Make sure the writer has established the number correctly. Also make sure he or she has punctuated documentation within the sentences involved. For example (bracketed references first; parenthesized, second; superscripted, third):

Jones [2] found it.
See Jones [2, p.5].

We know that (2).
We know that (2, p. 5).

We know that.[2] We[2] (p. 5) know that.

14.16 *Superscript numbers and footnotes.* AIP, MLA, MSH, Turabian, and many specialized systems of documentation—for example, of congressional and legal documents—require superscript numbers and footnotes to show documentation. Check the notes for consistency. Most commonly, the characteristics of this style of documentation are:

1. Numbers in sequence, according to position in manuscript.
2. Name in normal order.
3. Article titles placed within quotation marks, and book titles italicized. Capitalization follows Section 13.48.
4. Date near the end of each reference.
5. Commas, not periods, between the elements in the reference.
6. Page numbers preceded by "p." or "pp."
7. Abbreviation of journal names by a standard list, such as the American National Standard for Abbreviation of Titles of Periodicals. Some manuals, such as that by the AIP, include the list.

14.17 Be sure to specify:

□ Whether the notes go on the bottoms of text pages or on a separate page, entitled *Notes*.
□ Whether notes are to be double-spaced internally or single-spaced.
□ Whether typist is to double- or single-space between notes.

Substantive Notes

14.18 In form, substantive notes are much like documentation notes. Make sure the writer has indicated clearly:

□ Whether the notes go on the bottoms of text pages or on a separate page, entitled *Notes*.
□ Whether notes are to be double-spaced internally or single-spaced.

□ Whether typist is to double- or single-space between notes. When a document contains notes of both kinds, make sure the writer has integrated them in order of occurrence.

Tables

14.19 *General requirements.* Make sure tables are properly located, and mark whether they are to be typed on a separate piece of paper. When tables are separate and the manuscript is to be printed, make sure the writer has inserted a "table call" to show the typesetter about where the table is to be put in the text. The best place for the indicator usually is immediately after the first mention of the table. Examples of typed indicators are:

> [Table 2 about here]
> (Table 2 about here)

A typed indicator may go either between paragraphs or between lines of a paragraph. When the writer has used variable spacing to group columns (Sections 5.33 through 5.37 explain how), write a note to the typist.

14.20 Next, make sure the writer has:

□ Lined up numbers by decimals, expressed or implied. Figure 5.1, Chapter 5, shows examples.
□ In a column of dollar amounts, placed a dollar sign in front of the top entry even when the column head also indicates dollars. The sign is an additional help to readers.
□ In a column of percentages, put a percent sign (%) after the top entry even when the column head also indicates percentages. The sign is an additional aid to readers. In table titles, column heads and row stubs, use "percentage," not "%" or "percent."
□ Used the following conventions for empty cells and cells whose entry is zero (0):

1. No entry = the column head and the row stub are mutually inapplicable.
2. . . . . = the column head and row stub are mutually applicable, but no data exist. Leaders may run all the way across the column

or across the same horizontal space as the widest entry in the column. Figure 5.1 shows an example of the second option.

3. Zero (0) = the quantity entered is a numerical 0.

There is no need for dashes or n.a. (not applicable). Many writers don't know these conventions, so you may need to ask writers what they mean by a particular entry. The source of this convention is Section 12.22 in the University of Chicago Press's *A Manual of Style* (1969).

14.21 *Variations.* Next, check all tables for consistency. Figure 5.1 shows the parts of a table. In the body of the table:

- Look for consistency in use of vertical and horizontal lines. Most styles prohibit vertical lines and limit horizontal lines to positions beneath the title, boxheads and column heads, and the body of the table.
- *Never* add lines without asking the writer's permission.
- Check consistency in capitalization of row stubs and column headings. Also check consistency in treatment of second lines in stubs and headings. When the writer has no preference and the style guide expresses none, follow the style in Figure 5.1.

14.22 Also look for consistency in treatment of notes. Specifically:

- Check division between body and notes. Most styles require a line between these two elements.
- Check the order for source, general, and specific notes. Also check capitalization and underlining. In the absence of instructions, follow the model in Figure 5.1.
- Check the designation of notes that pertain to only one part of a table. Some styles require superscript numbers like those shown in Figure 5.1. Other styles require superscript letters (a,b,c) or symbols (*, **, etc.).
- Check indentation. In general, type notes flush with the left margin, as in Figure 5.1. However, some styles require indentation of the first line. In such cases, check the number of spaces required for the indentation.
- Check superscription. In general, "Source" and "Note" belong on a line with what follows. Superscripts for specific notes should be raised one-half space.

Illustrations

14.23 Check text for a location note. When the document is not to be printed, you may need to mark the text to remind the typist to leave enough space for the illustration to be inserted.

Bibliographies and Lists of References

14.24 *General rules.* Bibliographies and lists of references start on a separate page. Different styles have different rules for typing references. The references for this book (the bibliography at the end) are typed in MSN style. The basic characteristics of this style are:

- ☐ Names reversed, initials only (no full first or middle names), followed by a period.
- ☐ Order alphabetical, by author's last name.
- ☐ Date after name, followed by a period.
- ☐ Article and chapter titles without quotation marks; caps on only the first word and first after a colon.

In general, use full page numbers, such as 208–210, and not 208–10. Full numbers leave no room for misinterpretation. Figure 14.1 shows references in a style other than MSN.

14.25 *Variations.* Check reference lists for consistency on the following items. (If you don't have to ask the writer for clarification at least once, you will probably have set a world's record!) Section 11.20 lists full names for the styles abbreviated here. On all references, check capitalization of and punctuation around all of the following elements. Also check:

- ☐ Name; use of initials, reversal of name order, the word and or ampersand between names of coauthors, use of dashes or a short line to replace author's name for second and subsequent listings by an author.
- ☐ Date; order, from earliest to latest (ASA), or latest to earliest; placement either immediately after the name (ASA) or near the end of the reference (APA, ASTM).
- ☐ Titles of articles and chapters; omission; use of quotation marks (ASA but not APA).
- ☐ Titles of books; underline (APA) or not (ASA).
- ☐ Ed. and eds.; placement before or after the editor's name.

References

[1] Researcher, A. C., "A Report," Agency Report Number, Agency, Chicago, June 1969.

[2] Adam, A. T., <u>A Book</u>, Rev. ed., Wiley, New York, 1969, p. 3.

[3] Lee, A. G., in <u>A Monograph</u>, C. P. Excellence, Ed., Wiley, New York, 1974, Chapter 6, pp. 99-108.

[4] Student, S. K. and Lee, S. P., <u>A Journal</u>, Vol. 8, No. 6, April 1974, p. 8.

DISTINGUISHING CHARACTERISTICS

<u>Numbers</u>: consecutive, in order of mention in text; in brackets.

<u>Names</u>: reverse order, initials only.

<u>Article and chapter titles</u>: omitted; article title included only if journal is foreign or hard to obtain.

<u>Publishers' names</u>: brief form only for well-known publishers; for others, give name, city, and state (abbreviated).

<u>Page numbers</u>: complete; at end.

<u>Date</u>: near end.

FIGURE 14.1 Example: List of documents in ASTM style.

□ Journal titles; underline (APA, but not ASA); abbreviation.

□ Page numbers for articles and chapters; required (ASA) or not (APA); if so, placed after title of chapter (ASA) or at end of reference; preceded by "pp." or "Pp." (ASA).

□ For all page numbers; expressed as briefly as possible, for example 341–9 (ASA); or not, for example 341–42(MSN) or 341–342 (APA).

□ For books, information on city, state, publisher; all three required or some omitted; brief form or not.

Cover Sheet

14.26 Check the cover sheet for:

- Required items; most often, title, writer's name and position, organization, and date. Your organization might also require a release statement, abstract, acknowledgment of sponsorship, or other items.
- Style; capitalization, centering from left to right, space between title and name and between coauthors' names, and between name(s) and date.

To help with this task, design a model cover sheet for your organization and use it as a boiler plate form (described in Section 9.4).

Checking Language

14.27 When you check language, examine the way the writer expressed ideas; pay no attention to either format or mechanical style. Make changes on the basis of specific, identifiable standards and not personal preference. The more important the document or the more public it will become, the more necessary such a check is.

Items to Check

14.28 Consider items such as the following:

- Spelling; follow either *Webster's Third New International Dictionary* or the dictionary required by your employer. Choose the first spelling listed when the dictionary gives two or more accepted versions.
- Grammar and syntax; follow a good grammar book, such as Perrin (1972).
- Punctuation; follow a recognized standard, such as that in *A Manual of Style* (University of Chicago Press 1969).
- Usage; follow a recognized standard such as Fowler (1965), Bernstein (1965), Follet (1966), or Morris (1975).
- Fluency; check transitional words and phrases. Remove unnecessary transitional clauses, sentences, and paragraphs (for help see Sections 12.16, 12.18, 12.19, and 13.3 through 13.5).
- Conciseness; eliminate wordiness (for help see Sections 13.56 through 13.64).

□ Verb sequence; check for proper sequence of verb tenses in description, exposition, narrative, and argument.

□ Terms; identify wrong terms and terms used inconsistently. When the manuscript is on a word processor, use the string location function (described in Section 4.17) to help with this task.

□ Abbreviations, acronyms, and symbols; make sure that all abbreviations, acronyms, and symbols have been defined at least once, and that each is used in the same way each time it occurs.

□ Equations; check completeness and parallel expression.

14.29 Do these checks to insure parallel language:

□ Symbols, words, and phrases; in lists, headings, and subheadings, and column heads and row stubs, look for expressions that are not grammatically and syntactically parallel. For example, *anger* and *hunger* are parallel, as are *angry* and *hungry; anger* (a noun) and *hungry* (an adjective) aren't parallel.

□ Parallel structure; when an outline, list heading, or other category has one subordinate element, make sure it also has a second (ideas need company, Section 7.13).

Differences from Other Checks

14.30 Language checking differs from substantive editing (discussed in Sections 14.31 through 14.34) because the goal is to discover flaws that are visible without understanding the text. However, the lack of, say, parallelism in language often is a nonverbal clue that the writer's thoughts aren't parallel. In fact, the writer may need to rewrite one or more sections to clarify the thinking. Language checking differs from checking the mechanics of style because the focus is on the substance and not on mechanical expression. For example, the checker asks whether the first-level headings are grammatically and syntactically parallel, and not whether all are centered, underlined, and given initial caps. The latter is a question for mechanical checking.

Substantive Editing

14.31 Substantive editing helps to produce a first-class document. As with a language check, the more important and public the document, the more important and necessary substantive editing is.

In one sense, it is not possible to isolate substance from other targets of editorial checking; even the clarification of mechanics can directly affect substance by affecting nonverbal messages (discussed in Sections 12.7 through 12.13 and 11.19 through 11.33). Nevertheless, in contrast to the steps listed above, the topics in the rest of the chapter are primarily substantive.

Checking the Whole Document

14.32 Make sure the document presents the topic completely. Note gaps, items out of order, and redundancy. Specifically:

- Title; make sure title accurately reflects content of document.
- Abstract; make sure abstract is concise, is the proper length, and contains enough information to help readers understand the general content.
- Relation of headings to text; make sure the introduction, subsequent sections, summary, and conclusions contain the substance their headings say they contain (for help see Sections 12.15 through 12.17).
- Appendixes; make sure the text in appendixes is appropriate for an appendix and ought not to be either in the body of the report or eliminated completely (for help see Section 12.24).
- Divisions; make sure divisions and subdivisions make sense (for help see Chapter 7 and Sections 5.23 through 5.25).
- Emphasis, parallelism, and subordination; make sure emphasis is appropriate to significance. Also make certain parallelism and subordination suit the content and are reflected in the structure of headings and subheadings.
- Repetition and redundancy; in general, eliminate repetition and redundancy (for help see Sections 13.56 through 13.64).
- Inconsistencies; resolve apparent contradictions and inconsistencies among different sections of the document.
- Missing material; check for missing material—especially factual data and elements that the sponsoring organization requires.
- Irrelevant or inappropriate material; identify irrelevant and inappropriate material so the author can eliminate or rework it.
- List of definitions; decide whether the document has enough symbols and abbreviations to require a list of definitions. If so, recommend a list to the author.
- Undocumented text; make sure writer has documented all statements that require documentation.

□ Permissions; when writer has reproduced copyrighted material, make certain he or she has obtained permission (for help with permission forms, see Sections 12.43 through 12.49 in Mullins 1977).

Checking Tables

14.33 In checking the clarity and correctness of tabular material:

□ Text versus tables; check relation of text to tabular presentations. When conversion from table to text or text to table would make text clearer, make the conversion (for help see Section 5.3).
□ Design; make sure design of table is correct and that units of measurement appear in column heads and not in data fields.
□ Completeness of information; make sure information is complete. Also make sure column heads and stub columns clearly identify units of measurement.
□ Parallel form; make certain the writer used parallel forms to present similar information in the same table and similar information in tables in a series.
□ Titles; make sure titles are adequate, appropriate, and not excessive. Make sure the writer used a parallel form for the titles of tables in a series (for help see Section 5.6).
□ Powers; make sure the writer expressed clearly the powers of 10.
□ Columns and rows; make sure the writer grouped and ordered columns and row stubs in a manner that will enhance comprehension. Make sure the order highlights important similarities and differences (for help see Section 5.7).
□ Placement in order of use; make sure writer has inserted tables, or called for insertion, as close as possible to the places where he or she uses them.

Illustrations

14.34 Check arrangement and presentation of illustrations to ensure that they enhance the message of the document.

□ Identification; make sure writer has clearly identified all curves, data points, and axes (for help see Sections 6.37 through 6.46).
□ Elimination of detail; make sure illustrations contain no excess

detail. When the detail is important, find a place in text to incorporate it.

- Scales; make sure photographs that need scales have them. Also check illustrations with double scales, such as may be needed to express both SI and English units. Make sure the presentation is simple, clear, and consistent.
- Powers; make sure writer has clearly expressed powers of 10.
- Consistent structure; make sure writer has arranged consistently similar parts of illustrations with several parts and similar illustrations in a series.
- Relationship with text; make sure illustration suits the significance of the data as expressed in text.

Returning Results to Writer

14.35 Keep notes and comments in order of the text. Sometimes it helps to type or write notes on paper, cut them off, tape an end to the back of the page to which a comment applies, and then fold the tail over the page. As you write comments, be tactful. Whenever possible, write constructive suggestions. Don't skip flaws in a misguided effort to be kind; just treat the writer as another human being with feelings like yours (for help read Sections 11.13 through 11.18).

15 Typing, Proofreading, and Finishing Touches

15.1 This chapter is not only for writers but also for office managers, head secretaries, and editors, who often find themselves mediating between writers and typists. In addition to this chapter, also read Chapter 14, especially beginning with Section 14.8. When possible, also have typists read Chapters 14 and 15 and Sections 11.19 through 11.33.

15.2 When all or part of a manuscript is ready for final typing, attach to the draft a checklist like the following to help you keep track of progress. After each step has been completed, check it off. The steps are:

1. Typed in proper style.
2. Pages properly ordered and numbered.
3. Pages proofread.
4. Errors corrected.
5. Illustrations prepared in camera-ready form (when required).
6. Duplicated in acceptable manner and in enough copies for the recipient and for your organization (for guidelines, see Sections 15.3 through 15.6).
7. If the document was typed on a word processor, file name and identifying index code for tape, disk, or cassette (if used) written on checklist.
8. Cover added.

9. Document bound or stapled.
10. Letter of transmittal prepared.
11. Letter attached to appropriate number of copies of document.
12. Envelope or box prepared for mailing.
13. When manuscript is a journal article, self-addressed and stamped return envelope and acknowledgment card enclosed.
14. For any manuscript intended for publication, a 3 × 5 card prepared with bibliographic information.
15. Mailed:
    First class ———
    Third class ———
    Certified ———
    Registered ———
    Date ———
16. Form filed with file copies of the manuscript.

Paper, Type, Ribbons, Corrections, and Masters

General Instructions

15.3 Tell typists not to use erasable bond or other highly glazed paper because it is easily smudged. Instead:

1. Specify white paper of appropriate quality and size—16-pound paper usually is the minimum acceptable, and 8 1/2 × 11 inches usually is the appropriate size.
2. Although this may seem obvious, tell typists to *type on only one side of every page.* Inexperienced typists sometimes type on both sides because they are trying to conserve paper.
3. Similarly, when your typist is working at home, make sure the typewriter has both upper- and lowercase letters!
4. Specify the same *pitch,* or type spacing, throughout the manuscript. Pica type has 10 spaces or characters per inch; elite has 12.
5. Also specify the same type *style* (for example, script, gothic, courier), especially when several typists are working on the same document.
6. When you need multiple copies, specify the type of master.

Mimeograph, multilith, and xerographic copies usually are preferred to spirit masters.

7. For manuscripts typed on white paper, remind typists to clean
   the type and use a new, black ribbon.
   CAUTION: Some masters require a carbon ribbon.
8. When the typist does not have a self-correcting typewriter or
   word processing equipment, ask that small corrections be made
   with a correction fluid such as Liquid Paper. When properly
   applied, the fluid dries quickly, completely covers errors, and is
   invisible. Also, the fluid does not damage the surface of the
   paper as erasing often does. As soon as the fluid is dry, type the
   correction.

Special Instructions for Masters

15.4 When you have an inexperienced typist, you may need to give
additional instructions on use of masters. (Even writers will find
these instructions useful if, sometime, they find themselves with a
rush job, no typist, and mistakes that must be corrected before
copies can be made.) With any kind of master:

□ Ask the typist to check the manufacturer's instructions for recommended type styles.

15.5 For mimeograph masters, instruct the typist to:

1. Shift the typewriter ribbon out of printing position.
2. Clean the type, put paper in the typewriter, and type each key
   once or twice to remove excess ink.
3. Set the paper position lever at 1 or A (depending on the brand
   and model of the typewriter). On a selectric typewriter, set the
   gear on the type ball at 5.
4. Use a "backing sheet" between the master and the sheet to
   which it is attached. The box of masters usually gives instructions.
5. To correct typographical errors, rub gently over the error with a
   paper clip. Paint a very small amount of correction fluid on top.
   Then type the correct letters or words. This technique minimizes
   the waxy build-up that can cause blurred corrections.
   CAUTION: Be sure to supply the typist with correction fluid!

15.6 For manuscripts typed on multilith offset masters, instruct the typist to:

1. Read the instructions. Multilith often requires a carbon ribbon and specific type styles.
2. Type with a light or medium pressure. A heavy touch will create hollow images.
3. Be very careful not to touch the typing surface. Fingerprints will reproduce along with the type. Simply grasp the master by the extreme edges.
4. Read the instructions on correcting errors before beginning to type. In general, use a multilith eraser or another eraser that is not gritty and is not made of oily rubber. Erase gently so as not to damage the surface of the plate. Clean the eraser frequently. When the erasing is done, type the correct character with a normal touch.
   CAUTION: Be sure to supply the typist with the proper kind of eraser.

Margins and Hyphenation

15.7 Consistent margins are particularly important to the good looks of a document. To obtain consistency:

1. Always specify the width of *each* margin. The minimum margin allowed is one inch on each side. For most bound reports, specify a left margin of at least one and one-half inches (to allow for binding), top and bottom margins at least one and one-quarter inches wide, and a right margin at least one inch wide.
2. Tell typists to use the line indicator on the typewriter to monitor the amount of space left on a page.
3. To prevent incorrectly divided words, tell typists *not* to hyphenate words at the end of a line. When the length of a final word on a line forces typists to choose between a short line and a line that would extend into the margin, tell them to choose the short line.

Many word processing systems automatically control margins. Once you have specified them, you needn't worry about human error, such as typing into the bottom margin.

Consistent Spacing

15.8 Consistent spacing is important because:

- ◻ It implies that you prepared the report or proposal carefully.
- ◻ It gives readers clues to organization that enhance the readability of text.

For example, when you center all first-level headings (explained in Sections 12.15 through 12.17) from left to right and leave two vertical spaces above them, the appearance on a page of this pattern of space tells readers that you are about to stop one major topic and begin another. Inconsistency loses this benefit and may even confuse readers. For more information read Sections 11.19 through 11.33.

Vertical Spacing

15.9 From top to bottom:

- ◻ Specify vertical spacing for the text—usually double- or triple-spacing for drafts and single-spacing for final copy.
- ◻ Also specify the spacing between all lines of all title pages, biographies, abstracts, prefaces, tables of contents, lists of tables and illustrations, quotations, equations, notes, tables, illustrations, captions and legends, appendixes, bibliographies, lists of references, glossaries, and indexes.

15.10 Some fairly common uses of space are:

- ◻ Triple-space between the text and the beginning and end of a blocked, indented quotation.
- ◻ Triple-space above first-order headings and above second-order headings unless there is no text between the second-order heading and the immediately prior first-order heading. In such cases, double-space.
- ◻ Leave two inches (12 vertical spaces) between the top of a page and the title of a short report, article, or chapter, and above the titles "Table of Contents," "List of Tables," "List of Illustrations," "Biography," "Preface," "Acknowledgments," "Notes," "References," "Bibliography," "Appendix," "Glossary," and "Index," when the manuscript includes those sections. *Quadruple-space* between the titles and the next typed line.

- Leave at least two inches between the top of the page and the first line of typing on the title page and the release page (sometimes combined).
- See Sections 5.33 through 5.38 for additional guidelines on spacing tables.

Horizontal Spacing

15.11 The conventions for horizontal spacing are:

- Indent the first line of a paragraph five spaces.
- Single-space after words, commas, and semicolons; after a colon when what follows is part of the sentence preceding the colon; and after a period, question mark, or exclamation mark when it is *within,* and does not mark the end of, a sentence. For example:

  > Wow! expresses surprise; such exclamations are not common in technical writing.

- Double-space after periods, question marks, and exclamation marks that end sentences. For example:

  > Wow! Was he impressed! He was so impressed he replied immediately.

- Leave no spaces between the letters of words, or between dashes and the words preceding and following the dashes. For example:

  > decision-making procedure
  > His goal—to finish the report—seemed unattainable.

- See Sections 5.33 through 5.38 for additional guidelines on spacing tables.

15.12 The conventions in Sections 15.10 and 5.11 are so common that you should never to have to mention them to an experienced typist. In contrast, many typists will need explicit instructions about how to space outlines and numbered lists. Probably the most aesthetically pleasing format is to line up the numerals (or letters) so that the periods after the numerals (or letters) also line up. Also line up the numerals (or letters) for subsections beneath the text of the previous section. Leave *two* spaces between the periods and the beginning of text in outlines and lists. For example:

Outline	List
I. Text	1. Text
A. Text	2. Text
1. Text	3. Text
2. Text	4. Text
a. Text	5. Text
b. Text	6. Text
(1) Text	7. Text
(2) Text	8. Text
(a) Text	9. Text
(b) Text	10. Text
B. Text	a. Text
II. Text	b. Text
III. Text	11. Text
IV. Text	12. Text

Text Symbols, Accents, and Equations

15.13 To prevent misinterpretation, tell the typist to handwrite symbols and accents, unless the typewriter is equipped with them, and to distinguish displayed equations from text in the following manner:

- □ Triple-space between them and the surrounding text.
- □ Indent at least seven spaces from the left margin. Some styles require that equations be centered from left to right on the page.
- □ Type any identifying numbers, usually within parentheses or brackets, flush with the right or left margin. Right is more common. For example:

(9)

[3]

Quotations

Integrated Quotations

15.14 For quotations that are integrated into the text, the correct typing format is:

- □ Double quotation marks at the beginning and at the end of the quotation.

242

□ Periods and commas inside the quotation marks; question marks and exclamation points outside.
□ Question marks and exclamation points inside only when they are part of the quotation.
□ Single quotation marks for quotations within the quotation.
EXCEPTION: British firms and publishers usually prefer single quotation marks around the quotation and double marks for quotations within the quotation. Place all punctuation outside the quotation.

For example, "Treat an integrated quotation this way." When you need more information on the relationship of punctuation to quotation marks, see Perrin's *Guide and Index to English* (1972, pp. 550 and 684–686), or any other good grammar book.

Blocked Quotations

15.15 When you want to block a quotation, tell the typist to:

□ Block the entire quotation five or seven spaces from the left margin; seven is more common.
SUGGESTION: When you follow these guidelines carefully in drafts, typists are more likely to treat quotations exactly as you wish.
□ Leave three spaces above and below the quotation to separate it from the surrounding text.
□ Use *no* quotation marks at the beginning or the end. When you use internal quotation marks, use double marks unless you are writing for a British firm or publisher.
□ Use paragraph indentation only on second and subsequent paragraphs in a blocked quotation. For example, in the quotation below, the first line of the first paragraph is not indented; the first line of the second paragraph is indented.

> This paper bridges the gap between theories (1) by specifying a model, . . . (2) by measuring causal relations, and (3) by comparing boundaries over time.
>
> Indent the first line of the second paragraph as is done here. Block the remaining lines *with the lines of the preceding paragraph,* again as is done here. (Emphasis added.)

Omissions, Changes, and Emphasis

15.16 Use the following conventions to show changes and emphasis in quotations:

- An ellipsis, three periods with a space between each pair, shows the omission of words within a quotation. Ellipses at the beginnings and ends of quotations are incorrect.
- Brackets show changes in the wording of a quotation, or words added.
- Underlining emphasizes certain words.

15.17 At the end of quotations with underlining, indicate the source of emphasis either in text or in a footnote. The quotation in Section 15.15 shows examples of ellipses, brackets, emphasis, and statement of source of emphasis. Furthermore:

- Place any needed punctuation before the ellipsis. For example, when you omit the last words in a sentence, place the period after the last word before the ellipsis. Leave one space, then type three periods with one space after each. See the quotation in Section 15.15 for an example.
- Be consistent in how you designate the source of emphasis. The most common designations are statements like:

  (Emphasis added.)
  (Emphasis in original.)
  (Smith's emphasis.)
  (Smith's italics.)

Proofreading and Corrections on Finished Typing

Instructions

15.18 Proofreading is the only way to assure that what you intended is what got typed. The best way to proofread is with a partner; you or an assistant read the rough copy out loud while the partner reads the freshly typed copy. When the freshly typed copy is on paper, do *not* write on it. Instead, write corrections on separate paper, identified by page, paragraph, and line number. This procedure allows the typist to correct the original without unsightly smudges and gives you a record against which to check the corrected manuscript.

EXCEPTION: When the document is on a word processor, typists will prefer that you correct the fresh copy because they will prepare a completely new copy after making corrections on the master cassette, disk, diskette, or file copy. Similarly, when you are proofreading multilith masters, ask the typist to give you a xerox copy of each master. You can mark corrections on the copy without fear that your fingerprints will damage the master.

15.19 Mimeograph masters require slightly different procedures. When you are proofreading mimeograph stencils, you must write corrections on a separate sheet, following the procedure for documents typed on paper. Usually you will have to proof directly from the stencil, but sometimes you will be able to proof from either the stencil back or the backing sheet that is usually between the stencil and the sheet to which each stencil is attached (when the typist used a new sheet with each stencil)

☐ Remember to keep your fingers off the typing and the masters away from heat. Warmth can soften the wax and blur the typing.

Proofreader's Marks

15.20 When you write corrections on a page of typing, use the proofreader's marks shown below. They have standard meanings and are printed in most dictionaries and many English grammar books.

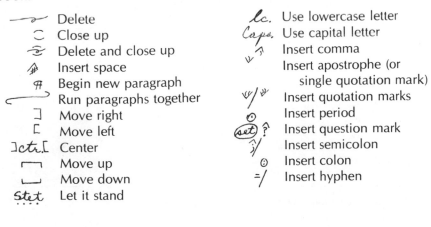

Mark	Meaning	Mark	Meaning
⟿	Delete	*lc.*	Use lowercase letter
⌒	Close up	*Caps.*	Use capital letter
⌒̃	Delete and close up	⌃	Insert comma
#	Insert space		Insert apostrophe (or
¶	Begin new paragraph		single quotation mark)
⌒⌒	Run paragraphs together	ᵛ/ᵛ	Insert quotation marks
⌐	Move right	⊙	Insert period
⌐	Move left	(set) ?	Insert question mark
⌐ctr⌐	Center	/	Insert semicolon
⊓	Move up	⊙	Insert colon
⊔	Move down	=/	Insert hyphen
Stet	Let it stand		

Instructions for Making Corrections

15.21 Whether the typing is on bond, stencils, or masters, when the document is not on a word processor, you may have to give the typist specific instructions for long, involved corrections, such as:

1. No matter how small the correction, require that it be typed. Otherwise, some typists will give you neat, handwritten corrections.
2. When you need to insert one or more words on a completely typed page, tell the typist whether you want the page retyped or whether you prefer to have the correction typed above the line and to use a caret ($\wedge$) to indicate position. Figure 15.1 shows examples.

316

52

```
When you need to insert one or
more words , use a caret (∧) to
indicate position.
```
(p. 52a follows)

52a

```
on a completely typed page, ask
whether the writer wants you to
retype the page or type the
correction above the affected
line and
```
(Insert on p. 52 as shown.)

51

```
        black
Use a new∧ribbon.  For some
publishers and some masters,
you will need a new carbon
ribbon.
```

FIGURE 15.1   Examples: ways to insert words on typed pages

3. On intermediate drafts or drafts for approval before a final copy is typed, sometimes you may need to ask that extensive corrections be typed on a separate page. Assign that page an "a" number and note, on the original, that the correction follows. Figure 15.1 shows an example.

Ways To Improve Typing on Future Manuscripts

15.22 To improve typing on future manuscripts:

1. When you proofread, list errors a typist makes frequently and ask that, in the future, he or she try to eliminate them.
2. Also give typists copies of finished manuscripts to keep in a notebook, with a general style sheet, to use as examples for future manuscripts in those styles.

Reproduction of the Manuscript

15.23 When you specify requirements for reproduction:

□ Request the highest quality paper that will give a clear, dark copy.
□ Check requirements for number and kind of copies. When the manuscript is for publication, remember that publishers and editors prefer photocopies or xerographic copies to carbon copies. Most need at least two copies, and some need five or six. With other kinds of document, you might need hundreds or even thousands of copies.
□ Check the clarity of reproduction on each page of each copy.
□ For journals and other publishers, *reproduce on only one side of each page.*
□ Check the number of other copies needed. You will need a copy for each critic, and *always* keep at least one file copy.
□ *Don't* staple copies for a publisher without first asking whether you should do so. Particularly when a manuscript is to be put into production, publishers prefer that you fasten copies with a paper clip or paper press.
□ On other documents, add cover (if any) and have document bound.

Packaging and Mailing

15.24 When the manuscript is not for in-house use, you or your assistant will need the instructions in this section. To make sure the document arrives in pristine condition:

- Place the letter of transmittal on top of the copies of the manuscript.
- When the document is to be considered for publication, include a return-addressed, stamped, 9 × 12 envelope (nicknamed the SASE, used for articles only) for return of the manuscript. Also include a postcard, addressed and stamped, whose return will acknowledge that the manuscript has arrived.
- Wrap the manuscript securely.
- Check mailing instructions.

15.25 For small documents, such as journal articles, a heavy brown envelope, about 9 × 12, usually is adequate. For a book manuscript or thick report with several copies:

- Wrap the manuscript in stout cord.
- Make sure no edges are sticking out.
- When the document is intended for publication, you will probably need to tie the illustrations in a separate bundle. Send photographs separately. Mark the package "Photographs. Do not bend." Insure these for the cost of replacement.
- Stack copies of the manuscript in a sturdy cardboard box. For bulky manuscripts, use one box for each copy.
- Wrap the box in heavy paper, seal it tightly, tie with stout cord, and address the package.
- When time is short, check the variety of same day and next day delivery services.
- When you want to guarantee an acknowledgment, register or certify the parcel.

Preparing a Record Card

15.26 When the manuscript is being submitted for publication, prepare a 3 × 5 record card with the manuscript title and date of submission, and the publisher's name. If the document was typed on a word processor, add the document's file name and the index name of the disk, tape, or cassette that contains the electronic copy of the manuscript. Use the card to record the manuscript's subsequent history and, eventually, complete bibliographic data for it.

Appendix:
Sample Pages
for Style Sheet

The enclosed pages are from the manuscript for this book. Their purpose is to show the kind of example typists need. In addition, readers might find it interesting to compare the typed pages with their counterparts in print.

THE COMPLETE WRITER'S GUIDE TO PREPARING REPORTS,

PROPOSALS, MEMOS, ETC. . . .

Guidelines, Techniques, and Checklists to Work Smarter, not Harder:

Word Processing, Standardized Outlines, Boiler Plates, Schedules,

Nonverbal Messages, Tables and Illustrations, Computer

Programs, and Much, Much More

Carolyn J. Mullins

SAMPLE PAGE 1   (Title page)

TABLE OF CONTENTS

SAMPLE PAGE 2   (Table of contents)

LIST OF TABLES

SAMPLE PAGE 3   (List of tables)

LIST OF ILLUSTRATIONS

SAMPLE PAGE 4   (List of illustrations)

PREFACE

Brilliant research, useful inventions, and ingenious proposals benefit no one unless their creators can explain them to others. When you don't write clearly and persuasively, good ideas don't bring either raises and promotions or the satisfaction of seeing your work get results. Technical writers and editors can help with writing, but they can't take full responsibility because they didn't do the work.

Even if you have always had trouble with writing, set aside the unpleasant experiences and try again with this book as a guide. Readers accept neat, crisply and precisely written documents as the result of sound reasoning and careful observation; they reject poorly written documents as the result of carelessness or incompetence. Readers form these opinions solely on the basis of writing, not on the quality of your work or thinking.

The students in my night classes have convinced me that most books on technical writing are too detailed and too concerned solely with writing. Most writers lack the time to sift through detail; a deadline is nearly upon them and getting the document written in any form is more important than getting it written effectively. To help resolve this problem, this book is shorter than most others on similar topics. It presents necessary steps in order (and thus acts as a checklist), summarizes information on support systems, and provides many outlines, examples, and time-saving suggestions.

I am grateful to Indiana University's Wrubel Computing Center for providing the text processing system on which I wrote the book; and to IU's Institute for Urban Transportation, where I developed and tested

---

SAMPLE PAGE 5 (First page of preface)

256

PART I

Support Systems

CHAPTER 3

DATA GATHERING, RECORD-KEEPING, AND ANALYSIS

3.1   Regardless of length, most documents require some data gathering even if nothing more than a quick look at a file folder. For example, when you are writing a progress report on a project, you will only need to find out how near completion the various parts are and what problems still exist. However, if you were in charge of selecting word processing equipment for your office, you would have to keep records to determine the number, length, and frequency of different kinds of document; read articles, books, and advertising literature; talk with people in organizations that   already have   word processing   equipment; see demonstrations; and test equipment.

Data Gathering

3.2   This section briefly reviews sources of data that will be used primarily by writers of longer, more formal documents. When yours is one of several   reports in a series (other than the first one) or a report somewhat like others done previously in your organization, lists of data sources and   requirements for analysis probably already exist. Ask co-workers or a supervisor where to find this information.

Sources of Data

3.3   Information in libraries. General information on a topic comes from encyclopedias, basic textbooks, and newspapers. More specialized

SAMPLE PAGE 7   (First page of chapter)

prepared outline, plus a section for random thoughts. Chapter 8 gives many examples of possible outlines.

++ For a report on word processing equipment, use sections on office needs, demonstrations (subdivided by vendor, when necessary), costs and capabilities, office organization and reorganization, random thoughts, and conclusions and recommendations.

3.11   When you must develop the outline from scratch:

++ Make a guess about divisions and then see how they work out.

++ Expect, when you begin, to make considerable use of the "random thoughts" section.

++ Periodically sort the notes and change the names of categories. You will find fewer and fewer changes necessary as work progresses.

Interview and Survey Notes

3.12   Researchers doing surveys sometimes need an additional section in the notebook for observations about administration of the instrument or behavior of respondents--questions that seem to evoke unusual responses, words that consistently are misunderstood, and so forth. This section is _not_ for recording responses; they should be recorded on specially prepared response sheets.

3.13   When you do only a few interviews, one section in a notebook probably will be adequate to record information either in place of or in addition to information on a tape recording of the interview. When you expect to do more than five interviews, get a separate, spiral notebook. Also:

SAMPLE PAGE 8   (Nontitle page of chapter, with headings)

31

++ Make appointments in advance, preferably an hour or so after opening time in the morning or an hour after lunch so your time won't be nibbled away by the questions, mail, and telephone calls that often occur at those times.

++ When you intend to record an interview, always let the interviewee know when you make the appointment. A few will object, and you will want to be prepared to take detailed written notes.

++ Before each interview, write at the top of the page the interviewee's name and job title; the date, time, and place; and your goal for the interview.

++ Write the date and interviewee's name on a label on the tape, and dictate that information into the microphone so it is recorded just before the interview information. Should the external label fall off, you still will have a way to identify the interview.

3.14   Sometimes a interviewee will refuse to be taped, yet a verbatim transcript is essential. For example, you may be recording the statement of someone who witnessed an accident, and the statement is essential to establish who caused the accident and which insurance company will pay damages. In such cases, arrange to take a court reporter with you.

Taking Notes from Documents

3.15   When you take information from sources other than your own primary data, record accurately both the factual information and complete bibliographic information.

3.16   Factual information. Record factual information on either 4 x 6 or 5 x 8 file cards. Keep them in a file box and separate them by

SAMPLE PAGE 9   (Nontitle page of chapter, with headings)

260

<u>How to LOG ON to TEST CICS</u>

Begin with either Step 1 (when small square contains a question mark) or Step 2 (when small square contains a cross).

<u>Actor</u>		<u>Action</u>
Operator	1.	When small square contains question mark,
	1a.	Pushes down ALT key.
	1b.	While holding down ALT, pushes SYS REQ key.
Computer	1c.	Changes question mark to cross. (If small square continues to contain question mark, calls 000-0000 for help.)
Operator	1d.	Goes to step 12.
	2.	When small square contains a cross,
	2a.	Presses and holds ALT, then pushes SYS REQ key.
Computer	2b.	Changes square with cross to solid
Operator	2c.	Goes to Step 3.
		OR
Computer	2d.	When cross changes to question mark, had no link to CICS.
Operator	2e.	Repeats Step 2a until computer responds with a cross.
	2f.	Goes to Step 12.
Operator	3.	To find out whether link is to PROD or TEST, types: CLME
	4.	Presses ENTER key.
Computer	5.	Responds with message in Figure 1, Part A, which says terminal is fully linked to PRODUCTION CICS.

FIGURE 11.2 Example: Text page that lists instructions

SAMPLE PAGE 10 (Sample illustration, treatment of instructions)

TABLE 5.1

TITLE OF TABLE TO SHOW PARTS OF A TABLE

Stubhead	Example of Boxhead[1]		
	Cost in Dollars	Column Head	Percen-tages
Spanner Head (Goes <u>Below</u> Column Heads)[1]			
Row stub	$ 10	4	1.0%
Row stub	110	100	15.3
Subordinate stub	1250	64	112.2
Second subordinate	1540	. . .	14.6
Row stub	3	1.2	.1
Second Spanner Head			
Row stub	$ 1567	0	2.6%
Subordinate stub	12	. . .	27.9
Subordinate stub	278	1765	281.0
Row stub	1567	0	0.0

Source: Mullins (1980, p.6).

Notes: General notes apply to the entire table.

[1]Specific notes apply only to the designated entries. Subordinate stubs and spanners are not present in every table.

FIGURE 5.1.   Illustration of parts of a table

SAMPLE PAGE 11   (Sample table)

Table 5.4 Associations Between [Independent Variables] and Dependent
          Variables 1 and 2 (Two Measures Each)

	Dependent Variable 1			Dependent Variable 2		
		Coefficients			Coefficients	
	Corr.	Unst.	Stnd.	Corr.	Unst.	Stnd.
Variable	2	2	3	3	2	2
Measure	2	2	3	3	2	2
Measure	2	2	3	3	2	2
Variable	2	2	3	3	2	2
Measure	2	2	3	3	2	2
Measure	2	2	3	3	2	2
Variable	2	2	3	3	2	2
Measure	2	2	3	3	2	2
Measure	2	2	3	3	2	2
Variable	2	2	3	3	2	2
Measure	2	2	3	3	2	2
Measure	2	2	3	3	2	2
Variable	2	2	3	3	2	2
Measure	2	2	3	3	2	2
Measure	2	2	3	3	2	2

SAMPLE PAGE 12 (Sample regression table)

BIBLIOGRAPHY

Aaronson, S. 1977. Style in scientific writing. <u>Current Contents</u> 9 (January 10):6-15.

> This article highlights the flaws in much technical, and especially scientific, writing.

American Psychological Association. 1974. <u>Publication manual of the American Psychological Association</u>. 2nd ed. Washington, D.C: American Psychological Association.

> The style guide for journals of the American Psychological Association, the <u>APA Manual</u> is one of the finer style guides on the market.

Anderson, D. R., Sweeney, D. J, and Williams, T. R. 1978. <u>Essentials of management science: Applications to decision making</u>. St. Paul: West.

> Chapter 14, "Project Scheduling: PERT/CPM," pp. 398-438, discusses use of PERT and Critical Path techniques.

Andres, W. C. 1978. The business systems proposal. <u>Journal of Systems Management</u> 29 (202, Feb.):39-41.

> This brief article describes an outline for business systems proposals.

Belnap, N. D. 1978. BINDEX: a book indexing system. <u>Scholarly Publishing</u> 9(January):167-170.

> This article describes a computer program, written in FORTRAN,, that can index text not prepared on a word processing system. Writers who want a copy of the program can get it by sending Belnap a blank magnetic tape.

Bernstein, T. M. 1965. <u>The careful writer: A modern guide to English usage</u>. New York: Atheneum.

> This highly readable and entertaining classic, which deals with common errors in usage, is one of the few books that teaches usage, entertains, <u>and</u> exposes readers to good writing. It even makes good bedtime reading.

SAMPLE PAGE 13   (First page of bibliography)

Bibliography

Aaronson, S. 1977. Style in scientific writing. *Current Contents* 9 (January 10):6-15.

This article highlights the flaws in much technical, and especially scientific, writing.

American Psychological Association. 1974. *Publication manual of the American Psychological Association*. 2nd ed. Washington, D.C: American Psychological Association.

The style guide for journals of the American Psychological Association, the *APA Manual* is one of the finer style guides on the market.

Anderson, D. R., Sweeney, D. J, and Williams, T. R. 1978. *Essentials of management science: Applications to decision making*. St. Paul: West.

Chapter 14, "Project Scheduling: PERT/CPM," pp. 398-438, discusses use of PERT and Critical Path techniques.

Andres, W. C. 1978. The business systems proposal. *Journal of Systems Management* 29 (202, Feb.):39-41.

This brief article describes an outline for business systems proposals.

Belnap, N. D. 1978. BINDEX: A book indexing system. *Scholarly Publishing* 9 (January):167-170.

This article describes a computer program, written in FORTRAN, that can index text not prepared on a word processing system. Writers who want a copy of the program can get it by sending Belnap a blank magnetic tape.

Bernstein, T. M. 1965. *The careful writer: A modern guide to English usage*. New York: Atheneum.

This highly readable and entertaining classic, which deals with common errors in usage, is one of the few books that teaches usage, entertains, *and* exposes readers to good writing. It even makes good bedtime reading.

————. 1958. *Watch your language.* New York: Atheneum.

This book compiles the sins of writers at the *New York Times,* together with corrections. It also contains many well-written passages, which Bernstein celebrates. All samples come from *Winners and Sinners,* which Bernstein used to issue once or twice a month from the "southeast corner" of the *New York Times* news room (p. 1). Like *The Careful Writer,* this book entertains as well as instructs.

Bostick, G. W. 1979. *The effects of selected graphic design variables on the readability of multiple-line graphs.* Doctoral Dissertation. Bloomington, Ind.: School of Education.

This dissertation reports Bostick's research findings on the readability of graphs. Writers who use graphs frequently would find its 50 pages well worth reading.

Breslin, D. 1973. Better personnel data for proposals. *Proposals and their preparation,* Anthology Series No. 1 (May). Washington, D. C.: Society for Technical Communication.

Breslin tells how to use to resumé-writing aids to organize and simplify the task of getting relevant, organized copy written by the resume subjects. With these aids information can be gathered, rewritten, and edited before it is needed for a proposal.

Brown, L. 1973. *Effective business report writing.* 3d ed. Prentice-Hall, Inc.: Englewood Cliffs, N. J.

This book contains a wealth of carefully organized detail about all phases of writing and presenting reports.

Buffa, E. S. 1976. *Operations management: The management of production.* New York: John Wiley.

Chapter 14, "Large Scale Projects," pp. 531–557, describes the use of PERT and Critical Path techniques. The chapter concludes with a two-page bibliography.

Caird, K. A. 1973. Publishing the mammoth proposal. *Proposals and their preparation,* Anthology Series No. 1 (May). Washington, D. C.: Society for Technical Communication.

This article gives many useful tips on how to prepare a huge proposal in a relatively short time (an accompanying photograph shows the 54 volumes of one proposal).

Datapro Research Corporation. 1978. Current word processing systems. A10-200-101, The current Office. Delran, N. J.: Datapro Reseach Corporation.

This 15-page report describes the different kinds of word processor, the general features of equipment, applications, advantages, tradeoffs, the marketplace, the outlook for the future, planning considerations, and salient features (in the form of a useful glossary of terms).

Davis, J. A. and Jacobs, A. M. 1968. Tabular presentation. *International Encyclopedia of the Social Sciences.* New York: Macmillan and Free Press.

This article shows many ways to present tables of percentages.

Day, R. A. 1979. *How to write and publish a scientific paper.* Philadelphia, Pa.: ISI press.

This small, well-written book describes features of successful scientific writing; examples from biology and chemistry.

Domitrovic, R. 1977. *How to prepare a style guide.* Washington, D. C.: Society for Technical Communication.

This 11-page pamphlet, available for a small charge from the Society, tells how to plan a style guide and what to include in it.

Eames, R. D. and Chesnut, D. J. 1973. Managing the proposal group. *Proposals and their preparation,* Anthology Series No. 1 (May). Washington, D. C.: Society for Technical Communication.

This article, which discusses qualification and motivation of personnel, management, and estimating cost and schedules, gives many helpful suggestions for managers of proposal groups.

Fischman, B. L. 1975. *Business report writing.* Providence, R. I.; P. A. R. Inc.

Fischman's elementary book on report writing begins with analysis and moves through the various phases of writing. Primarily a textbook, it includes a range of workbook exercises.

Flesch, R. F. 1974. *The art of readable writing.* New York: Harper & Row.

This book describes Flesch's readability measure, which is the basis of the computer program STAR.

Follet, W. 1966. *Modern American usage.* New York: Hill & Wang.

Follet's is one of several books on usage; all offices need a copy of at least one such book for editorial checkers (see Chapter 14).

Fowler, H. W. 1965. *A dictionary of modern English usage.* 2d ed. Rev. by Sir Ernest Gowers. Oxford: Oxford University Press.

Fowler's is the classic guide to usage. Every office should have a copy.

Frankenthaler, M. R. 1976. Utilizing the computer to prepare a manuscript. *Scholarly Publishing* 7:61–68.

A graduate student in Spanish with no experience in computer use, Frankenthaler typed and edited her dissertation in Spanish on IBM's Administrative Terminal System. This short article describes her experience in terms any novice can understand.

General Motors. n.d. *S.T.A.R.* Detroit: General Motors Public Relations Staff.

This booklet describes the computer program that General Motors wrote, in BASIC, to help its staff write good instructions for mechanics. Available free from

GM Public Relations Staff, 3044 W. Grand Blvd., Detroit, MI, 48202. Ask also for the sample program.

Gunning, R. 1968. *The technique of clear writing*. Rev. ed. New York: McGraw-Hill.

This book, written by a former journalist, gives many useful suggestions and examples, and includes a helpful appendix on technical writing.

Hall, K. R. 1979. *E. B. White: A bibliographic catalog of printed materials in the department of rare books, Cornell University Library*. New York: Garland.

White's writing is among the most enjoyable and readable that is available. Take your pick of children's stories, essays, letters, or books.

Hirsch, E. D., Jr. 1977. *The philosophy of composition*. Chicago: University of Chicago Press.

This book explains academic theories of composition and readability, and some of the limitations of readability formulas.

Hurwitz, J. 1979. Merging data processing and word processing. *Mini-Micro World* (July):26, 31.

Hurwitz describes companies that have begun to make computer equipment capable of both word and data processing. She describes general shortcomings as well as the specific inadequacies of specific systems.

Krathwohl, D. R. 1977. *How to prepare a research proposal*. Available through Syracuse University Bookstore, 303 University Place, Syracuse, NY, 13210. $3.45, including postage and handling.

A helpful resource for writers of research proposals on topics in psychology and social psychology.

Jet Propulsion Laboratory. 1976. *The levels of edit*. Pasadena, CA: Jet Propulsion Laboratory.

This 27-page booklet analyzes the process of technical editing, details nine types of editing, and provides an excellent model for organizations that want to develop their own prodedure manuals. The second edition, released in 1980, is available for $2.00 from the Superintendant of Documents, Government Printing Office, Document #003-000-00785-0.

John, R. C. 1976. Improve your technical writing. *Management Accounting* (September):49–52.

One of several good articles on use of plain language to improve writing.

Lesikar, R. V. 1974. *How to write a report your boss will read and remember*. Homewood, Ill.: Dow Jones-Irwin.

Lesikar's excellent book on report writing discusses at length analysis, organization, qualities of effective writing, techniques of readable writing, correctness, use of graphics, physical presentation, and references. Try this book when you need additional help on writing reports.

Linton, M. 1972. *A simplified style manual: For the preparation of journal articles in psychology, social sciences, education and literature.* New York: Appleton-Century Crofts.

This book is useful primarily to psychologists and others who use psychological statistics. Many of the style requirements now have been changed, but pages 99–106 still are extremely useful to writers of technical manuscripts that report psychological statistics in tables, text, or illustrations.

Lockwood, A.. 1969. *Diagrams: A visual survey of graphs, maps, charts, and diagrams for the graphic designer.* Vista, N. Y.: Watson-Guptill.

This book is a well-respected reference on graphics.

McCabe, H. M. and Popham, E. L. 1977. *Word processing: A systems approach to the office.* New York: Harcourt, Brace, Jovanovich.

This excellent book explains the development of word processing systems in detail, yet with the clarity and simplicity that every manager and secretary will appreciate. Included are sections on changes in job titles and office organization, various dictation and typing systems, human factors in word processing, case studies, computer word processing, management information systems, and paperless offices of the future.

McGraw-Hill Book Company. n.d. *Guidelines for equal treatment of the sexes in McGraw-Hill Book Company publications.* New York: McGraw-Hill, Public Information and Publicity Department.

This publication, one of the best available guides for writers who want to avoid sexist language, is available free from the Publicity Department, McGraw-Hill Book Company, 1221 Avenue of the Americas, New York, N. Y., 10020.

MacGregor, A. J. 1977a. Graphics simplified: Charts and graphs. *Scholarly Publishing* 8 (January):153–164.

This article, the first in a series of four, explains what kinds of chart or graph to choose for various kinds of data.

———. 1977b. Graphics simplified: Preparing charts and graphs. *Scholarly publishing* 0 (April).270–279.

This article describes how to prepare charts and graphs simply and effectively.

———. 1977c. Graphics simplified: Media specifications and artists' aids. *Scholarly Publishing* 8 (July):367–376.

This article describes how to prepare graphics for television, slides, film, and print.

———. 1978. Graphics simplified: Choosing illustrations. *Scholarly Publishing* 9 (April):270–279.

This article tells how to decide when to use a drawing or painting, a chart, graph or diagram, or photographs, and what qualities make a good illustration.

McLaughlin, G. H. 1969. SMOG grading—a new readability formula. *Journal of Reading* 12:639–646.

This article describes the simplest of the readability formulas and tells how it works.

Matthies, L. 1977. The task outline. *The Technical Writing Teacher* IV (Spring, 3):107–109.

A companion to Matthies's 1963 article, this article describes how to write instructions for a single worker's task.

————. 1963. Preparing a playscript procedure. *The Systemation Newsletter,* No. 115. Available from Systemation, Inc., Box 730, Colorado Springs, CO, 80901.

Playscript is a useful procedure for giving instructions on use of complicated procedures.

Menzel, D. H., Jones, H. M., and Boyd, L. G. 1961. *Writing a technical paper.* New York: McGraw-Hill.

Although 18 years old, this small book still gives timely and clearly written guidance for writers in the hard sciences.

Morris, W. and M. 1975. *Harper dictionary of contemporary usage.* New York: Harper & Row.

This book is one of several on usage. Somewhat harder to use than books like Bernstein's, sometimes it tells readers much more than they need to know to make a decision.

Muller, J. A. 1978. What consultation and freelance writing can do for you and for your students. *The Technical Writing Teacher* V (Spring, 3):74–77.

This article and others in this same issue of TTWT describe the benefits of a variety of consultative arrangements. Organizations that want to try apprentice technical writers can get a copy of this issue by writing to Nell Ann Pickett, English Department, Hinds Junior College, Raymond, MS, 39154. In 1979 the cost was less than $10.

Mullins, C. J. 1980. The computer as nitpicking copy editor. Paper given at 27th International Technical Communications Conference, May 14–17, Minneapolis.

This paper explains the use of computers for the editing tasks described in Chapter 13 and gives programs for a CDC 6600 computer.

————. 1977. *A guide to writing and publishing in the social and behavioral sciences.* New York: Wiley-Interscience.

This comprehensive handbook discusses writing, revising, and getting published. The book discusses in detail publication of both books and articles.

Murgio, M. P. 1969. *Communication graphics.* New York: Van Nostrand Reinhold.

Newman, E. 1974. *Strictly speaking. Will America be the death of English?* Indianapolis: Bobbs-Merrill.

Newman's book, which pokes fun at the foibles of American usage, is excellent for sensitizing oneself to bad writing.

1933. *The Oxford English dictionary.* Oxford: At the Clarendon Press.

For writers whose employers and publishers are British, the *Oxford* dictionary is the primary reference on correct English usage.

Pearsall, T. E. 1975. *Teaching technical writing: Methods for college English teachers.* Washington, D. C.: Society for Technical Communication.

This 23-page booklet, complete with a bibliography and available from the Society for a small charge, helps teachers make the transition from teaching standard composition to teaching the specialty of technical writing. Pearsall includes writing assignments and class activities.

Perrin, P. G. 1972. *Writer's guide and index to English.* 5th ed. Rev. by W. R. Ebbit. Glenview, Ill.: Scott, Foresman.

This excellent college textbook includes an easy-to-use index and is available in paperback. Try this book if you need more help with writing, and especially with grammar, than *The Complete Writing Guide* gives.

Pournelle, J. 1979. Writing with a microcomputer. *onComputing* 1 (Summer, 1):12–19.

Pournelle, a best-selling science fiction writer, describes the initial pains and ultimately seductive pleasures of writing on his own personal computer.

1974. *Publication manual of the American Psychological Association.* 2nd ed. Washington, D. C.: American Psychological Association.

This excellent style manual has been accepted by more than 200 journals, and the number continues to grow well outside the boundaries of psychology. The manual gives information on organization, clarity, grammar, construction of tables and illustrations, style, and journal procedures.

Richards, T. O. and Richardson, R. A. 1941. *Technical writing.* Warren, Mich.: General Motors Research Laboratory, reprinted by the Society for Technical Communication.

This 36-page pamphlet, available for a small charge from the Society, explains the pressing need for good technical writing, gives helpful hints and outlines, and has good illustrations that enhance the points the authors make in text.

Sachs, H. L. 1976. *How to write the technical article and get it published.* Washington, D. C.: Society for Technical Communication.

This readable, 64-page booklet gives many useful suggestions for technical writers who want to write and sell articles.

Schnitzler, R. K. 1973. Making your technical proposals more effective, sections 1 and 2. *Proposals and their preparation,* Anthology Series No. 1 (May). Washington, D.C.: Society for Technical Communication.

These articles, included in a general anthology on preparation of proposals, give advice especially for writers of highly technical proposals.

Shaw, J. G. 1976. *Teaching technical writing and editing: In-house programs that work.* Washington, D. C.: Society for Technical Communication.

This 76-page booklet describes a variety of ways organizations can help staff members improve their writing.

Spear, M. E. 1969. *Practical charting techniques*. New York: McGraw Hill.

Like Lockwood's book, Spear's is a classic source of information on how to design charts.

Stoddard, E. L. 1973. Producing the overnight proposal. *Proposals and their preparation,* Anthology Series No. 1 (May). Washington, D. C.: Society for Technical Communication.

Stoddard discusses some very useful shortcuts for producing even large proposals on short notice. Many also apply to writing reports.

Teigen, D. K. 1973. Documenting and retrieving your company's related experience for proposals. *Proposals and their preparation,* Anthology Series No. 1 (May). Washington, D. C.: Society for Technical Communication.

This article describes the history, development, and implementation of a Project Experience File (PEF).

Tichy, H. J. 1966. *Effective writing for managers, engineers, scientists*. New York: Wiley.

Tichy's excellent book is devoted wholly to writing. When you need more help on writing than *The Complete Writing Guide* gives, you might find Tichy's book useful even if you aren't a manager, engineer, or scientist.

Tukey, J. V. 1972. Some graphic and semigraphic displays. *Statistical papers in honor of George W. Snedecor.* ed. T. A. Bancroft. Ames: The Iowa State University Press.

This chapter, by one the U. S.'s best and most creative statisticians, suggests many novel ways to display statistics.

Turabian, K. L. 1973. *A manual for writers of term papers, theses, and dissertations.* 4th ed. Chicago: University of Chicago Press.

This book contains a wealth of information about writing and documenting research papers; includes detailed information on treatment of citations.

Ullman, L. L. 1973. Shortcuts to proposal preparation. *Proposals and their preparation,* Anthology Series No. 1 (May). Washington, D. C.: Society for Technical Communication.

Ullman discusses more shortcuts, such as modular boiler plate, use of input forms and preprinted sheets, and dual-purpose checklists.

University of Chicago Press. 1969. *A manual of style*. 12th ed., rev. Chicago: University of Chicago Press.

This book contains information on writing, manuscript typing, editing, indexing, and a host of other topics related to publishing. A must for technical editors and writers and for offices that produce documents for publication. A revised edition is due for publication in July 1981.

van Leunen, M-C. 1978. Scholarship: A singular notion. *Atlantic* (May):88–90.
   This article thoughtfully discusses the case for use of the first person singular.

Vaughn, J. 1979. A prescription for programming's least popular phase. *Datamation* (January):185–186.
   This short article tells why good user documentation is necessary and gives specific guidelines for writing, testing, and maintaining it.

Vector Graphic. n.d. A word about the WORD MANAGEMENT SYSTEM from Vector Graphic. Westlake Village, Calif.: Vector Graphic Inc. 7 pages.
   This pamphlet describes the WORD MANAGEMENT SYSTEM in readable detail.

Warren, C. 1978. Wordprocessing: A major factor in small business computing. *Interface Age* (December):64–69.
   Warren explains how word processors work, lists and describes several systems, and tells where to get more information.

Annual. *Webster's new collegiate dictionary*. Springfield, Mass.: G. & C. Merriam.
   Although *Webster's Third* is the ultimate source of information on American English usage, the *Collegiate* is the dictionary that most offices can afford. Replace your copy every two or three years.

Webster's third new international dictionary of the English language, Unabridged. Springfield, Mass.: G. C. Merriam.
   Webster's Third is considered by many to have the most nearly correct information on American usage.

Weir, A. M. 1973. The coordinator/editor and the strawman: A winning proposal combination. *Proposals and their preparation,* Anthology Series No. 1 (May). Washington, D. C.: Society for Technical Communication.
   Weir tells how to use "strawman" proposals to plan in advance the material needed to respond to an RFP (request for proposal).

Zeisel, H. 1968 *Say it with figures*. 5th ed., rev. New York: Harper & Row.
   This book discusses many aspects of using figures. Chapter 9 shows many ways to present cross-tabulations and explains the logic behind cross-tabulation procedures.

Style Guides and Aids for Typists

American Chemical Society. 1967. *Handbook for authors of papers in the journals of the American Chemical Society*. Washington, D.C.: American Chemical Society Publications. [1]

American Institute of Physics. 1970. *Style manual*. Rev. ed. New York: American Institute of Physics. [2]

American Mathematical Society. 1970. *A manual for authors of mathematical papers.* 3rd ed. Providence, R.I.: American Mathematical Society. [3]

American Medical Association. 1971. *Style book and editorial manual.* 4th ed. Chicago: American Medical Association. [4]

American Psychological Association. 1974. *Publication manual of the American Psychological Association.* 2nd ed. Washington, D.C: American Psychological Association. [5]

American Society for Testing and Materials. 1973. *ASTM style manual.* Philadelphia: American Society for Testing and Materials. [6]

American Sociological Association. Notice to contributors. Inside front cover of every issue of the *American Sociological Review.*[7]

Council of Biology Editors. 1972. *CBE style manual.* 3rd ed. Washington, D. C.: American Institute of Biological Sciences.[8]

1977. *JASA* style guide for authors. *Journal of the American Statistical Association* 72 (September):696–702. [9]

Laird, E. S. 1967. *Engineering secretary's complete handbook.* 2d ed. Englewood Cliffs, N. J.: Prentice-Hall.

———. 1973. *Data processing secretary's complete handbook.* West Nyack, N. Y.: Parker Publishing.

Modern Language Association of America. 1977. *MLA handbook for writers of research papers, theses, and dissertations.* New York: Modern Language Association. [10]

Sage Publications. n.d. *Journal editorial style, Sage Publications.* Beverly Hills, Calif.: Sage Publications. [11]

Standing Committee on Publications of the British Psychological Society. 1971. *Suggestions to authors.* Rev. ed. London: Cambridge University Press. [12]

Turabian, K. L. 1973. *A manual for writers of term papers, theses, and dissertations.* 4th ed. Chicago: University of Chicago Press. [13]

United States Government Printing Office. 1973. *United States Government Printing Office style manual.* Rev. ed. January 1973. Washington, D. C.: U. S. Government Printing Office. [14]

University of Chicago Press. 1969. *A manual of style.* 12th ed., rev. Chicago: University of Chicago Press. [15]

Index